The Terror of Terre Haute

Bud Taylor and the 1920s

John D. Wright

© 2008 John D. Wright
All Rights Reserved.

No part of this publication may be reproduced, stored in a retrieval system, or transmitted, in any form or by any means, electronic, mechanical, photocopying, recording, or otherwise, without the written permission of the author.

First published by Dog Ear Publishing
4010 W. 86th Street, Ste H
Indianapolis, IN 46268
www.dogearpublishing.net

ISBN: 978-159858-761-6

This book is printed on acid-free paper.

Printed in the United States of America

Table of Contents

Dedication v
Acknowledgments vi
Introduction 1
Little Terror 5
A Boxing Past 11
It Wasn't me, Mom 21
Use of Leverage 28
Banks of the Wabash 32
Enter Eddie and Eddie 38
Felling a Tree 43
Nothing Human 47
"Inarticulate Sounds" 51
Ringside in Terre Haute 58
Saved by the Bell 65
Mayoral Support 70
Money Gets Good 74
Nailed by Gordon, Love 79
Christening a Terror 83
Frankie Jerome 89
Punching with Pancho 96
The Shoulder 102
Boxing's Dr. Frankenstein 111
The Prime 114
A Hero's Welcome 123
Bushy, and the Timber Wolf 127
The Dirty Sock 134
The Chase Continues 139

Accused of Fix 142
Clever 146
Reeling in Rosenberg 152
Champion, by Appointment 156
For the Honor of Terre Haute 165
Preparing for Tony 167
First Defense 170
A Taylor Toboggan? 178
The Big One 182
Honored at Home 186
Sangor Gains Edge 188
Changing Times 191
A Straight-Punching Nemesis 196
Ellen's Choice 199
Title Departs 201
A Changing Face 204
A Time to Retire 207
Losing With a Grin 210
The Slide Continues 214
Battles in Ring, Court 216
A Freakish Ending 218
Battling Bat, Fidel 221
Getting Pounded 225
Booed in Philly 227
Adjustment 229
Sammy's Big Chance 231
L.A. Descent 235
The Final Rounds 238
Legacy 244
    Notes 247
    Bibliography 299
    Bud Taylor Fight Record 302
    Index of Names 308

Dedicated to the memory of H. Rendall "Ren" Wright, whose wisdom guides me

Acknowledgments

Thanks to all those people around Terre Haute who helped me with this project, sometimes by merely stopping me to say, "Hey I heard you were working on a book. I knew an old boxer who ...," which would lead to a good interview.

In the "Notes" section of the book are the names of people I interviewed for this book, and without their facts and perspective, this would be an awfully boring read. A special thanks to two helpers in particular. First, Dick Brokaw, in his mid-eighties at this printing, my boxing guru, who welcomed me into his apartment about 10 times for interviews. He drew on his 50 years as a boxer and referee to educate me on the nuts and bolts of the game. Brokaw also was of great help because he knew Bud Taylor more than just in passing, since Taylor had been a good friend of his older brother. Brokaw's only request in return for all his help on this project was that I tell the world that Terre Haute's Cleveland Brown was the best fighter he ever saw. There you go, Dick. Secondly, special thanks to Bud Taylor Jr., whose encouragement and interest in this project inspired me to finish. I only wish I could've finished in time for Bud Jr. to read the product, but he died in 2006.

Thanks to the people at ProQuest Historical Newspapers, whose full-text online archive of newspaper articles from six major dailies provided a vital source of information for this biography. For all writers and history buffs, I hope the online compiling of newspaper archives continues with newspapers from other cities.

The press covered Bud Taylor thoroughly during his career, and I relied heavily on newspaper articles for sources for this biography, although aware of the pitfalls of trusting the accuracy of 1920s sports reporters who tended to skew and sensationalize. When possible, I substantiated the facts that appear in this book with other sources, published and living, and I put more emphasis on those that could be verified.

There are people I thank whose names may not appear in the Notes section who helped either by referring to me to a valuable source or enlightening me about some facet of history or the publishing business. Thanks to historian B. Michael McCormick for sharing his private collection of Bud Taylor newspaper clippings, not available on microfilm. The surviving members of Taylor's family and his descendants were of invaluable help, and especially gracious at the 2005 International Boxing Hall of Fame's induction ceremonies. Many of the photographs used in this book come from copies made available to me by his family members.

Thanks to Richard Roth and Tom Reck for hiring me to my first journalism job. Thanks to all the city editors in the formative stage of my journalism career who took the time to help me with my writing, in particular, Joe Baker and much later, Jim Lewers, valuable mentors both. Thanks to my mother, Sara, for instilling in me a lifelong love of words with all those word games we played at home when I was a grade-schooler, and to my parents for a lifetime of love and support. To my friend, David D. Goodwin: thank you for your reaction to the parody of the television series "Lost in Space" that I wrote in the fifth grade When I read it to my fellow fifth-graders during our classroom show-and-share time, Dave laughed hysterically while everyone else in the room yawned. I don't know if my writing career would have survived a unanimous rejection at that impressionable age. A special thanks to my brother, Mark, for providing insightful edits for this book, and to Roseanne Toulson for her web expertise.

Employees of the Vigo County Public Library were of tremendous help in this project, especially David Lewis and Nancy Sherrill in Special Collections. I thank www.boxrec.com for its valuable reservoir of information about boxers of the past, especially their fight records. Finally, thanks to the many teachers of the world who take extra time to encourage their students to write creatively and imaginatively. I had some of these fine educators, and they made a difference. In particular, at Fuqua Elementary, Duane Miller; at Sarah Scott Middle School, Alice Everly; at Terre Haute South Vigo High School, Faye Donald; and at Indiana State University, John Christie and Warren Loveless.

Introduction

It was a chilly morning, that 26th of March, 1927, but then as now, brisk air does nothing to lessen the excitement felt by schoolchildren as they hop out of bed for a Saturday of play. And, this particular day carried a bonus to the typical slate of spring activities on a boy's weekend agenda—a father's treat. The youth would join thousands lining the streets of Wabash Avenue in Terre Haute to listen to a makeshift blow-by-blow account of their hero's first defense of his world bantamweight title.1

Bud Taylor, the local hero they had seen and touched and shouted at dozens of times, was about to make history. Although his boxing match with Tony Canzoneri was being staged 200 miles away in Chicago, Illinois, his local pull was such that the *Terre Haute Tribune* had sent two reporters to Chicago, one to call the fight, and the other to telegraph the call back home, where an announcer with a megaphone, standing in the window of the newspaper's upstairs offices, would relay the details to the throngs in the street below.2

The people of Taylor's hometown in Indiana adored him, and throughout his career he rewarded them by boxing as if the honor of all its residents were at stake in the outcome of every bout.

Bud Taylor was no ordinary fighter, but one whose physical talents and work ethic marked a path to the International Boxing Hall of Fame. When he died in 1962, the testimonies about his boxing career were spoken in superlatives usually reserved for the likes of a Jack Dempsey, Joe Louis or Sugar Ray Robinson. "Pound for pound, Bud Taylor was the greatest fighter of all time: greater than Jack Dempsey, Gene Tunney, Harry Greb or Benny Leonard, fighters who will be remembered long after he is forgotten," said Tom Doyle, former matchmaker for the Los Angeles Olympic Coliseum.3

Taylor's fights sold out the 10,000-seat Olympic six times, and Doyle marveled at Taylor's performances there over some of the best in the world in his weight class.4 Taylor's audiences believed they had seen the core of the man revealed with such special efforts as the evening in 1924 when he lost the use of one arm in an early round, let it dangle in excruciating pain, then proceeded to defeat his foe single-armed.

With two good arms, Bud Taylor was for a time in the mid-1920s, unquestionably, the best in the world at the 118-pound weight limit. By then, the press nationwide had referred to him for years as The Terre Haute Terror. "Taylor was the most vicious little man the game has ever known," said Hayden "Wad" Wadhams, Doyle's partner as matchmaker at the Olympic Coliseum. "… He had everything: boxing skills, punching power and an indomitable will to win."5 Bill Miller, a boxing press agent in the 1920s, once drove 50 miles in a driving snowstorm just to see Taylor fight.6

The 1920s was a time of prosperity for Americans, a playground age of flappers, speak-easys and motorcars, and one in which such sports notables as Babe Ruth, Bill Tilden, Bobby Jones and Red Grange enjoyed godlike status. The public craved boxing and Taylor swept in with the tide of its popularity. His give-it-all performances inside the ring and pleasant personality outside made him one of the brightest stars of the Golden Era of Sports.

For all the glamour and glory in his career as a celebrity athlete, Taylor the human being struggled with its side effects. The deaths of two opponents from his punches, marital problems, drinking, obesity and financial difficulties burdened him, especially in the thorny period of readjustment after he quit the ring. In many ways, Taylor's life seems to follow the course of the times: a decade of prosperity in the 1920s, a struggle in the 1930s and early 1940s before a postwar period of redirection.

I first became aware of the name "Bud Taylor" as a child in the mid-1960s from my father, an amateur boxer out of Sullivan, Indiana, from 1949 to 1951. Dad would talk about notable boxers of the past, and he always spoke the name "Bud Taylor" with a reverence in his voice that, eventually, beckoned me to learn more. In 2004, seven years after dad died and 43 after Taylor passed, I looked for a biography of Taylor, and found no book, and few articles of substance. So

I began to dig. I sat inside a Terre Haute library, threading a spool of microfilmed newspaper under the glass platelets of a reading machine, beginning four years of research and interviews across the nation that would, at last, provide a detailed account of his life.

I would find that Taylor overcame great odds in reaching the pinnacle of his profession, and in this regard his story is one with universal appeal.

Chapter 1

Little Terror

The bell rang, signaling a day's end for Estella East. Her 41 third-graders headed for the classroom door, spilling into the hallway and out onto the inner-city streets of Terre Haute, Indiana, for the walk home.

Soon, East would follow, released for the day from all the clamor and clutter that tested the dedication of a $500-per-year public-school teacher in 1912.[1] As she completed her final duties of her day, some of the children came running back into McKeen School to her classroom.

"Bernard is having a fight in a vacant lot," they exclaimed, referring to the boy the children knew as "Bud" Taylor. East rushed outside and to the lot to break up the fight, but arrived to find the affair had passed and the crowd dispersed.

The next day, 9-year-old Taylor trudged into class with a scratched and swollen face, and East sat him down for a chat. She asked what had caused the fight. A new boy in town had bragged he could "lick" Taylor, he said.

Taylor, although smaller than the new boy, won that tussle, and many others in a career of fighting that began long before he ever set a sneaker inside a roped enclosure.[2] The new boy's consolation would be the mounting toll of victims over the years at the hands of the kid he had underestimated.

Taylor lived about eight blocks from the school with his parents, Samuel W. and Matilda "Tillie" Taylor. Bud also shared the house with older siblings Edith, born in 1897, and Orville, born in

1900. Bud entered life July 22, 1903.[3] They had named him "Charles Bernard," but the name soon gave way to the easier nickname. In his childspeak, Orville called his younger brother "brudder," later "brud," and eventually "bud," which stuck.[4]

Tillie Taylor, whose maiden name also had been Taylor, had grown up on a farm east of Terre Haute. Sam Taylor had been reared in Pennsylvania and probably moved to Indiana as an adult.[5] In whatever the circumstances Sam Taylor and Tillie Taylor met—perhaps at a dance, or a market, or through acquaintances, or in a chance encounter—they had found their lasting companions. They married in 1894 in Terre Haute.

Sam Taylor worked as a teamster,[6] which in 1903 meant he hauled goods by driving a horse- or mule-drawn wagon or carriage (thus the term "team"-ster). The job ranked near the bottom of all professions in earning capacity and working conditions.[7]

"In a teamster's life, work was scarce, jobs were insecure, and poverty was commonplace. In 1900, the typical teamster worked 12-18 hours a day, seven days a week for an average wage of $2 a day," according to a historical account by the union. The organization known as International Brotherhood of Teamsters did not form until 1903,[8] and early teamsters' locals were mostly decentralized groups, years away from being strong enough to elevate the lot of their members into what is commonly thought of as society's "middle class."

Tillie Taylor stood about 5 foot 5 inches, and had a pleasant, round face with features that she passed to her youngest son.[9] By the time of the birth of Charles Bernard, she was 34 years old. Sam was 45, well beyond the years of his youth and the blond hair that he passed to his son.[10]

By all accounts, Bud cared dearly for his mother. A 1922 newspaper article about the family refers to her as Bud's "best pal." It quotes Edith as saying, "he will grab up mother in his arms and waltz her all over the house, but when he wins a bout, he breaks his neck home to tell mother about it." He also liked to treat his mother and sister with gifts, especially boxes of candy.[11]

Sam Taylor was remembered as a hard-working and honest man, although gruff and humorless.[12] A newspaper photograph accompanying the 1922 interview appears to capture the Taylor family in character. Bud stands with an arm around his mother affectionately. Bud, Tillie and Edith each are smiling, with Tillie's the most revealing—a pursed-lip grin of pride. Sam Taylor stands disconnected from his wife on his left and his daughter on his right, glaring at the lens.[13]

Working as a teamster around the turn of the century would have subjected Sam to the fickle state of industry in America. Seasonal employment and unemployment were common, and as Noel Kent wrote in his book *America in 1900*, "part of the laborers are overworked and have no time for enjoyment and culture, the other part have no work."[14]

Sam Taylor's roughly $700 annual income would have put the family at or near the national poverty level during Bud's childhood,[15] and he likely struggled to pay the rent. From 1900 to 1915, Sam Taylor moved his family to seven different residences, all within about an eight-square-block area of Terre Haute, centered about 10 blocks northeast of downtown.[16]

Tillie Taylor may have handled the ache of poverty with a wave-off; she had grown up as one of seven children of a poor farmer.[17] Sam, about whose early life less is known, no doubt felt the pangs of frustration over the challenges of earning a living for his family.

The streets of the Taylors' neighborhood, such as Tippecanoe and Liberty avenues, were lined with mostly single-family dwellings rented by railroadmen, industrial laborers, bricklayers, motormen, janitors, porters, and their families, about 75 percent Caucasian.[18] Decades later, such occupations afforded workers and their families a comfortable, middle-class existence, but in the urban America of 1900-10, these families lived paycheck to paycheck, with few of life's amenities. These were not the folks whose names appeared in the newspaper's weekly Society Page.

A lack of time, money and transportation would have limited these families' ventures beyond the confines of their section of the city, thus the character of the neighborhood must have exerted tremendous influence on the socialization of its youth. It seems likely that few people, if any, from the Taylors' neighborhood owned any of the 600 automobiles that chugged on the streets of Terre Haute in 1914.[19] Youth organizations existed in the city, such as a growing Boys Club and many Boy Scouts troops, but no evidence exists that young Taylor ever belonged to either.

Instead, little Bud Taylor and the other restless youths ran the streets, and when they engaged in disputes, they settled them in the dirt and cinders of alleys and back lots.

"You had to know how to fight in my neighborhood," Taylor is quoted as saying,[20] and that he lived in an area "where a kid protected his rights with his fists."[21], "Taylor had more street battles than any of the lads in his neighborhood," according to a sportswriter.[22]

Taylor's small stature would have made him a target for older, predatory boys in the area and he may have learned to use his fists out of fear or humiliation. Children often fight to bolster self-esteem, and Bud's may have suffered from shame over being poor, a lack of male role models, or disinterest in school.

Floyd Patterson, heavyweight champion for most of the late 1950s, remembers a poverty-laced upbringing in which his exhausted father, a longshoreman, would come home at night so tired he would fall asleep at the dinner table before he could eat. The family's plight made him feel terrible. Young Floyd's self-esteem was so low he would point to a photograph of himself on a wall in his house and say, "I don't like that boy!"[23]

Likewise, boxing history is filled with examples of great champions whose fondness for fighting begins before they learned their fractions. Joe Frazier became so tough that at a mere age eight, he accepted gifts of sandwiches or money from schoolmates in exchange for Joe's protection from bullies.[24]

Taylor's fisticuffs began at as early an age as Frazier's, and McKeen School's overburdened and underpaid teachers didn't seem to know what to do with him. In one year alone, school officials expelled Taylor 13 times, all for fighting.[25] "Gosh, it was a lonesome day when I didn't have a fight with some other kid," Taylor said in 1925.[26] He could not have learned much in school, except perhaps a geography lesson about respect for boundaries: *Fighting on school property is especially forbidden. You must cross the street before you pop the other kid.*

The extent of Taylor's delinquency apparently ended at fighting. No evidence exists that he ever stole anything, and in his entire adult life he seemed honest and forthright in all financial matters.

Aside from using his fists, Bud mastered one other athletic skill as a boy: roller skating, then a popular pastime for children.[27]

Merely six blocks from his house stood the grand palace for such activity: a former National Guard Armory that had been converted into an 8,000-square-foot rink.[28] The place was a house of thrills for junior speedsters, racing around turns and weaving in and out. The activity suggests an adrenaline rush that approximated a fistfight—and without the resulting bloody nose.

By age 10, Bud had entered the job market, working part time after school and in summers. First, he sold the *Terre Haute Post-Telegram* newspaper on the streets. The job gave him his first lesson that muscle can translate into enterprise: he beat up the other kid sellers to overtake the busiest corners. Later, he delivered messages for Western Union. He also worked as a delivery boy for Max Frank, who owned a downtown shoe repair service and advertised himself cleverly as the "Sole Saver."[29]

The timing of Bud's entrance into the work force corresponded with a family tragedy: the death of older brother, Orville. The 13-year-old fell ill with a stomach problem in November 1913, and underwent surgery. Physicians who operated on him found that gangrene had already set in. They closed the incision, and Orville died soon afterward of what doctors blamed on appendicitis. His playmates then reported that Orville had suffered a kick in the stomach from a bigger boy at school while playing football. County Coroner F.W. Jett opened an investigation, and surgeons confirmed that the wound appeared to have been caused by the kick. The funeral was conducted out of the Taylor home, then at 1612 Locust St.

"On Tuesday, his schoolmates viewed the body and a delegation escorted the funeral to the cemetery, the Taylor boy being popular with his classmates ..." the *Terre Haute Tribune* reported.[30] The document with the coroner's findings is missing from the county archives, but family members apparently accepted the finding that the kick inflicted the injury that caused the death.[31]

Throughout his life, Bud Taylor seldom talked about Orville's death. Bud's son, Bud Jr., did not learn until 43 years after his father's death that his father had a brother. "I am absolutely flabbergasted that nothing was ever said, all these years," Taylor Jr. said in 2005, shortly after being told about his uncle Orville.

Charles Rutz, who was married to Bud Taylor's daughter for more than 40 years, also had no knowledge of the family tragedy.

In thousands of interviews with the press over the course of his life, Taylor is known to have mentioned the death only twice,[32] and then only briefly, perhaps finding the tragedy too difficult to discuss.

It is impossible to gauge the long-term effects of Orville's death on Bud Taylor. He could have carried residual guilt as a result from any number of scenarios surrounding the death, or the effects may have been inconsequential.

What was certain was that at age 10, Bud lost a companion just 2 1/2 years older, the originator of his nickname, a confidante with whom he probably shared a bedroom, ate the same meals and discussed fears and dreams. By age 10, Taylor already had evolved into a street-tough, fighting kid, and the death of a brother so close in age certainly did nothing to soften his view of the world.

In his own life, little Bud Taylor's scuffles continued into adolescence, and gradually, bruise by purple bruise, he emerged from being the bullies' prey to becoming the one nobody messed with. He got tough, and became known for it. "He was the champion of the neighborhood," Taylor's sister, Edith, told a reporter in 1922, "and whenever some girl got the worst of it, or some smaller boy, they always said, 'I will tell Bud Taylor on you' and that settled it."[33]

Chapter 2

A Boxing Past

Prizefighting. The sport has existed for centuries, from its roots among the Greeks and Romans to the popular bare-knuckle contests of the 19th century British Islands.1

By the early 1800s, it had reached the shores of America, for a long-lasting stay. In the 1880s, the weekly publication *National Police Gazette* helped create modern boxing by promoting and popularizing the sport.2 Men such as John L. Sullivan, the first "heavyweight champion of the world," became famous for their prowess with their gloved fists inside the ring.

Still, in 1900, the sport was illegal practically everywhere in the states.

The communities that allowed it—and there were many—did so on the particular preferences of the mayors, police chiefs, prosecutors and others in power.3

Welcomed in some cities, shunned in others, men who tried to make a living out of boxing followed the roads or rode the rails to wherever promoters sought their services. The fighters often were treated like sideshow curiosities, tolerated long enough for the locals to make some money off of and provide a measure of prurient entertainment, then shown the city limits. It was a nomadic, inglorious existence, fraught with the risk of jail time, crippling injury and for little pay.

Fighters of this era were paid by all ways imaginable—if at all—by percent of the paid admissions, by side bets placed by their handlers or themselves, by percent of net receipts, by the contents of a hat passed among spectators ...

As Hall-of-Fame boxer Jack Blackburn put it, "Sometimes you got a guarantee and sometimes you didn't but you didn't have any guarantee that you'd be able to find the promoter after the fight."[4]

Blackburn grew up in Kentucky and Indiana, and in the late 1890s began learning the ring skills he would later teach to fighters such as Bud Taylor, and more famously, Joe Louis, while serving as their trainer.

As an active fighter, Blackburn partook in a series of bouts in Terre Haute in 1902-03 about which published accounts illustrate the unpredictable nature of the business.

Local entrepreneurs staged the three fight cards over four weeks beginning Dec. 16, 1902, setting up a ring in a downtown club. Many of the same boxers performed in all three shows, including 20-year-old Blackburn in two main events against Eddie Gardner of Minneapolis. Newspaper accounts say the first fight card drew 500 spectators, the second 100, the third unknown. Blackburn and Gardner were paid by a percentage of the net receipts, while the fighters in the preliminaries received about $10 each.[5]

A few days after the third fight card, the city's Mayor Henry Steeg ordered the police to break up any more bouts. On Jan. 14, four of the pugilists were all spotted at the same time at the Terre Haute train station, leaving the city.

"You can say that we have been royally treated in Terre Haute, and we are sorry to leave," Gardner said, adding that the fighters hoped to return.[6]

Boxers would, indeed, return to Terre Haute, which became one of the sport's more accommodating outposts. In 1906, a Chicago sportswriter cited Terre Haute and Indianapolis as the two biggest boxing cities in Indiana.[7]

The public always has been particularly fascinated with the heavyweights, those towers of power whose champions could boast of achieving the ultimate in male machismo: toughest man in the world.

Heavyweight champions John L. Sullivan, Bob Fitzsimmons, Jack Johnson and Jack Dempsey each visited Terre Haute along their travels.[8] Most of their visits were for exhibitions; none of them has a fight in the city listed on his boxing record. Fitzsimmons' wacky stay was particularly memorable. The Englishman, world champ 1897 to 1899, came to Terre Haute in February 1905 to appear in a vaudeville production. He brought his wife, child and two pets—a poodle and a lion.9 Not surprisingly, he had trouble finding a room. Innkeepers accustomed to accommodating the occasional tabby or dachshund apparently drew the line at sharp-toothed carnivores. After Fitzsimmons finally settled in, he took the leashed feline with him for a walk downtown. At one point, the lion relieved itself. Fitz responded by kicking it in the ribs. Luckily for Fitzsimmons, the lion did not take exception to his master's method of discipline, but a Humane Society officer did. The officer had been following Bob and beast, and upon seeing the boot, ordered Fitzsimmons to stop. During the ensuing fight, Fitzsimmons at one point grabbed the officer by the coat lapel and "shook him until his teeth rattled."

Police arrived at the scene and arrested the ill-mannered boxer. Fitzsimmons never went to jail, but he did have to appear before the justice of the peace and pay a $1 fine for assault and battery. He apologized for the incident.10

In 1909, as Taylor tangled with his grade-school peers, Marvin Hart came to Terre Haute to fight Mike Schreck. Hart, a Kentuckian who claimed the heavyweight championship in 1905-06, is best known for a 20-round decision over Jack Johnson in 1905. He was past his prime when he fought Schreck on July 29, 1909. Schreck broke Hart's jaw before Marvin's friends stopped the fight in the fourth round.11 When Indiana Gov. T.R. Marshall heard about the fight, he complained, and Terre Haute authorities accordingly issued arrest warrants for 11 of the principals involved in the show, including the two fighters and the promoter. Apparently, the outcome had violated one of the requisites for a legal prizefight in Indiana: that the match run only as an "exhibition," in which athletes merely exhibit their skills.12

Ultimately, the case against the 11 men went to a grand jury. Grand juries are comprised of citizens, not politicians, and this particular panel voted with a message that foretold the future of boxing, not only for Terre Haute but nationwide: they refused to indict.13

Near the end of the decade, the fight game in America gathered momentum. Teddy Roosevelt, president of the United States from 1901 to 1909, counted Sullivan and Fitzsimmons among his personal friends and made no secret of his fondness for the sport.[14] Johnson's title defense against the "Great White Hope," James J. Jeffries, in 1910 in Nevada made headlines across the nation for months in advance. In Terre Haute, 2,000 spectators watched a fight in 1911 between nationally known middleweights Jack Dillon and George Chip.[15] In that same year, the nation's most populous state, New York, legalized boxing matches of 10 rounds.[16]

In 1904, the *Terre Haute Tribune* newspaper had hired an 18-year-veteran sportswriter named Ralph White, who cultivated a keen interest in boxing.[17] By the middle of the 1910's, White had begun supplying the readers with tidbits about prizefighting in the community, even venturing so far in his daily column as to inform his readers the status of permissiveness—or as White put it, when "the lid" was "on" or "off" in the city.[18]

Under the Terre Haute mayoral administrations of Louis Gerhardt (1910-1914) followed by Donn Roberts, boxing flourished. The lid was not only "off," it seemed to have been discarded entirely, and at least three men in the city actively promoted fights. Promoters Jack Tierney, George Grammell and Charles Johnson were ex-fighters who held other jobs in the community but remained huge boxing fans and organized fight cards on the side for extra cash.[19] These part-time promoters not only mined the local talent, they tried to entice the big-timers; in December 1913, Grammell was sending out wires trying to return Chip and Dillon to Terre Haute for a rematch.[20]

In a sensational scandal, unrelated to boxing, the city's Mayor Roberts was convicted in 1915 of conspiring to fix the county's 1914 election. He had wanted a certain judge elected and sent his cronies around to ensure victory. One of their recruits testified he was allowed to vote 22 times. A federal judge sent Roberts to prison in Leavenworth, Kansas,[21] and the succeeding Terre Haute city administration stifled boxing.[22] Grammell and Tierney tempered their efforts to promote the sport and Charles Johnson moved to Youngstown, Ohio, to promote fights.[23]

The lid, however, would not stay on long.

When Jack Dempsey fought Jess Willard for the heavyweight championship on July 14, 1919 in Toledo, Ohio, for a million dollar purse, it ushered in what Paul Gallico, sports editor of the *New York*

Daily News, called the "Golden Age of Sports."[24] In the decade that followed, participant and spectator interest in boxing soared, thousands of young men made a living in the game and the most talented fighters found wealth. But the game didn't just magically take wing as if directed by the wand of some grand god of pugilism. It owed its surge to World War I.

On April 6, 1917, the United States declared war on Germany, and the ranks of the military branches swelled. Before the raw recruits were shipped across the ocean for the trenches, however, the boys of the Stars and Stripes needed bayonet training. Since young men cannot joust with such weapons without carving up one another, military officials sought alternative methods of training. The head of the War Department's commission on training camp activities, Joseph E. Raycroft, endorsed the teaching of boxing to the troops as the solution. Military officials became convinced that the skills required by boxing best simulated bayonet fighting, and that the conditioning and training involved in the fistic game also built endurance and discipline in the troops.[25]

To teach the GI's, dozens of well-established boxing professionals from around the nation volunteered their services, such as Willie Ritchie, Johnny Kilbane, Joe Welling, Mike Gibbons and the world lightweight champion, Benny Leonard.[26] By the time the war ended on Nov. 11, 1918, the War Department estimated that *3 million* GI's had received instruction in boxing.[27]

"A lot of tough kids were coming out of the service," says boxing writer Bert Sugar. "You had people like Benny Leonard teaching kids to fight. 'The war's over, what the hell are we gonna do with this skill'? So you had a ready-made group of fighters."[28]

When these 17- to 22-year-olds returned to their hometowns, jobless, and into a booming post-war spectator market for sports entertainment, the enterprising Mr. Boxing Promoter approached and said, "Let's talk." Boxing presented itself as a viable career choice.

In January, 1919, the Knights of Columbus, a national organization that promotes Catholic education and charity, began organizing one of the biggest boxing tournaments in the world in Paris, France, for the entertainment of the U.S. troops remaining overseas.[29]

In a statement that held significant implications for boxing in Terre Haute, the national K of C's overseas activities director announced: "The Knights of Columbus is strongly in favor of boxing, professional or amateur, if conducted under proper regulation, and it is to be hoped that before long laws will be passed permitting the sport in every state in the union."[30]

The K of C boasted a strong membership in Terre Haute. Its headquarters sat downtown since about 1905 in a converted home/office building formerly owned by a construction company.[31] By 1919, the main attraction of the two-story brick structure at 828 Ohio St., was its upstairs gym/auditorium, which the Knights donated or rented out for basketball, indoor baseball, dances and other uses. "It was originally a ballroom," said Dave Winters, who in 2005 was chairman of the K of C's club committee. "Some people convinced the Knights they had a need for a kids' area, and so they remodeled it as a gym."

The K of C gym had served as the site of a few boxing cards in the years before World War I, and with the sport's newfound popularity, the promoters in 1919 began inquiring about its availability.[32] Four of the seven professional fight cards put on in Terre Haute in 1919 were staged in the K of C's upstairs gym.[33]

When Bud Perrill of Terre Haute fought Don Curley of Indianapolis on March 27, 1919, the 1,800 seats of the K of C auditorium were filled and 200 additional patrons watched while standing.[34] Boxing had begun its postwar growth spurt, and capacity crowds at the fights soon became commonplace across America. In Terre Haute, boxing in 1919 even became a mandatory part of the instructional curriculum at Rose Polytechnic Institute, an engineering college at 13th Street and Eighth Avenue (later relocated and renamed Rose-Hulman Institute of Technology).[35] Statewide, legislators proposed making the sport legal in a boxing bill before the Indiana House, although the attempt failed.[36] Nationally, a 23-year-old Dempsey, scheduled for his summer date with Willard for the heavyweight championship, was cashing in on his popularity by touring the nation fighting exhibitions. Dempsey would make Terre Haute one of his stops in April.[37]

Dempsey, who would knock out Willard and hold boxing's top spot until 1926, was to boxing what Babe Ruth was to baseball. John

L. Sullivan paved the runway for boxing's takeoff a generation earlier, and Dempsey piloted it into the sky. The blustery Sullivan, unchallenged in his day, had people talking boxing in taverns, billiard halls and cigar stores. Dempsey's popularity put that talk into the soda fountains and bakeries and across the dining-room tables of America. A ferocious bull inside the ring and a modest Everyman out, he became an American idol and a household name. Men respected him because of his work ethic and his climb from poverty; women were drawn to him by his rugged, movie-star features, wavy hair and quiet charm.

In the spring of 1919, Dempsey was the No. 1 contender for Willard's title as they prepared for their championship bout, and Jack would have been content to train in seclusion.[38] His manager, Jack Kearns, induced him instead to take a monthlong tour of cities, to box exhibitions.[39] A show in Terre Haute's Grand Opera House on April 19, 1919, served as the 15th stop on the tour.[40]

Dempsey had a standing offer of $1,000 for any man along the stops who could last four rounds with him. If no one challenged, his show consisted of Dempsey boxing a few exhibition rounds with the heavyweights traveling in his entourage.[41] In the first 12 days of the tour, 12 challengers stepped forward to go for the thousand bucks. All either fell, or, more wisely, quit before being felled.[42] Three days before the Terre Haute show, Dempsey flattened two comers in one appearance in Columbus, Ohio.[37] An article in a Terre Haute newspaper mentioned the feat in Ohio, which probably dissuaded any locals tinkering with the idea of impressing their girlfriends.[43] The newspaper accounts do not mention if the offer came up inside Terre Haute's Grand theater. If it did, silence must have followed.[44]

The heavyweights of boxing always have been the sport's most financially successful. But as the game gained popularity after World War I, the wealth spread to the lighter fellows. Benny Leonard, who boxed in the 135-pound "lightweight" division, earned $200,000 in 1919.[45] The money and fame associated with the sport began to attract more men of small stature, with dreams fueled by published reports of the financial successes of fighters such as Leonard.

One of these men was Clifford "Bud" Perrill, who would later influence Taylor's decision to enter the fight game. Perrill, who had served as an infantryman in the Army, needed a job after he returned to his hometown of Terre Haute from France in March 1919.46 He had excelled in boxing at Camp Shelby, Mississippi, winning the lightweight championship of the 38th Division and later was champion of his regiment.47 He had arrived at Camp Shelby with the advantage of having partaken in a dozen or so small-time professional fights as early as 1914.48

Born in 1897, Perrill had grown up on Terre Haute's far east side. Like Taylor, Perrill had an emblazoned reputation around the city as a tough street fighter. "I think he actually took up boxing to help his parents, moneywise," said his daughter, Jane Mauk.49 Those parents, Adolphus and Catherine Perrill, struggled to raise 13 children on a steelworker's wages. By 18, Perrill had progressed to pro boxing preliminaries, picking up five bucks here and 10 there to help his father support the home.50

Returning from the war, Perrill took a job in a factory and began boxing part time, and usually won. To make the kind of money as a Benny Leonard, a fighter had to ascend beyond regional success and draw national attention. Based on the typical amounts paid to fighters in 1920-21, Perrill earned between $50 and $300 for main-event bouts in Terre Haute and around the Midwest, and seldom fought farther from home. Nonetheless, boxing was a lucrative part-time job for men of Perrill's means. At the time, a coal miner earned $873 a year, about the same as a public school teacher, and Perrill's part-time job in a factory paid about 40 cents an hour.51

Perrill and Taylor became friends, and Perrill offered 16-year-old Bud a suggestion: Try boxing.52

By this time, Taylor had been disciplined so many times for fighting his schoolmates that he had been expelled permanently from public school.53 He had enrolled in Terre Haute Vocational School, a three-year program of about 150 boys in training to become journeymen mechanics, carpenters, electricians and other tradesmen.54 Taylor also was working part time in the steel stamping mill at Columbia Enameling as a machinist's apprentice.55

In early January 1920, Taylor was blazing circles around the skating rink one evening when a 22-year-old local pro boxer that he knew named Leo Roberts approached and asked him if he wanted to fight. Taylor, thinking Roberts meant duking it out with boys from a rival neighborhood, replied, "Sure, sure! Where are they?"

"No, not here," Roberts said. "I mean do you want to box in the ring about two weeks from now?"

"Why not?" was Taylor's comeback.[56]

Despite his mother's disapproval, Taylor began training to become a boxer. Lest she badger him about it at home, he chose carefully when and where he trained. He worked out downtown in the YMCA and enlisted help from a friend, Leo Light, in hiding his aspirations.[57]

"Leo Light's father owned a saloon, and they had a room up above the bar, where he snuck up there and trained," Bud Taylor Jr. said in 2005.[58]

"We all tried to persuade him not to train at first," Bud's sister, Edith, told a reporter 1922, speaking on behalf of her parents. "In fact, we felt dreadful because he was so set on making a boxer out of himself ..."[59]

Charles "Bud" Taylor in his mid-teens.

Chapter 3

It Wasn't Me, Mom

Charles E. Johnson loved boxing, and stayed close to the fight game although fate seemed to direct him elsewhere. He had been a lousy fighter, a puny stick figure of a fellow who wisely hung up the gloves while he still had his molars.[1] Then he became a manager of fighters in Terre Haute and suffered the misfortune of watching one of them die in the ring. The victim, "Greek" Jimmy Ryan (John Pappakeriazes), fractured his skull falling into a metal ring post in 1909 in Savannah, Ga.[2] Johnson eventually turned to promoting fights, where he found success. He was about 30 years old when he left Terre Haute in 1915, after the city administration changed and the sport fell out of bureaucratic favor. He moved to Youngstown, Ohio, where he made some money organizing fights.[3]

After World War I, Johnson hoped to extend that good luck in a return to Terre Haute.[4] The city had a customer base built for boxing that Johnson hoped to harvest, with its thousands of railroadmen, miners and manufacturing workers. In their weekly escapes to the bleachers, they could act out their contempt for the long hours and shoddy working conditions of their daily routines vicariously by screaming for their local heroes to pound the opponent into submission. Johnson secured the K of C as a venue and put on shows in October and December 1919.[5] He priced seats at $2 floor and $1, balcony.[6] When the second show, Dec. 2, 1919, drew only 800 fans, and most of them in the buck balcony seats, the disappointed promoter blamed the low turnout on a miners' strike.[7] Johnson also had erred by not signing a quality Terre Haute-area fighter to headline the card. Instead, he had relied on two out-of-towners with little local fan support. For a third show, in January 1920, he signed popular Bud Perrill to fight Tommy Teague of Muncie, Indiana in the main event, and then set off to line up his three preliminary bouts.

For the opener, Johnson secured the services of Davy Templeton, 21, of nearby Linton, Indiana, for a flyweight (112-pound limit) bout. Johnson decided to test the skinny kid from the skating rink as Templeton's opponent—Bud Taylor.

At the Taylor household, Sam Taylor had warmed to the idea of allowing his son to box, but Tillie stayed firmly opposed.[8] In newspaper previews that appeared in the days preceding the K of C boxing card in January 1920, one story lists Bud as "Bob Taylor," another "Bob Martin."[9] It seems likely that Johnson intentionally misidentified Taylor to the press to keep Tillie Taylor from finding out.

Shortly before the 8:30 p.m. opening bell on Jan. 26, a gangly, 16-year-old blond climbed up to the ring in the K of C. His long arms lacked muscle definition and at a string-bean 106 pounds, he would have eased through the ropes with the clearance of a cat through a rail fence.[10] He was announced as "Bud Taylor," then turned any smirking faces into smiles by winning his debut as a professional fighter. The published accounts of the four-rounder merited only a few lines in the next day's city *Tribune* and *Star* newspapers;[11] sportswriters seldom devoted much space to four-round preliminary fights. Taylor never forgot what he got paid: $3. To train for the fight, he had spent $7 for liniment and rubdowns, so the fight had cost him money. Taylor had not known his pay beforehand, since he had been too shy to ask.[12]

On the morning after the fight, Tillie Taylor picked up the newspaper and saw her son's name as the winner of a boxing match. She called Bud over and showed him the article. Bud denied it, and told her it wasn't he, but his cousin, George "Bunny" Taylor, who had fought under the name "Bud." Tillie believed the fib until the next day, when an insurance salesman rapped on the Taylors' door. Bud opened it, and the insurance man immediately recognized Taylor from the fights. The peddler peppered Bud with praise, thinking it might help him sell Bud's father a policy. "That sure was a great battle you fought, Bud," the caller said. Bud tried to signal him to stay quiet, to no avail.13

Just one night after the card that introduced Bud Taylor to pro boxing, a four-bout boxing card played in the Grand Opera House in downtown Terre Haute, organized by a different promoter.14 Nationwide, the sport of boxing had entered a phase during which the public couldn't seem to get enough. Johnson landed a pair of heavyweights to highlight his fourth show, which ran Feb. 16, 1920. Taylor fought in the first preliminary, three bouts ahead of a headliner of prominence: Sam Langford. Langford is appreciated by boxing experts as one of the all-time greats. He had started boxing in 1902 at a much lighter weight, and grew into the heavyweight ranks through the years. Langford had defeated such notable fighters as Joe Gans, Peter Jackson, Stanley Ketchel and Jack O'Brien. He never landed a title shot with Jack Johnson or Jack Dempsey, despite his efforts.15

In the K of C, Charles Johnson paired Langford with Jeff Clark in what one sportswriter estimated was the 11th career bout between the two black men.16 In the decades ahead, blacks would come to dominate boxing in numbers of participants and champions, but the segregated 1920s gave no such hint. (Taylor fought 119 pro contests over 7 1/2 years before he ever opposed a black man.) In the '20s, boxing's white promoters seldom matched a black fighter against a white one, meaning that a black fraternity, of sorts, developed in which talented fighters such as Langford, Clark, Harry Wills, Joe Jeanette and Sam McVey were relegated to fighting one another repeatedly in venues across the nation. Prejudice, of course, figured into the promoters' matchmaking choices.

"There was a whole thesis on that," says Bert Sugar, boxing Hall of Fame journalist. "When a black man fought a white man inside the ring in those days, no matter *who* wins, they were equals. In 1920, it wasn't what [white establishment] wanted. And when you look at Indiana ... Indiana had the largest Ku Klux Klan of any state."17 When Terre Haute established a city boxing commission in 1924, it specifically forbade "mixed" bouts.18 It wasn't that the city was a hotbed for bigotry. The segregated condition of boxing merely reflected the attitude of 1920s white society all across the nation.

Indiana law required black children to attend separate schools. The state also did not permit interracial marriages.[19] In Terre Haute, people of color who wanted to swim publicly had to do so in their own, segregated public pool;[20] and in the K of C as in fight arenas across America, blacks were seated together in segregated sections. Black men who wanted a spot on a fight card often had to settle for the "battle royal." The battle royal consisted of a match with four or five black men in the same ring simultaneously, usually blindfolded. At the bell, they were turned loose to wail at one another until the last one standing "won" the match, to the amusement of the audiences. In the 1920s in the Terre Haute area, there are at least 15 published accounts or indications of battle royals; promoters often opened their evening's card with one.[21]

Taylor had been matched against Paul Sheehan for a four-round preliminary Feb. 16 on the Langford card.[22] Instead of Sheehan, however, Taylor found himself staring across the ring at Everett "Jack" Shepherd of West Terre Haute, a late substitute. The stand-in, apparently the only guy whose services Johnson could enlist on short notice, weighed 128, Taylor later recalled. Bud weighed 106.

"He knocked me down so hard twice that I saw stars—dozens of them. They didn't float by me, either, they whizzed," Taylor said, recalling the bout five years later. Good judgment dictated staying down after the second knockdown, but ego insisted otherwise. Taylor not only rose, he attacked the bigger guy, and knocked Shepherd down. Shepherd, too, managed to regain his feet to continue the brawl, but he walked into a windmill. "I wailed away and hit him square in the back ..." Taylor recalled, Shepherd decided he wanted no more from the wild kid and "... walked to his corner begging to be excused," according to the *Terre Haute Tribune's* brief account.[23] Taylor was ruled the winner by technical knockout, or "TKO," the term used when the referee stops a bout prematurely.

The fan turnout for Feb. 16, 1920, had proven the best of the four shows Charles Johnson staged over the winter of 1919-1920 and he immediately announced plans for a fifth show.[24] Johnson followed the practice of paying paltry sums to his fighters in the prelims so he could afford to dish out the far better money to the main event-ers. Taylor, consequently, made $5 for his second fight and would be paid similarly for the third.25 Taylor kept his day job at the Columbia Enameling stamping mill and trained during evenings.26

In the previews for his third bout, on Johnson's March 15, 1920, card, the local scribes began to hype Taylor. The *Tribune* showed his photo and noted that he has "flashed a lot of natural ability, and is probably the most promising youngster in our midst in recent years."27 The *Star's* writer opined that Taylor "had exceptional promise."28 These reporters hardly were prophets; they wrote similarly about Terre Haute boxers such as Johnny Lucas, Billy Long, Larry Mahaney and a host of others of the 1920s who failed to advance beyond local fame.29 Ralph White of the *Tribune*, in particular, unashamedly promoted the fighters and their bouts instead of writing objectively. White operated under the apparent premise that since the fights sold newspapers, he must sell the fighters. But as the months passed and the body count at Taylor's feet rose, the blond guy's name alone did the selling.

In the main event on March 15, lightweights Tommy Teague of Muncie and Clint Flynn of Chicago squared off in Terre Haute before a meager 500 fans.30 The lesson had been reinforced to Johnson that if he wanted the turnstyles to click, he needed strong local talent in the main event. Taylor won his preliminary over Walter Gering by fourth-round TKO.31

Taylor landed his first road bout in April in Dugger, Indiana, about 35 miles south of Terre Haute, but he pulled out after he injured his finger in an accident in the stamping mill. Organizers found a replacement for Bud and the card drew an attendance of 400 in the mining town of 1,800.32 Taylor also underwent surgery for an unspecified problem with his nose. The *Tribune* ran a short piece about his recovery and that this boxer of "exceptional merit" would miss Johnson's boxing show May 11 at the K of C.33

In late-May, Taylor traveled 100 miles northeast to Muncie to fight Jack Edwards of Marion, Indiana. Taylor dominated with his right-hand punch, his favorite, and the referee stopped the fight in the second round to save Edwards from further punishment.34 The only "knockout" on the four-bout card in Campbell's Auditorium came from among the spectators, when boxer Don Mullen's wife fainted and had to be carried from the premises.35 Edwards, 19, went on to a so-so career of 30 or so fights, then became one of the most memorable political figures in Marion's history as a two-term mayor, a judge, and finally, in his eighties, a city councilman.[36]

The date of the Taylor-Edwards fight, May 24, 1920, stands as a landmark date for the status of boxing nationwide. New York Gov. Al Smith signed into law the Walker bill, strengthening the boxing laws in the most populous state in the nation. New York would have a three-member commission to supervise the sport under specific rules. Fifteen-round matches would be allowed, with two judges deciding the winner, (and with the referee deciding, in case of disagreement).[37]

The new law meant boxers and their fans would have the luxury of an official decision attached to every professional fight in New York. In most states in which boxing was illegal, including Indiana, a match that went the distance simply ended with no winner announced, thus the term "no decision." That meant no acknowledgment of a victor, even in one-sided contests. Fans that didn't attend but wanted to know who won these fights of the bygone days had to read the next-day's newspaper account for their favorite sportswriter's call. The writers, however, often differed widely in their opinions. Gamblers also relied on the papers to settle their bets, so a reporter's opinion could not always be trusted as being accurate. Sportswriters, who often earned minuscule salaries, might be on the take. The writers also tended to spin their stories to favor the hometown combatant out of a sense of community duty or more likely, in the interest in selling more papers.

With the sport's blast-off in New York, boxing enthusiasts in other states tried to legalize the sport, mostly without success. A bill in Indiana early in 1921 died by a close vote and states such as Wyoming, Kansas, Texas and Illinois either failed to act on, or rejected, bills to legalize boxing in 1920-21.[38] Because of the demand for the sport, city officials often took it upon themselves to circumvent state law. Cleveland, Ohio, and the Twin Cities in Minnesota, for example, enacted ordinances either licensing the staging of fights or setting up boxing commissions to oversee them.[39]

In Terre Haute, the county's prosecuting attorney in 1920, Noble Johnson, advised the local pugilistic circle that while Indiana law outlawed prize fighting, it did not distinguish between "prize fighting" and "boxing." He stated publicly that he believed that two men who were paid depending on the *outcome* of the fight constituted prize fighting—they fought for the prize, thus, the contest was illegal. For example, a promoter was forbidden to offer a pre-fight guarantee of $50 to the *winner* and $10 to the *loser*. But a bout between two men to fight for a stipulated amount of money, whether from prenegotiated guarantees or from percentage of the gate, did not constitute a prize fight, thus was legal.[40]

Figuratively, Prosecutor Johnson's endorsement clanged like the timekeeper's bell that ushers in an evening's slate of fights, signaling the all-clear for the sport to flourish in Terre Haute.

Chapter 4

Use of Leverage

Bud Taylor's TKO victory over Jackie Edwards marked the first bout in a four-month stretch during which Taylor fought five times in venues around Indiana. Taylor got away with fighting professionally at age 16 because the sport in most places was illegal, with no oversight, thus, no rules. In boxing jurisdictions with age limits, 18 generally was the minimum. If asked his age, Taylor simply lied.1 Sportswriters seldom reported the ages of boxers.

Taylor began his jaunt across Indiana by KO'ing Davy Templeton in a four-round rematch in Vincennes, Indiana, 50 miles south of Terre Haute. Taylor picked up 25 bucks for the effort.2 He scored a KO in Clinton and followed it two weeks later with a TKO in Muncie before an audience of 400, crammed into a tiny arena at $1 a head.3 He fought two semifinals in Vincennes, where he was billed in promotions as "the Fighting Fly."4 Promoter Charles Johnson, serving as Taylor's manager, probably conjured the nickname.

The nickname referred to Taylor's weight division, flyweight, (112 pounds maximum), the lightest of the principal boxing divisions in the 1920s. In boxing, the combatants are required to fight at like weights to eliminate the obvious advantage in punching power that a heavier man carries over his opponent. The heavyweights are the only class with no weight limit; therefore one boxer could tip the scales at 280 pounds, for example, with the other at 210. Otherwise, in the light-heavyweights, the limit in 1921 was 175 pounds; middleweights, 160; welterweights, 145; lightweights 135; featherweights 125; and bantamweights 118.5 The weight classifications would break into many more divisions as the decades passed, such as junior lightweight (130-pound limit), and junior middleweight (154 pounds), but for most of the 1920s, only the aforementioned basic classes were recognized.

Boxers are required to make the weight limit at an official "weigh-in" ceremony, usually on the day of a fight. Fighters typically weigh right at, or a pound or two below, the designated limit to take full advantage of the strength associated with being at maximum weight. Boxing promoters required that boxers post "forfeit" money in advance, to protect the promoter financially if one fighter does not make the weight and the bout must be canceled. If one fighter weighed over the weight limit designated for the bout, his opponent typically had the option of pulling out of the contest.

October 1920 stood as a great month to be a spectator in Terre Haute, not only for boxing, but for national politics.

In a span of one week, three of the four principals in the presidential election of 1920 campaigned in Terre Haute. New York Sen. Franklin D. Roosevelt (Democrat for vice president), Ohio Gov. James M. Cox (Democrat for president) and Ohio Sen. Warren G. Harding (Republican for president), visited the city on separate stops. Cox far outdrew the two future presidents when he spoke Oct. 9 before 25,000 spectators at the Vigo County Courthouse.6 Vigo County and the nation, however, would choose Harding to serve.

Five days earlier, Taylor fought his first main event, a 10-rounder in the K of C for which he would earn $50 against Artie Armstrong of Cincinnati.7 Armstrong had 11 years of ring experience, but he decided early in the bout to cover rather than trade punches with Taylor.8 He wanted no part of Bud's wallop and offered very little in offense, content to hunch and block while Taylor teed off with his right.9 The *Terre Haute Star* newspaper's Olin McAfee, one of the more objective of the Terre Haute writers, scored the bout 8-2, Taylor.10

Taylor already had forged the fighting style he would employ unwaveringly throughout his career, that of the stalker, always willing to take a punch for the opportunity to throw one. To him, a fight was a fight, a bloodletting exchange of blows until one man dropped, and nothing resembling a minuet or a fencing match. Throughout his career, Taylor often complained about opponents who avoided mixing it up, the ones who tried to win the bout tactically.

Although he weighed 106 to 112 pounds in his first year of pro boxing, Taylor stood 5 feet, 6-and-a-half inches tall—taller than nearly every opponent in his career, and his reach measured an impressive 68 inches.[11] Observers found him odd-looking, so lean and long, with blond hair and light skin, like some Scandinavian adolescent pushed into the ring as a joke.[12] Then the bell would ring and Taylor would stun those same onlookers with his viciousness.

"Bud Taylor is a freak," Los Angeles sportswriter Ed Frayne later would write. "He has the bones of a featherweight and the build of a lightweight. But he only weighs 118 pounds."[13]

Taylor moved with extraordinary quickness and flexibility, and in his wiry build he tapped the same power source as Bob Fitzsimmons, the lanky heavyweight champion of the 1890s.

"Leverage," accounts for that power, says boxing writer Bert Sugar. "The same as [baseball power hitters] Roy Campanella or Harmon Killebrew, it was how much they can get into their hips. Sometimes, power comes off speed. Guys like [boxing champions] Sandy Saddler, Bobby Foster were able to propel themselves and crack their punches, and a lot of it came off of leverage. I would put you the same with Bud Taylor."

Taylor's punching power would serve as the great equalizer on the many occasions in which his opponent outweighed him.

On Nov. 1, 1920, Jimmy Burns of Indianapolis scaled 114 to Taylor's 108 for their scheduled 10-rounder in the K of C.[14] To the public, six pounds may not seem like a significant difference in weight, but to fighters, especially in the lighter weights, the difference is substantial. Burns brimmed with confidence and on the morning of the fight jabbered to a reporter, "Taylor will be a sadder and wiser boy when I get through with him …"[15] Taylor, bashful around reporters early in his career, seldom contributed to the pre-fight hype with comment. He may have been simmering under the surface, because he administered a severe beating to Burns over nine rounds. He toppled him twice in the ninth before Burns' seconds surrendered their man by tossing a sponge into the ring.[16] Taylor earned

$50 for the massacre and Burns probably near the same, although Burns had to forfeit his $20 weight-guarantee money for scaling two pounds over the weight limit.17

In the first week of November, election stories saturated the newspapers across Ohio, the home state for opposing presidential candidates Harding and Cox. Buried in the *Cincinnati Enquirer* sports pages was the mention of an upcoming six-round boxing match Nov. 8 between Tom "Whitey" Murette of Columbus and his Indiana opponent, mistakenly referred to as "Fred Taylor."18

In the third round, Murette caught Bud with a right cross that knocked him over the ropes and out of the ring. Ringsiders caught Taylor and tossed him back in for their man Whitey to finish the job. Taylor, however, rallied and eventually floored Murette for a 7-count—in the same round. Taylor won every round thence. By the time Bud left the city, members of the press were citing his name correctly.19

As the Midwestern breezes shook the leaves from the sycamores and ushered in a change of seasons, Charles Johnson encountered a change of his own as he lined up boxing matches for the winter. Terre Haute's main boxing promoter now was referred to as "Tex" Johnson, after nationally known boxing promoter "Tex" Rickard. Taylor fought in all four of Johnson's cards in the winter of 1920-21, 10-rounders that filled the K of C. He won them all, including a rematch with Murette on Dec. 13. The fight lasted the full 10 rounds, "a long, sizzling journey," wrote one writer, and from which Taylor gained the local newspaper decisions.20

"It was one of those rare bouts that caused the adherents of the sport to go crazy. I have heard some long and loud rooting at other ring shows, but last night's vocal efforts took the cake," Ralph White wrote. When ring announcer "Cy" Pfirman announced Taylor's next opponent, Frankie Mason, one of America's best flyweights, the cheers were long and loud.21

Taylormania in Terre Haute had begun.

Chapter 5

Banks of the Wabash

As 1920 ended, undefeated boxer Bud Taylor's contingent of followers had swelled to encompass members of the community from all walks of life. A generation earlier, boxing had been the fancy of the working class. The more prominent citizens stayed away, finding the fights at best a mild embarrassment and worst, a crude form of entertainment unsuitable for a "proper" person. By the '20s, boxing had gained the kind of social acceptance that brought business owners, men of profession, politicians and women to the arenas in greater numbers.

As for Terre Haute, its people always had rallied around their own kind. In the earliest days of the community, its settlers needed one another just to survive.

Terre Haute (rhymes with "wear a coat,") in Vigo (Vee go) County exists because of the Wabash River, the chief mode of transportation through the area for the explorers and fur traders of the 18th century. The French had encamped on the Wabash as early as the 1600s and referred to land near where the city would grow as "*la terre haute*."[1] The phrase referred to the high bluffs the French noticed when they paddled by the area's river banks. The American infantry built Fort Harrison on this *terre haute*, or "high ground" in 1811[2] to defend against Indians. Settlers soon followed. Many of them were American-born adventurers originating from New York, up from Kentucky or, as with Taylor's maternal grandparents, Andrew and Margaret Taylor, over from Ohio.[3] They mostly were a rugged lot challenged by Indians and malaria but determined to forge a living by farming or trading on the broad, fertile plain near the fort.

By 1835, the community had 1,200 residents, weekly mail and more than 50 buildings.4

By 1890, 30,000 people called Terre Haute their home, and the industrial revolution had begun to transform the riverside city into a boom town.5 The area's rich coal deposits, strong railroad center and wealth of manufacturing swelled the population to 60,000 by 1903 and 75,000 by 1915.6 Wealthy benefactors such as Chauncey Rose (1794-1877) and the Hulman family beginning with Herman Hulman (1831-1922) poured hundreds of thousands of dollars into hospitals, colleges and churches.7

In 1920, the city smelled of factories, rumbled with street cars and teemed with pedestrian traffic downtown. Off the main roads, the character of its people shown in its neighborhood gatherings, musical programs in its parks and company picnics.8 The city's Collett Park, for example, routinely drew thousands for community gatherings organized by churches and featuring orchestra music and speeches by civic leaders.9

That type of community spirit owed itself in part, to the times. Urbanites interacted more than their grandchildren of half a century later and beyond. Jobs in the 1920s were less mechanized and citizens relied on one another at work, and in leisure. A visit from a neighbor or a family get-together was more a welcome event in the age before television, Internet and central air conditioning.

When a resident named Guy Jackson, for example, hosted a barbecue in the summer of 1921 for residents of Kent Avenue, the event attracted hundreds.10 Jackson, 31, had grown up in Terre Haute and in 1920 worked as a butcher. Jackson was an avid sports fan, and could be seen ringside watching Bud Taylor.11

Not surprisingly, the community backed its sports stars with verve. They loved their own Terre Haute Tots, the minor-league baseball team. In Bud Taylor, a product of their own city, they felt a special attachment. First, Taylor looked like the common guy. His slight build resembled the banker, street car conductor or hotel bellhop more than a professional athlete. The city's attraction to Taylor also owed itself to the underdog factor: he had grown up poor and worked hard to succeed. Perhaps most importantly, Taylor was a native

Hautean. Not until 60 years later would the community's excitement over a sports star reach as giddy, when Larry Bird brought his amazing basketball act to Indiana State University. While Bird's accomplishments roused the sports-minded, it touched Hauteans only superficially. Bird had been reared in French Lick, a town a hundred miles south; Taylor, however, was *theirs*. His successes were Terre Haute successes.

Terre Haute also served as the hometown for Eugene V. Debs (1855-1926), activist, labor leader, social critic, supporter of women's rights and racial equality, and a catalyst for change who gained national attention with his efforts helping unions to organize. Debs' tenacity, individualism and strength of character emboldened the community with the kind of can-do attitude that leads to extraordinary feats.

Grace Evans, a Debs supporter, provides an example. In 1918, the Terre Haute woman showed up at the city's Indiana Theater with a ticket entitling her to a main-floor seat for a vaudeville show. The problem was that Evans was black, and blacks were allowed only in the theater's balcony—it had always been that way. Evans refused an offer by theater management to refund her money; she insisted she be allowed the seat for which she showed a ticket. When management would not budge, she left. Then she took an even more brazen step for a black woman of the times: she filed suit in a Vigo County court against the theater for racial discrimination.[12]

Evans lost the case, of course—the jury took just 30 minutes to decide—but the woman's effort to challenge racial injustice nearly a half century before the peak of the American civil rights movement underscores an uncommon courage among the Terre Haute populace.[13]

Perhaps it is a stretch to suggest that Debs' accomplishments kindled the type of ambition that leads to success in athletics, but Bud Taylor was not the only 1920s sports superstar reared in Vigo County. Art Nehf pitched a shutout against the Babe Ruth-led Yankees in the final game of the 1921 World Series; and bicyclist Clarence Wagner set world record times pedaling coast to coast in 1927, and from Canada to Mexico.[14] In Terre Haute, dreams sprouted wings.

In 1920, Frankie Mason was a boxing name associated with the big time, and known nationwide. Mason fought 42 pro bouts in 1919, or about one every nine days. It was astounding frequency, even for the times, when the busiest boxers answered the bell about twice a month. (Taylor averaged 17 fights a year in his first five years, a higher-than-average number for a pro.) Mason hailed from Fort Wayne, Indiana, but his real home consisted of the passenger cars along the C&E, Pennsylvania and New York Central railroads and hotel rooms of Springfield, Illinois; Lima, Ohio; Battle Creek, Michigan; and other cities and towns of his flyweight encounters.[15]

Mason had kept up the breakneck pace of bouts since 1910, and when his train rolled into Terre Haute in 1921, he was 30 years old. While most fighters in the lighter weight classes gain weight with age and move up in weight divisions, Mason stayed a flyweight. He usually weighed about 108 pounds.[16]

Mason carried the informal title of "American flyweight champion." He had fought the acknowledged world champion, Jimmy Wilde of Britain, in March 1920 in Toledo, Ohio. Mason lost, but the fight drew 39,000 fans and Frankie collected a check for $5,000.[17] The pay amounted to enough money in those days to help Mason retire to a quiet life in the country, which he often talked about.[18] But he couldn't stay away from the ring.

Mason was meticulous about his appearance, and in training wore protective devices to keep from being struck in the face and head.[19] It was written that his seconds avoided fanning him between rounds so they wouldn't spoil the part in his hair.[20]

A smitten newspaperwoman named Louise Fritz, covering a Mason bout in 1919, actually wrote in her story in the *South Bend News-Times* that she was glad he won "because I think Frankie is cute."[21] Mason read the article, marched into the *News-Times* offices and introduced himself to her. The couple married the following year.[22]

In the ring, Mason boxed patiently, specializing in the left jab and expert defense.

For Taylor, Mason represented his first opponent with a bona fide national reputation in the sport. Taylor's won-loss mark had reached 14-0, but his victims had ranged from nobodies to those with only a modest measure of success in the Midwest. Tex Johnson, hearing the talk around Terre Haute's Nash's and Puff's cigar stores and in the gyms, found local fans as worried about the fight as excited.23 Old Jack Tierney, at various times a boxer, promoter and gym owner in Terre Haute since roughly the turn of the century, didn't think Taylor had a chance against Mason. Boxing fan Ed Baker, one of the city's best bowlers, also thought Taylor would lose.24 For Johnson, the matchup was a gamble. As promoter for the card, his mouth watered at the prospect of a huge turnout. But as Taylor's manager, he certainly didn't want to rush him into a career-stalling defeat.

In a warm-up for Mason, Taylor won every round of a 10-rounder in the K of C on New Year's Day 1921 against Bobby Moon of Gary, Indiana.25 Taylor's growing constituency sold the place out for the Moon fight.26

Taylor enlisted the help of an Indianapolis boxer, Don Curley, who had once served as Mason's sparring partner. Curley trained with Bud to help him learn the nuances of Mason's style.27

Mason had been advised about Taylor's dangerous right-hand punch. "I'll probably polish him off in four or five rounds," he said two days before the fight. "He won't even touch me with that supposed crack right hand of his."

"One thing for sure," Taylor said, "I'm going after him from the first bell and I'll stop him in one round if I can …"28

The fight on Jan. 17, 1921 stirred the boxing community with the kind of anticipation that puts circles on calendars and prompts lively chatter in offices and restaurants.

Taylor fans filled all 1,800 seats in the K of C, so Johnson instructed his ticket workers to sell standing-room-only stubs. Even the SRO ducats sold out 30 minutes before the first preliminary started!29

Tierney plopped down in his ringside seat, eager to see if Taylor could pull it off. Baker was there, $102.50 richer after bowling a 678 series in a tournament the night before in Indianapolis. Guy Jackson, the butcher, dependably arrived among hundreds in Taylor's expanding legion of supporters.30

The cautious, unspectacular fight did not justify all its attention, but the bout did establish that Taylor carried the skills to compete with the best in his weight division. Early on, Taylor's punches failed to break through Mason's guard, but in the eighth and ninth rounds, they found their mark. White wrote that Taylor won the bout, and published the comments from a dozen spectators who agreed.[31]

Mason fought on for four more years, with declining success and far less frequency. His career and Taylor's had met like skyrise elevators, side by side for an instant, then vanishing in opposite directions. Shortly after Mason quit the ring, his body, weakened by more than 200 professional boxing matches, contracted tuberculosis. He struggled with the illness for four years before dying in 1929.[32]

Chapter 6

Enter Eddie and Eddie

Bud Taylor's boxing exploits began to gain notoriety throughout the Midwest in 1921, and his "sweetheart" commands credit for much of his success. "Sweetheart" was Taylor's pet name for his coveted right-hand punch.[1] As he pursued a foe, he constantly looked for an opening through which to propel his right, like Babe Ruth at the plate seeking the belt-high fastball he could drive out of the ballpark.

In St. Louis, Taylor found the path in the opening round, flooring Jimmy Murphy for a 3-count. Murphy recovered and mounted a comeback in the same round, landing left hooks and inciting his hometown crowd of 2,500 into wild cheers.[2] Murphy fought strongly in the second and third rounds and by the fourth, Bud's impatient Terre Haute fans tried to exhort their hero with the chant "TAY-LOR, TAY-LOR."[3] Taylor won the final round, the sixth, and the newspapers called the bout a draw.[4]

Starting strong and finishing strong became a hallmark for Taylor's performances. "I always fought harder in the first and last rounds," he said. "I fought hard in the first round to intimidate my opponent. It worked many and many a time. The fellow lost heart and began to think only of getting out alive." Taylor said he pressed hard at the finish to impress the judges, hoping to gain their favor in a close fight.[5]

As Taylor retreated to the dressing room of the St. Louis Armory, fans swarmed around him in appreciation. He managed to make it through the doors, where three police officers took up post to keep the unwanted out. After dressing, Taylor tried to rush to his train, but he and supporter Ed Baker were "cornered in the big building and fairly mobbed by 1,000 fans, all of whom tried to shake his hand." A woman kissed him on the lips, "and our Bud blushed red as a rose," wrote Ralph White.6

One constant in Taylor's early career is that he trained hard. He knew that all the sweat and sacrifice in the gym produced results when the lights dimmed, the fans shifted in their seats and the bell signaled go. He jogged daily, punched the bag, skipped rope ...

Even in street clothes, boxing dominated his agenda. On fight nights when he wasn't on the card, he helped by swinging the towel or carrying the spit bucket in the corner of his friends or sparring partners, Don Curley, Jackie Barnhart, Dick Barnett ... Taylor tagged along when they fought on cards in the nearby towns of Clinton, Indiana; Sullivan, Indiana; or Paris, Illinois, and farther trips to Gary, Indiana, or Detroit.7

If Taylor sat among the audience, the ring announcer in Terre Haute occasionally "introduced" him to the crowd, as if those in their seats wouldn't recognize their blossoming superstar out of his boxing trunks. Taylor would acknowledge the ovation modestly, but as the months passed he apparently grew embarrassed by the attention and would decline to hop up into the ring and wave.8

Taylor signed for a rematch with Murphy for the K of C, welcoming the thought of a return to a smoke-free arena. In their first bout, smokers had turned the air so thick in the St. Louis Armory that Taylor had struggled to breathe.9 He could count on clean air in Terre Haute—the fire chief had outlawed smoking in the K of C.10

The 10-round rematch on Feb. 28, 1921, played to a capacity crowd, but Taylor took more punches than ever and again came away with a draw.11 A Murphy punch split his lip so badly that he required stitches. He laid off boxing for two weeks while the pucker healed.12

A third fight with Murphy, March 21 in St. Louis, settled the matter of superiority. Taylor slugged his way to an early lead and maintained the edge to win the newspapers' decisions.13 At the final bell, fans struck up the TAY-LOR chant for their warrior.14

Since his ring loss to Taylor in August 1920, "Dutch" Davison of Muncie had been clamoring for a rematch, spouting off about how he could whip Taylor. In their first encounter, Davison fell through the ropes in the third round, twisted his ankle and couldn't continue, resulting in a third-round TKO for Taylor. Davison had managed to land some punches early in the fight and had been boasting that he deserved a second chance. Tex Johnson decided to appease him, and set the rematch for April 4, 1921, in the K of C.[15]

"He can't hit as hard as I can and I am out to stop him in a hurry …" Davison claimed. "We'll see tonight who is the best flyweight in the state."[16]

Two punches provided the answer. Taylor decked Davison with the very first one. The knockdown surprised sportswriter Ralph White, who did not believe Taylor's blow landed cleanly. After Davison rose, Taylor hit him again—this time for real. Davison sunk to the canvas, blood flowing out of his ear. Jack Tierney, refereeing, didn't even bother to count him out.[17]

For the card, Johnson had raised the price of the balcony seats to $1 from 50 cents[18] and still the affair drew well. Johnson had started the evening by putting two 10-year-olds, Joe Ryan and Buddy Walker, in the ring to maul each other for three rounds. The crowd enjoyed it so much they showered the ring with $11.75 in change, leaving it to the referee to scurry about the canvas between rounds, picking up coins.[19]

Johnson surely recognized what most promoters know: boxing fulfills a basic need within its spectators that cannot be satisfied by other forms of entertainment. Then and now, most fight fans care little about scientific boxing, defense and strategy. They want to see leather meet face, bodies reeling from blows, streams of blood, and heads bouncing off canvas. They want fearless fighters who seldom back up and *never* clinch—the style exemplified by Bud Taylor.

One particular bout on a spring evening in 1921 inside Terre Haute's Grand Opera House proved pivotal for Taylor's career. Fans accustomed to watching their blond bomber go all out, bell to bell, would not have considered the evening extraordinary, as Taylor provided his usual thrills. Two men watching the 10-rounder from the near-sellout crowd, however, noted the performance with more than a casual interest. Eddie Kane and Eddie Long had never seen the slender kid before this date, April 29, 1921. The two men managed Tommy Gibbons, a St. Paul, Minn., light-heavyweight fighting in the main event that evening in the Grand. Chicago-based Kane and Long were known nationally in the boxing business. Their main client, Gibbons, would three years later fight for the heavyweight title against Jack Dempsey.

The two Eddies studied the skinny kid named Taylor in action against "Battling Chink," and recognized the potential. They were especially impressed that he was fighting his tail off in a semifinal for a meager $50.

They found out his name, and inquired further at ringside. Taylor's friends encouraged the two men to shop Bud around Chicago for bouts. Long, more so than Kane, liked what he saw in the kid. Taylor, however, was only 17, and the pair balked at signing him.[20]

Boxing was illegal in Illinois in 1921, but as in Indiana and elsewhere, the matches played discretely in various towns where political bosses allowed them. The 2.7 million people of Chicago included a substantial crop of tough kids looking to punch their way to the top and into the big boxing money. Taylor had seen some of these fighters in action on trips north to watch his sparring partners in bouts in the vast metro area. He wanted to break into the region's fight market. On one trip, Taylor had visited south-side Chicago to talk with Jack O'Keefe, a popular boxing manager in the area. Ted Ross, a fighter in O'Keefe's stable, said in a 1962 interview that Taylor wanted O'Keefe to manage him. O'Keefe declined.

"He told him he couldn't find the time for him," Ross said. "He was a puny, skinny kid who O'Keefe thought wouldn't amount to anything. O'Keefe some years later told me it was his greatest and biggest mistake ..."[21]

On July 18, 1921, in his 22nd professional boxing match, Taylor lost for the first time. Eddie O'Dowd of Columbus, Ohio beat him in a 10-rounder in Louisville, Kentucky. It was a close bout officially recorded as a "no decision," but one in which all four of the Louisville newspapers scored the victory for O'Dowd.[22] In defeat, Taylor's gameness so impressed the Broadway Athletic Club of

Louisville that its people immediately signed him for a bout there one week later.[23] In that follow-up, Taylor fought to a draw with Battling Chink, whose real name was Johnny Samuels. The audience at the Taylor-Chink rematch demonstrated boxing's growing appeal to mainstream America: about 400 of the 2,000 in attendance were women.[24]

On July 22, 1921, Bud Taylor turned 18 years old and within six weeks, he would join the stable of Eddie Kane and Eddie Long.[25] Taylor had 19 wins, one loss and three draws, and would belong to the same managerial group as the nationally known boxing Gibbons brothers, light-heavyweight Tom and middleweight Mike, and a promising lightweight from Rockford, Illinois named Sammy Mandell. Taylor now could break into the Chicago fight scene. If he could win with regularity, the possibilities were limitless.

Chapter 7

Felling a Tree

The "knockout" punch, coveted by the boxers who possess it, feared by those without, reigns as the most decisive single act in all of sports. In baseball, a game-ending home run can happen only in the last inning, and in basketball, a victory-snatching jump shot only near the final buzzer. A KO can occur *at any time* in a boxing match, granting an edge-of-your-seat uniqueness to the sport. The careers of thousands of talented boxers have fallen short of glory because they didn't have a KO punch.

Put plainly, a knockout results when a punch causes a boxer's brain to smack against the inside of his skull, resulting in a temporary concussion and loss of consciousness. Boxers aim for the chin because a solid impact there effectively snaps the head back to propel the brain. A side blow to the chin or lower jaw, rather than a direct hit, is ideal because the neck muscles can't brace as well to fend off the impact. An angled blow to the nose also provides an effective snap of the head, though to a lesser extent. Boxers seldom aim for the temple and never the forehead, the hardest bone in the human body and one in which off-center hits can bruise or fracture a hand.[1]

In the fall of 1921, an Indianapolis bantamweight named Solly Epstein carried a distinction rivaled by few. In an estimated 200 bouts, he had never been knocked out, nor even knocked off his feet.[2]

Epstein had taken the best shots from great fighters, among them nationally known Joe Lynch and Pal Moore, yet Solly had never gone down. The feat stood as even more remarkable considering Epstein's style. Like Taylor, Epstein stalked his opponents, inviting blows just so he could dish out his own.3

Taylor had not been knocked out, either, in 26 fights, so the fans figured something had to give when Taylor and Epstein uncoiled on each other Oct. 10, 1921, in the K of C.

Epstein's ring experience would give him the edge over Taylor, according to speculation in the press.4 Epstein certainly thought so.

"I didn't dream I could get Taylor inside the ring and now that I have him, I'll show him who is the best in the state," Epstein boasted. "I'll kayo that bird, see if I don't." Taylor's response: "If anyone takes the count Monday, it will be Mr. Epstein, not I."5

The fans, who turned out in droves, watched an action-packed bout with little holding—and, stunningly lopsided. For all the fight except the first round, Taylor pounded Epstein around the ring. Finally, Epstein fell, like a maple hacked by woodsmen's axes that inevitably, topples.6

"I believe his jaw is made of iron," Taylor said later, "for I know I landed at least 30 times squarely on that portion before he went down."7

One published account attributed the knockout to a "bombardment of punches from all directions," another account to a left to the pit of the stomach and right cross to the chin and still another account, to body blows and six hard rights.8 Epstein probably never remembered how or where he got hit. He stayed unconscious for two hours.9

Harold Smith lived in an area Chicagoans referred to as "the stockyards." The smoke-stacked, industrialized section of the urban south side emitted a stench that, on a breezy day after a prolonged dry period, reached the nostrils of residents far west into the suburbs.10

"Harold Smith of the stockyards" the sportswriters referred to him, maybe because it sounded tough. They did not write "of Chicago," or "south side," just "of the stockyards," as if he slept on a pallet and ate out of the trash bins with the rats. In reality, Smith had been born in Ohio, and was the son of a newspaperman who just happened to live in the working-class area.11

Smith is one of those better-than-average boxers of the 19-teens and early '20s all but forgotten from an era when boxing was illegal, win-loss records were not officially compiled and published accounts of fights are scarce. It was against Smith that Taylor made his Chicago debut on Dec. 3, 1921. The pair would crash blows on each other in four bouts over nine months. These were thrilling encounters long-remembered by fans and journalists.[12]

In their series, they slugged it out in Chicago's old West Side Auditorium and in Jimmy Keyes' club in LaSalle, Ill., the latter where it was legal to render decisions. The four bouts, about which few details were published, resulted in two narrow newspaper victories for Taylor, a draw and a loss.[13] Like the earlier series with Jimmy Murphy and Battling Chink, the Smith bouts served to educate and toughen Taylor, a bloody apprenticeship for the trials ahead. It also won for Taylor a vast set of new fans.

"I'll always remember him as one of the cleanest fighters in the ring. He never went in for that dirty work and was well-respected," Smith said of Taylor, many years later.[14]

By "clean," Smith meant that Taylor did not rely on the use of illegal tactics to win fights. Boxers bent on winning at all costs have an array of dirty tricks at their disposal. They range from minor infractions such as hitting on a break or while holding, to egregious ones such as head-butting, using the thumb of a glove to gouge an opponent's eye, or intentionally missing a roundhouse punch to follow through with a strike from the elbow.[15] The same sportswriters who extolled Taylor's ferocity as a fighter also noted numerous examples of his conduct and fair play, and how it swayed crowds in his favor.[16] Some fighters carried reputations for using all mechanisms, whether legal or forbidden, to win fights. It has been written that the light-heavyweight Harry Greb's idea of a "clean" fight was one in which he thumbed his opponent no more than a dozen times.[17] Taylor, a contemporary of Greb's, is known to have respected Harry as a fighter.[18] If Bud himself seldom cheated, he must at least have appreciated Greb's resourcefulness. As Fritzie Zivic, world welterweight champion 1940-41, once said, "You're fighting, you're not playing the piano, you know."[19]

Taylor's second fight against Smith, Dec. 29, 1921, closed out a year in which Bud fought a prodigious 19 pro bouts (including four times in December) and lost only once. Boxing writers in Chicago were beginning to notice the 18-year-old, especially Ed Smith of the *Chicago American*, who also worked as a well-respected boxing referee.

"... He seems to enjoy fighting more than anything else in the world, and boys of his age have huge appetites [for] everything," Smith wrote of Taylor. "... Is this boy ... going the way of the good prospects, or will he fall by the wayside and, as so many of the others have done, be relegated to the discards within a short time?"[20]

Chapter 8

Nothing Human …

To explain defeat to the members of the media, a professional boxer has a pool of common excuses from which to pull: He didn't train enough; he overtrained; he was weakened by having to make weight; he fought injured; he was wronged by the judges … The defeated fighter often follows his excuse with the suggestion of a rematch as the way to settle the matter of who is the better man.

Sometimes, a defeated fighter reaches deep into the blame bag to come up with a dandy. After Taylor sent Solly Epstein to the canvas in October 1921 for the first time in Solly's 200-bout career, the Epstein camp in Indianapolis blamed poisoning. They charged that someone in Terre Haute had slipped poison into Solly's water bucket in his corner.[1] The poison caused Epstein to collapse, not Taylor's series of punches, they said. Epstein and his handlers claimed they had medical evidence that a morphine derivative had been dumped into his water, resulting in his fall and the need for hospitalization in Indianapolis two days after the fight. When George Grammell, who had refereed the fight, heard the claims, he dismissed them as nonsense. Tex Johnson, who had promoted the fight, blamed Epstein's overconfidence.

"He came to Terre Haute expecting something soft, and found Taylor an altogether different boxer than what he expected …" Johnson also quipped that if Epstein had been poisoned, it must have been by his brother or manager, since they were the ones in his corner.

Taylor responded to the controversy tactfully. "I regret that he is ill, and that he did not train as he should, if that is true; for I believe I can beat him every day in the week. If he thinks he did not get a square deal, I will be pleased to meet him in any ring that a match can be arranged. I take no stock in the poisoning story."[2]

By December, Johnson had decided to grant the Indianapolis boxer a rematch, and set it for Jan. 5, 1922, in Terre Haute's Grand opera house. Taylor's stablemate Sammy Mandell traveled to Terre Haute to help train Bud for the fight.[3]

Mandell and Taylor instantly became friends. They were born in the same year and raised in Midwestern cities of similar size (Rockford, Illinois for Mandell), before legions of admirers. They had reached a similar stage of their careers toward a shared goal. They wanted to be world champions, at that time Taylor as a flyweight and Mandell as a bantamweight.

With his spaniel's eyes and olive complexion, Mandell was not merely good-looking, but *pretty*. Rather than boxer, he looked more like one of those pop-singer teen idols that would surface in the early 1960s—Frankie Avalon, Fabian, Paul Anka ... In public, Mandell often was mistaken for Rudolph Valentino, an internationally known Italian film star of the period over whom women swooned and whom men idolized.[4] Sportswriters thus dubbed Mandell "the Rockford Sheik," referring to characters that Valentino played in films. The print media also tabbed him with the nickname the "Rockford Flash," because of his extraordinary quickness. He owned one of the best left-hand punches of the times, a jab he peppered into opponents' noses while he sped about the ring.

While Mandell trained with Taylor in Terre Haute's YMCA in early January, Johnson watched his $1 to $3 tickets for Taylor-Epstein go fast in advance sale, both locally and in Indianapolis.[5]

"My friends who are coming," Epstein said, "will have enough long green to take all bets, for they, like myself, see a KO victory ahead."[6]

Taylor, too, spoke confidently about the fight. "His style of boxing is just what I like and I will land twice to his once all the way through," he said.[7]

As the rematch neared, Epstein backed off from the story of being poisoned. He personally had never used the excuse, attributing

Sammy Mandell, Rockford, Ill. *Winkler Collection, University of Notre Dame*

it to others in his party. He lost because he didn't train hard enough, he said.8

To sell more tickets, Johnson exploited the Terre Haute-versus-Indianapolis angle. He tried to arrange the fight card to pit a Terre Haute boxer against an Indianapolis one for each of the four bouts. Johnson also hired as a referee the most famous Indiana fighter of all time, retired light-heavyweight Jack Dillon of Indianapolis.

At weigh-in on the afternoon of the fight, Epstein tipped at 119 1/2 pounds, 3 1/2 pounds over the maximum stipulated by the contract, giving Taylor the option of pulling out of the fight. Taylor weighed only 113. Taylor agreed to go ahead with the fight, and Epstein agreed to forfeit the $100 he had posted as weight-guarantee money.

Fourteen hundred fight fans filled the Grand to capacity. They watched the Terre Haute fighters win in the preliminaries. A Taylor victory would make it a hometown sweep.

Referee Dillon summoned the fighters to the center of the ring to touch gloves in the traditional, symbolic handshake before the opening gong. In that instant of neutrality as they were supposed to step back before fighting, Epstein shot a punch that clipped Taylor on the nose. Ralph White, covering the bout from ringside, thought the blow amounted to a sucker punch and that it seemed to enrage Taylor. Taylor ripped a left uppercut that sent Epstein down for a count of 5. He rose, but Taylor tagged him with a right cross to the jaw. This time, it took 9 ticks for Solly to struggle to his feet. With the hometown crowd in a cheering frenzy, Taylor bombarded Epstein with rights and lefts and finished him off at 1:51 of the first round.

"Nothing human could have weathered the attack ..." White wrote.9

Chapter 9

"Inarticulate Sounds"

Chicago, 1922: a metropolis rife with the trappings of 1920s culture. Skyscrapers and traffic. Shoppers, flappers, gangsters. Mass transit, art deco architecture, jazz, The Loop ...

In the first three months of the year, Bud Taylor divided his time between Terre Haute and the mega-city 180 miles due north. In Chicago, his managers Kane and Long pitted him against the best available competition. More importantly, the co-managers hired Jack Blackburn to train Taylor and Sammy Mandell.[1]

Blackburn had nearly reached age 40 and was winding down his own fight career of 20-plus years. He had been a talented boxer at various weights, back in the days when fights lasted as long as 40 rounds and a fighter would be lucky to clear $35 a bout.[2] Blackburn's specialty had been his left, which he used to jab and hook in flashes, and about which he would impart his wisdom to understudies Taylor, Mandell and later, Joe Louis.[3]

Outside the ring, Blackburn liked to aim his lefts and rights to his own lips with bottles of beer, transforming an otherwise pleasant man—one who loved dogs, fishing and playing cards—into a belligerent drunk. Blackburn shot three people in 1909, one died, and he served four years of a 15-year prison sentence.[4]

Not surprisingly, a lot of people were afraid of Blackburn. Even in street clothes, he looked menacing, a balding man with a weathered face marked with a knife-scar lengthy enough to impress a pirate—the remnant of a bar fight. But inside a roped ring, the man was in his element. Blackburn knew boxing and he taught it tactfully. For example, he avoided criticizing fighters in the presence of other fighters, instead taking them aside to confer.5

Blackburn's tutelage suited the promising young talent before him—and more the greener Taylor than Mandell. Bud had considered his left-hand punch merely a setup for his "sweetheart" right, but Blackburn laid the groundwork to change that thinking.6

Eddie Long liked what he saw in the progress of his newest acquisition. "He's title bound, that's all there is to it …" he boasted about Taylor to a Terre Haute sportswriter early in 1922.7

The grooming to place Taylor in such contention continued Jan. 13, 1922, against George Corbett, a south Chicago brawler. The fight took place inside what the newspapers referred to only as a "suburban arena," its site undisclosed presumably to protect the principals from arrest.8

Corbett was a popular fellow among the stockyards crowd, and Taylor heard the strains of a hostile audience as the pair volleyed in the early rounds.9 The bout met its abrupt end in the middle of the third round, when Taylor rocked Corbett with a punch that broke his jaw in three places. The injury disfigured Corbett's face, but the wounded man gamely continued to flail away with his mouth open while the crowd yelled wildly. Boxing writer Ed Smith, refereeing the fight, saw that the front teeth of Corbett's lower jaw had been smashed back into his palate. When Smith heard Corbett making what Smith later described as "inarticulate sounds," Smith stopped the fight.10

In those days, a broken jaw ended a fighter's career. The injury forced Corbett to retire from the ring, the main source of his income. A month later, Corbett's friends organized a benefit boxing exhibition/party for him in the visitation hall at 54th and Peoria streets, Chicago.11 The event raised $1,000 for the disabled fighter.12 Taylor traveled to Chicago to box in the exhibition, paying for his own way and that of a sparring partner, winning many friends by his kindness.13

Only baseball surpassed boxing in the early 1920s in terms of sports media attention. Jack Dempsey's popularity had become ridiculous—if he caught a cold or caught a fish, the writers reported it. The saturation of boxing stories in the newspapers extended from the heavyweights on down to the lighter divisions, with plenty of ink for pugs such as Benny Leonard, Georges Carpentier, Harry Greb, and the fighter Taylor proclaimed as his personal favorite: middleweight champion Mickey Walker.[14] In the Terre Haute area, a pro boxing card popped up about every two weeks, with Tex Johnson waiting in the wings to count the money. Ring sports were even being promoted at the high-school level. In January 1922, the boxing and wrestling teams of Terre Haute's two high schools, Wiley and Garfield, could be found training hard for their big spring showdown in the K of C ring.[15] One of the businesses that sold tickets to Johnson's K of C shows was Eddie Nash's cigar store at 661 Wabash Avenue. Johnson leased two rooms in the same building as the store, installed a gym for fighters to train, and considered it the headquarters for his "Vigo Boxing Club."[16]

This makeshift gym sat in the heart of downtown, amid the bustle of street cars, automobiles and pedestrians. Less than half a block east sat the intersection of Seventh Street and Wabash Avenue, the point where the National Old Road (later known as U.S. 40) met Dixie B line highway (later known as U.S. 41). These two highways in 1922 served as the nation's main arteries of automobile traffic east-west and north-south across the continent. The citizens of Terre Haute were mightily proud of this distinction and referred to the intersection as the "Crossroads of the World."[17] Thus, the headquarters for boxing in Terre Haute had moved into a location symbolizing its elevated status as a sport: right at the center of the nation.

On Jan. 23, Sammy Mandell headlined a boxing card in the K of C, with Taylor helping in his corner. To train for the fight, the pair sparred in the downtown gym under Blackburn's supervision.[18] *Blackburn, Mandell and Taylor.* Lucky spectators could one day boast of seeing the three future boxing Hall-of-Famers working out together, long before anyone knew.

Taylor, who loved to dance, had planned to attend a dance after the fight and invited Mandell to join him. Mandell did not like to dance, but he didn't want to offend his friend, so ahead of time he wired his brother Joe in Rockford with a plan. Joe sent Sammy a late telegram with the bogus message that Sammy needed to hurry back to northern Illinois after the bout to sign some important papers.

Sammy broke the "news" to Taylor, avoided the dance and got away with the ruse.[19]

Over the next four months, Taylor entered Chicago-area rings against a succession of the city's best bantamweights. He gained newspaper decisions over Herbie Schaeffer and Ollie O'Neill, TKO'd Frankie Henke and battled to a draw with Harold Smith. A wide-shouldered, University of Notre Dame student from Chicago's west side named Jimmy Kelly provided his toughest challenge.[20] Kelly handed Taylor his second defeat in 36 bouts. An American Legion post promoted the bout, aboard the USS Commodore, a retired U.S. Navy ship formerly used for military training that was docked on Lake Michigan at the foot of Randolph Street.[21] The Legionnaires loved the fights, and organizers turned away more than 400 people after the ship's gymnasium reached its maximum occupancy on fight night Feb. 10, 1922.[22]

Kelly took a kiss from Taylor's "sweetheart" in the first round that dumped him on the seat of his trunks, but the Chicago fighter shook off the effects. In the second round, Taylor took a low blow and writhed in pain. He, too, recovered, and the pair went at it in what the *Chicago Daily Tribune* called a "savage battle." In the fifth round, Kelly smacked Taylor again with what appeared to be a low punch. In great pain, Bud was allotted a minute's rest in his corner, and complained to Long that he seemed paralyzed. Long refused to allow Taylor to answer the bell for the sixth, and the fight was over.[23]

The referee claimed he did not see any fouls by Kelly and despite protests from Taylor's corner, awarded the victory to Kelly by TKO. The crowd, which had sided with Kelly, deserted him with a shower of hisses and boos when he left the ring, and cheered the Hoosier.[24] Organizers planned a rematch for Kenosha, Wis.

Long, always the banner-waver for his fighters, (and, a master of hype), told the press Kelly was "yellow" and suggested he struck low to keep from being knocked out.[25] The rematch March 22 in John Wagner's Club in Kenosha drew 2,500 and considerable wagering from the fans on the result.[26] This time, no one disputed the outcome. Taylor won eight out of the 10 rounds and "gave his man a terrific lacing."[27]

The pain in Taylor's right hand bothered him so much over the course of three bouts into the spring of 1922 that he resorted to placing it in a cast for about a week, between bouts, to heal whatever the ailment.28

On the loosely organized pro boxing circuit of the 1920s, minor injuries were either ignored or dealt with by quick fixes. Boxers of this era typically fought 10 to 15 times a year, and they rarely canceled. Pulling out of a fight made for bad business relations. Promoters booked bouts months in advance, and their pre-fight preparations included renting the venue, scheduling fighters for the preliminaries, having the tickets printed and hiring all the help to put on the show. Consequently, they expected a fighter short of being bedridden or on crutches to honor his commitment.

Fighters constantly ached from any number of afflictions: fractures, infections, boils, strains, pulled muscles and other ailments. An infected wound upped the risk for blood poisoning, a potentially deadly affliction in the years before the penicillin mold was discovered in 1928.29

Hand problems were common, and no boxer of his day suffered more problems with sprains, cracks and breaks than Taylor.30 Like most fighters, he had his hands wrapped in tape before he put on the gloves.31 The tape steadied the hand to absorb the shock from off-center punches. Still, the hands of fighters meted out so much force that deep bruises and fractures were continual, and unavoidable. The boxing gloves of the 1920s did not pack the cushion of their 8-ounce and 10-ounce successors.

"They called them 6-ounce gloves, but they weren't no more than winter mittens," remembers Dick Brokaw, a Terre Haute native who boxed in the 1920s and '30s. "My hands used to hurt all the time."32

The human hand, a marvel of intricate tendons and muscles and delicate bones interconnected by ligaments, simply wasn't made to be rolled into a fist and crashed repeatedly into the skulls of other people.33

Broken noses were as routine for busy boxers as broken fingernails for switchboard operators. Brokaw's nose was broken about 10 times. "You never thought much about it," he said. "I would pack it with a string of cotton and two days later, I was boxing again."34

A fighter's pain asserts itself between fights, in bed, in the shower, at dinner—but seldom in the ring. During a fight, adrenaline dilutes it, because winning commands all the attention. Pain is relative to one's amount of idle time.

Taylor's ring successes in 1922 attracted the attention of Chicago promoter Jim Mullen, who signed him to fight "Memphis" Pal Moore on June 23 in Aurora, Illinois. A recently built arena in that Chicago-area city seated 8,000 and Mullen anticipated big numbers of fans with such a matchup.35 Moore, a boxer since 1913, carried a reputation as one of the top bantamweights in the nation. He had defeated former titleholder Pete Herman twice and held a 3-1 mark against former champ Joe Lynch. Against common opponents, Moore and Taylor were 5-0 at the time.36

Moore stands as one of the great masters of defensive boxing. To him, boxing was more like a lively dance than a fight, and he specialized in avoiding his opponent by scurrying about the ring. Nimble as a gymnast, Moore used all of a ring's space, bobbing, ducking and sometimes even leaping, but always *moving*. Forty years later, Cassius Clay/Muhammed Ali similarly dazzled audiences. Moore's bouts seldom ended in knockouts, but often ended in frustration for his chasers, whose punches found only empty space for 10 rounds. On evenings when Moore's jab missed or he couldn't pedal fast enough, he lost, but by 1922 it had happened only 17 times in more than 150 bouts.37

Walter Eckersall of the *Chicago Daily Tribune* referred to Taylor as the "Terre Haute Terrier" in previews for the Moore fight.38 Taylor had outgrown the flyweight division, so the "fighting fly" nickname no longer applied, and the sportswriters apparently thought that the attack dog moniker better described Bud's style. (Pit bull would have been more appropriate, and if Taylor had been born in Pittsburgh ...) The Terrier nickname stuck and would appear in print more times over the course of Bud's career than the more famous references, "Terre Haute Terror," and "Blonde Terror of Terre Haute."

Taylor knew a victory over veteran Moore would widen his acclaim in the boxing world. Taylor had defeated many of the best of the Midwest, but few outside that territory, and Moore hailed from Tennessee.

The Terrier trained hard in his hometown YMCA, then warmed up for Moore by winning a 10-round newspaper's decision June 14 in Indianapolis against Herbie Schaeffer of Chicago.39

In Aurora, 6,500 spectators turned out, the biggest crowd that Taylor had ever seen at one of his performances. About 65 fans drove the five-hour trip from Terre Haute.40

Moore started the bout by immediately demonstrating his intention to use drastic tactics to keep his distance. He not only ran, he *bounded*, "like a rubber kangaroo," as Taylor described it, recalling the fight many years later. When the bell ended the first round, Bud sulked in his corner, mystified.

Long leaned in with an idea. "Jump up and down like he does; shame him into stopping his monkey business," the manager advised.

"That's what I did," Taylor recalled. "I came out of the corner like a voodoo dancer. Moore stopped dead in his tracks. As soon as he started jumping again, I did the same. He finally settled down and fought a little, but not much."41

Taylor won the early rounds, Moore the middle ones. Taylor stung Moore with his best punch of the fight in the ninth, and won the final two stanzas. The Aurora boxing establishment had no local authority to render decisions in bouts, so the winner went undeclared. The *Chicago Tribune* scored it 4-4-2, a draw.42

Chapter 10

Ringside in Terre Haute

By the summer of 1922, Bud Taylor had not fought professionally in front of his hometown fans for six months. Tex Johnson arranged the grand return for July 4, 1922, securing Terre Haute's minor-league baseball park as the venue. For an opponent, Johnson recruited Johnny "Babe" Asher of Grand Rapids, Mich. He was no Pal Moore, but Johnson counted on Taylor's presence on the card alone to fill the seats. Asher and Taylor had fought common opponents in Eddie O'Dowd, Frankie Mason, Pal Moore and Jimmy Kelly, but among them, Asher had defeated only Kelly.[1]

Taylor rose as early as 5 a.m. to train, beginning with eight or 10 miles of roadwork.[2] Taylor often jogged down the tracks of the Vandalia Railroad line that ran east-west only a few hundred feet north of the home where he lived with his parents at 1904 Liberty Ave. He liked the jogging sessions that other boxers found so tedious, and on the tracks, he could run to a rhythm inside his head.

"Bud would run [on] every tie so he could get the timing on his feet—it was the only place he could get the timing like that," Dick Brokaw said. "And then he would change to every *other* tie."[3]

Taylor began his workout by running about half a mile down the tracks west to reach Union Station, the train depot for Terre Haute. Then he would follow the C&E Railroad line northbound out of the city.[4]

Discipline ruled Taylor's success. After his early-morning runs, he worked out in the gym by punching a sand-filled heavy bag, skipping rope, tossing a medicine ball and shadow-boxing with other boxers. He also would don the gloves for at least half a dozen, fast-paced rounds with whatever sparring partner was available.[5] In preparation for Asher, he sparred with Bud Perrill, Billy Long and Ward Sparks, all regulars in the local boxing rings. For the Asher fight, Taylor varied his routine to include rowing a canoe on the Wabash River, believing the activity would help accustom himself to exertion in the July heat.[6]

The rowing also provided the benefit of burning calories. Making weight is a constant worry for fighters. Fight managers and trainers become experts at shedding pounds in short amounts of time and know all the tricks. Billy Gibson, a renowned boxing manager of the 1920s, used to apply cold water towels to the heels of a fighter's feet just before weigh-in, a practice he said fooled the scales into reading a half-pound or pound lower than a man's actual weight.[7] Fighters who didn't constantly watch their diets resorted to starving themselves in the days before a weigh-in and ran the risk of entering the ring robbed of their strength. The light-heavyweight Stanley Ketchel once brought a pound of chocolate crèmes to a weigh-in, then lustfully wolfed them down after showing he was under the limit.[8] Taylor's favorite post-scales indulgence was chicken soup made by Eddie Long's mother-in-law, which Bud downed by the thermos.[9]

On fight day, 2,500 fans showed up at the ball park.[10] A Bud Taylor fight had become a big enough social event for the community that the *Terre Haute Tribune* sent a news and features writer, Anna Bowles-Wiley, to cover the bout along with sportswriter Ralph White.

Upon arriving, Bowles-Wiley noticed the jovial behavior of some men who appeared to have been drinking. Since 1922 fell during the Prohibition era, Bowles-Wiley's reporter's curiosity prompted her to ask one fellow where she could get some alcohol.

"Nothin' doin', the lid's on," came the whispered reply, meaning federal agents were, at least at the time, closely monitoring such activity.[11]

The Prohibition era had begun April 2, 1918, with federal law prohibiting the manufacture, sale or transport of alcoholic beverages. It was an odd time for such a restriction, when frisky Americans of the post-war 1920s were wearing stylish clothes, dancing to jazz

Eddie Long adjusts Taylor's headgear during training.

music and wanting to party.

    The Prohibition law, of course, did not stop people from drinking publicly or selling alcohol. The law's immediate effect on Terre Haute was to put out of work the many hundreds of people employed in its breweries and distilleries. It also stripped the city of $75,000 a year in liquor licensing fees from the booze retailers.[12] Some of Terre Haute's 300 taverns closed while others continued in business as joints referred to in the press as "soft-drink establishments." Most, if not all, of the proprietors of these places continued to sell liquor on the sly.[13]

As in cities all across America, the residents of Terre Haute knew which private residence or "soft-drink" parlor in their neighborhood they could slip into to buy a bottle.[14] The throngs of otherwise law-abiding citizens who were arrested for liquor-law crimes were given light sentences and merely clogged up the jails and courts. For the month of April 1922, for example, more than half of the 75 criminal cases before Judge John P. Jeffries in Vigo Circuit Court were liquor-law violations.[15]

During Prohibition, the brewer gave way to the bootlegger, and he seemed to be everywhere in the 1920s. In February 1922 alone, city police escorted 93 booze-makers to jail, and the police files were filled with reports that show the prevalence of the illegal business.[16] In one such example, on Feb. 17, 1925, police found a still lying in the middle of the intersection of a busy Terre Haute street during noon-hour traffic! The 100-gallon copper contraption found at 27th and Buckeye streets apparently had fallen off the bed of a truck, the authorities concluded.[17]

In another example, police in the summer of 1924 found a moonshine still ingeniously hidden in the city's crematorium, a facility used by the city to burn dead animals and trash. They arrested two city employees who had assembled the beer-making apparatus there.[18]

In nearby Clinton, Indiana, a Prohibition officer was quoted as saying that bootlegging was so common that one could smell the alcohol from the streets.[19]

A moonshiner or still operator could supplement his income handsomely. By 1920, a quart of bootleg whiskey with a fake label showing it had been bonded (meaning made legally, before Prohibition) could fetch as much as $15—the equivalent of about $150 in 2007 dollars.[20] Thus, men took grievous risks to undertake the enterprise. A homeowner at 23rd Street and Grand Avenue in Terre Haute blew up his entire house in 1921 when the still in his basement exploded. The man, who was not seriously injured, rushed to save his furniture by pulling it from the flames before police arrested him and carted him off to jail. He admitted to police he was just a beginner in the moonshining business.[21]

Prohibition, ironically, may have served to make the boxing audiences of America drunker. Instead of clutching open containers of beer bought from concessionaires, imbibing ticket holders simply carried concealed hip flasks with, presumably, harder liquor inside.[22]

At the Taylor-Asher fight, Bowles-Wiley also noted the presence of women in the crowd, estimated by reporter Ralph White as numbering 250.[23] Boxing had existed as a sport played exclusively by *men*, and for the entertainment of primarily *men* until the 1920s, when the winds of social change brought the smell of perfume into the arenas.

The national suffrage movement, after many years of being stonewalled by a male-led government, had succeeded in 1920 in securing for women the right to vote. The new freedom for women, coupled with the general prosperity of the times, led to an unfettering of inhibitions. Bobbed hair, curls, makeup and shorter skirts were signs of independence and allowed women to display their femininity. Self-assured women had a spring in their steps as they strode the sidewalks.[24] Some of these women were on their way to boxing matches.

The Terre Haute area produced its share of dedicated suffragists. Among them, Ida Husted Harper worked closely with nationally known activist Susan B. Anthony and later wrote Anthony's biography.[25] The suffrage law emboldened three Terre Haute women to run for the City Council in 1921, and one polled 2,184 votes to finish a respectable sixth out of 14 candidates.[26] Despite their gains, some women still found it necessary to sneak off to the fights. As one remarked to Bowles-Wiley, "Well, Tom don't know where I am, he would faint if he did. I can remember when he used to sneak off to go to a bout, but he likes to play pinochle or golf nowadays.'[27]

The presence of one woman, in particular, inspired Taylor—a brown-eyed, light-skinned femme who wore her auburn hair stylishly bobbed. Edith Taylor seldom missed her brother's bouts.[28]

Edith gradually had grown to like the bouts unlike the early days of Bud's ring career when she shared her mother's misgivings about her brother's choice of sport.

"I saw him first at the K of C hall and, of course, I worried then for I was afraid they would hurt him, but I do not worry much any more since I have seen my brother in action. He certainly can protect himself," Edith told a reporter, two weeks after the Asher fight.

Edith had traveled to her brother's fights in St. Louis and Louisville, and showed up without fail at the Terre Haute ones. Their mother, Tillie, still declined to attend and had never seen Bud in the ring.

"He is younger than I, but some way he seems older," Edith said of Bud. "He takes me every place and is so kind. Bud is a kid at that. He will grab mother up in his arms and waits her all over the house, but when he wins a bout, he breaks his neck home to tell mother about it."

"Someone said the other day that it would make him brutal," Edith said of her brother's involvement in boxing. "It certainly has not done anything of the kind. He is as tender as a baby to us all, and his boxing is science. Oh, yes, dad is proud of him, but not strong on boxing matches. I am the fan of the family outside of Bud."29

By 1922, Taylor had started to earn four-figure sums from his bouts, and he treated his parents and sister by buying them a home at 2011 Third Ave.30 He splurged on himself by acquiring a Cadillac roadster.31

People with all-consuming occupations often choose sedating activities for their free time, and for Taylor, it was camping along the Wabash River.32 In the 1920s, its banks in Terre Haute splashed with activity, with beaches and boating.33 Taylor's favorite river spots in summer 1922 included Camp Silverberg, where he earned a reputation among its frequenters as a strong swimmer and canoeist.34

Bowles-Wiley's account of the Taylor-Asher bout also carries the first-ever publicized mention of a love interest in Bud's life. Bowles-Wiley wrote that Bud's "sweetie" attended the fight, although the story does not provide her name. The girlfriend bawled as the fight began, and Edith Taylor comforted her. The girl need not have fretted over her beau's safety; Taylor floored Asher in Rounds 1 and 2 of the lopsided 10-rounder.35

Throughout his life, Taylor seems never to have encountered any difficulty attracting women. In his easygoing manner, women found him disarming. He was a polite, soft-spoken, unpretentious charmer. As for his appearance, he kept himself well-groomed, clean shaven and wore his hair slicked back in the style of the day. He dressed impeccably in the finest suits and collars—the latter a detached piece of clothing in the early '20s—and he was especially particular about his shoes and socks. He was fond of the short-billed, pancake hats common for the times, later known as "golf hats."[36]

A sportswriter once described Taylor's voice as a "nasal drawl,"[37] although those who remember Bud's speech do not remember it being drawly.[38] The press found him well-spoken, easy to interview and approachable. Their only knock on his behavior was that he became testy in the few days leading up to a fight, saying many things that he did not mean and later regretting the remarks.[39]

Chapter 11

Saved by the Bell

Babe Asher's hard head had caused more problems than his fists. Taylor emerged from the July 1922 fight with fractures in both hands. A physician wrapped them in plaster casts and Taylor took two weeks off from training.1 When he resumed fighting, he avenged his loss to Jimmy Kelly by defeating him convincingly as part of a Labor Day card in Terre Haute.2 In East Chicago, Indiana, promoter George Oswego wanted to sign Taylor to fight familiar foe Harold Smith, "of the stockyards." Smith had gone 5-0-1 since their fight in March.3 Taylor already held two decisions and a draw against Smith, and could gain little careerwise with a fourth bout, but Bud's managers Kane and Long accepted it.4 Kane thought that with a victory, he could land for Taylor a fight against Pancho Villa.5 Villa of the Philippines was considered "American Flyweight Champion," one notch under world champion Jimmy Wilde of Britain.6

"I am in communication with eastern promoters who want to put on the match ..." with Villa, Kane said. "We realize Bud must beat Smith, But I think he will do this rather handily. He is anxious to meet Villa for the flyweight title and we will close the match if suitable terms are offered."7 Oswego signed Smith and Taylor for Sept. 21, 1922, to battle in his open-air ballpark. Tickets sold briskly, including a single sale of a block of 50 to a packer from Chicago's north side wanting to treat his guests.8

Training in Chicago in the days before the fight, Taylor told the *Chicago American* about his desire for a title bout, either against flyweight Villa at 112 pounds or bantamweight champ Joe Lynch at 118.9

Smith, riding a win streak, but having not beaten Taylor in three tries, awaited the bout like a dog straining at his leash. He was, as he said years later, "out to murder" Taylor.10

For eight rounds, they laid into each other, neither with a clear-cut advantage. In the ninth, Smith found an opening around Taylor's right hand and tagged him on the chin with a left hook. He followed with a right to the chin and Taylor sunk to the canvas. He looked like he would not rise, but at the count of 6, the bell ended the round and allowed him a minute's rest. During the break, Bud recovered well enough to fight Smith even in the 10th, and the crowd responded wildly with approval. But when the papers hit the stands the next day, Smith had earned the decision.

A match with Villa would have to wait. Taylor blamed the knockdown punch on carelessness for leaving himself open, and resolved to learn from the mistake. As for Smith, his win streak soon ended. Though he continued to fight quality opponents until he quit the ring in 1927, he struggled with mediocre results.11

In the fall of 1922, Taylor twice volunteered his time to box exhibition matches for veterans' organizations in Terre Haute.12 The veterans' groups liked to include boxing matches for entertainment in their get-togethers, and many of the volunteering boxers were veterans themselves.

Taylor had been too young to serve in World War I, but he had seen older boys from his neighborhood march off to the trenches of France. Some were returned home in boxes, while others came back with crippling wounds, their lives forever changed. Regardless of his eventual status as a sports hero, Taylor never harbored any illusions about the nation's *real* heroes. He gave the same answer throughout his career when the vets called on him for help: if you want me, I'll be there.

On Sept. 26, the American Legion staged a convention in Terre Haute and presented six bouts of boxing for the veterans' entertainment. Sammy Mandell boxed an eight-rounder with Taylor in the third match. The pair wore extra-padded, oversized gloves while they mixed it up freely. Referee George Grammell clowned around by using a long board to break their clinches from a distance. In the final round, Mandell and Taylor turned on Grammell, backing him into the ropes for a mock attack from both sides. As Grammell managed to escape, the war veterans laughed and cheered uproariously.[13]

Despite his near knockout by Harold Smith, Taylor showed no cracks in his confidence. He stayed committed to his goal of winning a championship, and to investing the required effort to position himself for the chance. Boxing was his work and the gym his office, and he honored his appointments with the speed bag and jump rope conscientiously. "He is one of the few boys who thoroughly love to box and is a source of constant worry to his manager for fear he will hurt himself," Ed Smith wrote in the *Chicago American*.[14]

Taylor and Eddie Long, 16 years his senior, developed a solid friendship.

"There was a special relationship between the two," said Long's son, Jim Long. "There was an affinity, an older brother-younger brother type relationship. I remember from just listening to dad talk about him, there would be a gleam in his eye, a shift in his personality."[15]

Even as a boy, native Chicagoan Eddie Long seemed destined for notoriety. He made headlines in 1900 at age 13 when he plunged into a lagoon in the city's Union Park to save a drowning boy. He kept the larger boy afloat until a police dispatcher helped pull the boy to shore.[16]

By 1908, Long had begun his long career associated with boxing when as a friend, he accompanied Chicago fighter Eddie Coulon to the West Coast for a bout.[17]

Long was built stout and had a cheeky, expressive face with prominent dark eyebrows. He was chatty and outspoken with the press, and unflinchingly loyal to Taylor. Long generally carried a cheerful disposition and sportswriters enjoyed his candor. But he could be volatile and intemperate, almost to his undoing.

"If he was a friend, he was a friend for life, but don't dare cross him," son Jim Long said.[18]

In a 1962 column, Los Angeles sportswriter Sid Ziff related the story about once criticizing Taylor in print for being too hard on

Bud Taylor and Eddie Long.

a sparring partner. "Taylor didn't take offense, but Long wanted my hide," Ziff wrote. Long threatened Ziff, and although he did not carry out the threat, Ziff remembers a few days of cowering. "I imagined the worst every time an automobile backfired," Ziff wrote.[19]

Jim Long remembers hearing various accounts of an incident in which a Chicago police officer once had his father jailed overnight, in a case of mistaken arrest. Months later, Eddie Long exacted his revenge. He and Jack Blackburn were strolling down State Street when they saw the officer, out of uniform, hobbling along on crutches. Long, probably fueled by alcohol, knocked the policeman down, grabbed his crutches and threw them under a passing street car, apparently slipping away before the officer could determine the identity of his attacker. The incident stunned even the ex-con Blackburn, who ran off during Long's assault. Blackburn told and retold the story about the stunt that crazy Long pulled on State Street.[20]

Long and Kane scheduled the opponents and Taylor dropped them like dominoes in the fall of 1922—among them, Stanley Everett, Battling Chink, Billy O'Brien, Eddie Santry. Then on Dec. 22, Taylor boarded the old USS Commodore for the inevitable rematch with Pal Moore.

On a ship "packed to the rub rails" with enthusiastic fans, the pair replayed their first encounter.[21] "Bud chased him all over the ring for 10 rounds," said Billy Long, a Terre Haute boxer who attended the fight, then talked to a sportswriter.[22] Moore won most of the newspapers' decisions.[23]

"These two great little fighters had the crowd in an uproar and standing on their chairs for the entire 10 rounds," according to one account.[24]

Lovers of sports always have appreciated one-on-one contests that feature contrasting styles, such as baseball's junkball pitcher versus the slugger at the plate or tennis' steady baseliner against the attacking net player. A Taylor-Moore fight belonged in that genre.

1922 closed as boxing's most prosperous year to date. The nation's marquee fight for the year, Benny Leonard versus Lew Tendler for the world lightweight championship, drew a crowd of 70,000 in New Jersey. Jack Dempsey remained king of the heavyweights and an idol to millions of Americans. In New York, the thriving sport was governed by a three-man commission.[25]

On Dec. 28, Taylor learned that Eddie Kane had negotiated a deal with Milwaukee promoter Tom Andrews. Pancho Villa had accepted a guarantee of $7,000 to fight Bud on Jan. 15 in the Wisconsin city. Taylor patted his right hand, his "sweetheart."

"If I can only land this on the right spot, it means a championship, and that is what I will try and do," he said. "Just think of it, a chance at the flyweight title. I'll not kick the chance, either, if I can help myself."[26]

Chapter 12

Mayoral Support

The holidays are for giving, and on New Year's Day 1923, Bud Taylor gave away 6 1/2 pounds to Benny Vogel in an Indianapolis ring.

Vogel didn't last long enough to profit from the advantage—two minutes and 48 seconds to be exact—before a right cross knocked him senseless. He stayed unconscious for two minutes. An Indianapolis writer, apparently remembering how Taylor also had stretched out Solly Epstein, wrote: "Punches that pickle a fellow seem to flow out of the Terre Haute boy's anatomy." No attendance figures were reported, but it was called at that time the largest crowd ever to see a boxing match in Indianapolis.1

The Vogel bout served as a nice preparatory bout for Villa, but the Taylor camp soon learned that a match with the Filipino would have to wait. Villa had injured his hand and needed time to heal, nixing the bout with Taylor.5

A week later, Taylor was back in Chicago against familiar foe Jimmy Kelly. Kelly lost to Taylor again, and recalled the bout fondly in a 1927 interview:

A clear underdog, Kelly had decided to go all out from the opening bell. For nine rounds, he and Taylor threw punches at breakneck pace to an appreciative crowd. Kelly fought courageously, pulling from every ounce of strength inside of him despite being behind on points most of the way. At the end of the ninth, the exhausted Kelly could barely hold up his hands, but he figured

Taylor to be just as weary. When they came to the center of the ring for the glove-tap handshake at the start of the 10th round, Kelly remembered how it deflated him to hear Taylor urging him to speed up the pace. "C'mon, Jimmy, let's make a fight out of it," Taylor coaxed.[3]

Speaking about Taylor in a 1939 media interview, Jack Blackburn also recalled Bud's commitment to the performance.

"Man, he sure did like to fight," Blackburn said. "He'd come along to the eighth round of a 10-round fight so far ahead and he could have spent the next two rounds on the floor and won—and I'd tell him to take it easy. Bud would just grin and say as how folks had paid money to see a fight so he was gonna let 'em see one."[4]

In East Chicago a week after the Kelly fight, Taylor entered his third bout in 14 days, and it was his third career contest against the inimitable Pal Moore. Two thousand fans jammed into George Oswego's newly completed arena at 143rd Street and Todd Avenue for the building's inaugural event, most of them cheering their fellow Midwesterner. "There wasn't an idle minute in the whole fight," Ed Smith wrote in the *Chicago American.* The fight settled nothing between the rivals; the newspapers called it a draw.[5]

In Indianapolis, promoter Ed W. Harter likely had learned of the crowds attracted to cards led by Taylor-Moore. Harter, who went by his father's first name, "Steve," signed the two fighters for Feb. 13 in Tomlinson Hall. Taylor would be paid $2,000 for this fight.[6] Terre Haute-area fans eager to see their main man cleared their calendars and snapped up tickets. Joe Potts of Jasonville, Indiana, a huge fan of Taylor's, offered to give Bud a full-blooded Boston terrier puppy if he would stop Moore—a terrier for The Terrier.[7]

When the doors to Tomlinson Hall opened at 7 p.m., a double line of fans stretched two city blocks long. By main-event time, 5,000 souls had stuffed themselves into an arena that seated 3,700, an excess that did not go unnoticed by the Indianapolis fire department. Firefighters ordered the door closed even as the fans continued to pour into the Hall at East Market and North Delaware streets.[8]

More than 200 Hauteans had plopped into the seats of their Model T's and Essexes for the roughly 75-mile trip to Indy, at least a two-hour drive in those days with only about 50 miles of it over paved roads.[9] In the fight, Moore played his usual motion game, but took a few more chances than usual. "Often they stood toe to toe and slugged for dear life," read one account.[10] The Indianapolis newspapers the *Star* and the *News* scored it 3-3-4 and 4-4-2, a draw.[11] Joe Potts gave Taylor the puppy, anyway, and Bud quickly grew attached to his little friend.[12]

    The spectators at the Moore fight included a man whose fondness for sports helped foster a positive climate for boxing in Terre Haute: Mayor Ora Davis.[13] Davis had been raised in a town about 35 miles north of Terre Haute, served in World War I, then became an attorney and settled in the city.[14] When the 50-year-old ran for mayor in 1921, he promised to wipe out gambling, prostitution and bootlegging. This was no small task, as these enterprises had thrived in Terre Haute's notorious "red-light district" for decades. With a straight face, Davis phrased this promise to the public: "Give me four years to do it and if I fail, I want you to use my head for a football."[15] He got elected, left the whores and the horse-bettors alone, concentrated on upgrading the city's park system and other civic improvements, and became a well-respected leader. Among his accomplishments, he facilitated the building of the city's $400,000 Memorial Stadium in 1925, still a venue for athletic events 83 years later. Instead of kicking him in the temple, appreciative citizens tolerated the vice and re-elected him in 1925 for a second, four-year term.[16]

    The subculture of prizefighting in Terre Haute had an ally in Davis, who often attended the fights as did his police chief, Jack Smock.[17] In 1923, Davis slapped the official stamp of authority on boxing in the city by appointing a seven-member commission to oversee the fights.[18] The mayor seemed to love all sports, had played baseball earlier in life and was himself gifted athletically.[19] He enjoyed following the endeavors of the city's athletes and reveling in their team and individual successes. He could be counted on to throw out the first pitch for the minor-league Terre Haute Tots' baseball season opener.[20] When the city-owned Rea Park Golf Course opened on Aug. 1, 1924, Davis was handed a club for the honorary strike of the first ball. He whacked it 260 yards down the middle of the fairway, and from that tee it would stand as the longest drive of the day, even outdistancing some golf teaching professionals.21 When the women's state bowling tourney came to Terre Haute on May 9, 1925, organizers called on Davis to roll the ceremonial first ball. He had never been known to bowl, yet he honored his commitment by unselfconsciously lofting one onto the boards, then watching it fall off into the gutter a full 15 feet shy of the pins.22

The mayor's interest in Taylor extended beyond Davis' love for competitive athletics. In Taylor, he saw an image-builder for Terre Haute, a potential champion who was a clean liver and model of sportsmanship, whose publicity along his boxing travels could bring a wealth of positive attention to the city.23

Chapter 13

Money Gets Good

Taylor left Indianapolis with an aching thumb from the Moore fight, and the pain grew worse during sparring sessions in the days that followed. On Feb. 22, X-rays showed a fracture.[342]

The layoff from training meant he could catch up on the Terre Haute boxing scene. Taylor took an interest in Eddie Dyer, a wannabe pro who had been hanging out in the gyms, sometimes sparring with Bud. Dyer, 17, had blond hair, fast hands and an eagerness to learn, making it easy to surmise that he reminded Bud of someone. Taylor taught him how to generate more power by starting his blows from the shoulder, how to block punches, and other essentials.[2] Taylor agreed to manage him and served as his corner man on Feb. 23, 1923, when Dyer upped his record to 3-0 with a KO victory on a Terre Haute card.[3]

The next day, Taylor fell ill and checked himself into Union Hospital, where he was diagnosed with blood poisoning. Although the condition turned out not serious, Bud complied with doctors' orders to stay confined in a hospital room for a week.[4] Kept from his usual routine of training like an Olympian, these were restless days for Taylor. Dyer broke up the tedium with a phone call on one late night. After winning a fight at the K of C, the kid had hurried to call the hospital to gush the news to his mentor.[5]

On March 1, a Bronx-born fighter of Italian heritage named Frankie Genaro outpointed Pancho Villa to win the American flyweight championship. When Taylor heard the news, he declared his intention to chase Genaro everywhere, if he had to, to get a bout.[6] Taylor had been fighting at 114 to 118 pounds, but thought he could reduce to the flyweight max of 112 and still be effective. Promoter Joe Coffey promptly signed the pair for a 10-round bout in the Chicago Coliseum. Taylor, however, would not get his wish for a title bout, because the contract set the weight limit at 116.[7]

Genaro, 21, stood only 5 feet, 1 inch tall, but was thickly built. He threw an effective left hook punch, but knocked out very few men. "I know I am not a puncher, but I have the kind of blows that win points, and points win titles," he said. He also defended extraordinarily well, using his arms to block punches. Sportswriters called it Frankie's "pretzel guard," the way he positioned himself with both arms in front of him and tilted them at various angles.[8]

Taylor, aware that Genaro would merely counter-punch, planned to attack like a hungry mosquito. "I intend to go right after him with the first bell and stay right in there throwing gloves until something falls or breaks," a Chicago newspaper quoted Taylor.[9]

The bout's stakes shot higher when it was reported that Jimmy Wilde of Britain would visit the United States in the summer of 1923, and that the Genaro-Taylor winner might rate as his opponent for a world title fight.[10]

Interest in the Taylor-Genaro bout attracted 1,200 people downtown to Kid Howard's gym on Madison Street in Chicago, just to watch Taylor's training session April 2.[11] Taylor's understudy Dyer traveled to Chicago to work as one of his sparring partners.[12]

A few weeks earlier, boxing had been given a boost in Chicago with the passage of a citywide injunction keeping police from interfering with bouts.[13] For the first time in two decades, promoters could sell tickets publicly without fear of arrest. On fight day, April 4, 1923, a crowd estimated at 9,500 to 12,000 filled the Coliseum.[14] Scalpers sold $10 ringside seats for $40.[15]

Genaro boxed wisely, letting Taylor lead before retaliating with punches from all angles. Taylor won the first round, and gave it all he had in the final three minutes of the bout, but the vast in-between saw Genaro landing more blows, and avoiding Bud's. Genaro knocked two teeth out of Taylor's mouth in the fourth, and the bridge in the fifth. Taylor left the ring with solid evidence of a beating: swollen left cheek and nose, and puffed lips that trickled blood. Genaro showed only a cut lip. Five Chicago newspapers that covered the bout all gave the decision to Genaro, the closest being 4-3-3.[16]

One writer characterized Taylor's punching as extremely wild at times.[17] Taylor had taken a beating by a more efficient puncher whose compact shots pecked their target with precision.

The Taylor camp made $5,000 for the Genaro fight, Bud's biggest payday to date.[18] In those days, about 25 percent went to a boxer's manager. After his manager's cut, and smaller payouts to sparring partners and for equipment and travel expenses, Taylor made about $3,500 off the fight. Put in perspective, the mayor of Terre Haute made $5,000 *a year*, a junior high school teacher in Terre Haute with experience, $1,800 a year, and attending a major U.S. college for a year cost a little more than $800.[19] Taylor's income had soared from fighting $50 semifinals just 15 months earlier.[20] He might have been pinching himself to make sure it wasn't a dream—if he had any body fat to pinch. Except for buying the $5,000 Cadillac, which he later admitted was a foolish splurge, he generally took good care of his money.[21] In the aftermath of Taylor's fights, *The Terre Haute Tribune's* Ralph White wrote about Taylor visiting "the stone front," meaning, the bank.[23]

Taylor urged his dad, now in his sixties, to sell the horses and wagons that the hard-working elder used in hauling goods as a Teamster. He invited Sam Taylor to retire—at Bud's expense—and dad agreed. "But it wasn't long," Bud said, "dad got lonesome in just being retired and he hied away early one morning and brought back some of the horses and wagons to again enter business."[24]

Before he could rebound from the loss to Genaro, an injury forced Taylor to lay off fighting for eight weeks. In a sparring session with Sammy Mandell on April 22, Mandell buried a right into Taylor's side that cracked a rib.[25]

As Taylor's rib healed, baseball fans across the nation welcomed a new season. The diamond game reigned as the No. 1 sport in America throughout the 1920s. Thousands of men played on teams, from hometown amateur-level clubs sponsored by businesses or industry on up to the big leagues. Baseball fans daily scoured the box scores of their newspapers, cheering the progress of their heroes: Babe Ruth, Ty Cobb, George Sisler, Rogers Hornsby—household names in 1923.

In New York, a brand new ball park opened to host the American League's New York Yankees. With 74,000 fans looking on, Ruth christened the park April 18 with a home run into the right field bleachers. That same home run ball would sell for $1.26 million at auction in Sotheby's in New York in 2001, demonstrating the public's affinity for America's national pastime and the enduring popularity of its stars.[26]

In Terre Haute, the focus centered on the Tots, a professional minor league team. Baseball's 1920s minor leagues consisted of teams at divisions "A" through "D." One of the highest of the "B" division leagues was comprised of teams from Iowa, Illinois and Indiana; thus, it was known as the "3-I" League.

In 1923, the Terre Haute Tots' 3-I League park on the city's east side also served as the site of the occasional outdoor boxing promotion. On June 25, Taylor entered the ring against Tommy Murray for the first of three summer fight cards there in which Bud was featured in the main event.

Promoter George Grammell positioned the ring at home plate and charged $3 a ringside seat, $2 grandstand and $1 bleachers and sold all 3,400 tickets.[27] These were bargain prices, considering a ringside seat cost $10 for Taylor-Genaro in Chicago, (and, $7.70 in Indianapolis a month earlier when Taylor decisioned Johnny Shepard).[28] Taylor fans who failed to buy a ticket before the day of the Taylor-Murray bout walked up to the gate to find the bout sold out, so they resorted to clambering over the unguarded center-field fence. About 1,000 fans entered the premises this way and saw the bout free, standing or sitting in the outfield.[29] Taylor won the 10-round decision over Murray.

In the summer of 1923, Jack Dempsey defended his heavyweight title against Tommy Gibbons in Shelby, Montana. Since they shared the same manager, Taylor knew Gibbons well; they had worked out together and Gibbons had helped in Taylor's corner in the Jimmy Kelly fight in January.[30] Gibbons' successful fight career dated back to 1911, and Taylor had found Tommy's boxing advice helpful.[31] Taylor also noticed how Gibbons managed his money, investing much of his ring earnings in real estate instead of frittering it away foolishly, like others in the fight game.32

From the downtown newspaper building, *Terre Haute Tribune* employees announced by loudspeaker the round-by-round results of the July 4 Dempsey-Gibbons fight. A crowd outside the building ran for an entire downtown block. Guests in the 10-story Terre Haute House hotel, across the street from the newspaper building, opened their windows to keep current with the fight's status.33

Gibbons, 32, lost the decision, but historians generally consider it a victory for him just to have stayed upright for 15 rounds against Dempsey. The newspaper's fight story, in keeping with boxing's status at the time, ran on the front page of the *Terre Haute Star*—not page one of the sports page— but *page one*.34

Dempsey, by now accustomed to being paid in outrageous amounts, received $300,000 for the fight. Gibbons, a family man in Minnesota with three children under age 6, needed the money far more than the champion. But Eddie Kane had negotiated a contract for this bout that linked Gibbons' pay to the gate receipts. The remote Montana location drew a paltry 7,000 fans, so the challenger wound up with nothing. Gibbons' only payment came indirectly, from a months-long traveling vaudeville stint during which he earned an estimated $10,000 to $50,000. In these stage shows, he related to audiences how he stood up to the champ for 15 rounds. That a man could make that kind of money in 1923 for merely talking about how he went the distance with Dempsey effectively illustrates the champ's fame.35

Taylor, whose fame lay ahead of him, motored to Indianapolis on July 5, where he cruised to a 10-round win over Johnny Shepard, his second victory in six weeks over the Massachusetts fighter.

Chapter 14

Nailed by Gordon, Love

Harry Gordon owned a powerful right-hand punch, he just couldn't land it enough to win boxing matches. The New York bantamweight had lost to most of the better fighters in his weight class by the time he signed to fight Bud Taylor. About the best that can be said about Gordon's fistic career by 1923 is that Harry usually lasted the distance. Still, Gordon's shaky credentials mattered little to promoter Jim Mullen. Mullen needed a substitute to fight Taylor on July 20, 1923 in Aurora, Illinois after Herbie Schaeffer canceled a few days beforehand with hand problems.[1]

Taylor had won three straight since the Genaro loss, and Gordon seemed an unlikely candidate to end the streak. Opponents can be dangerous, however, when they have a big punch and nothing to lose.

Taylor had been training periodically for about a year under Jack Blackburn, master of the left jab and hook.[2] The hook is a powerful punch, with effects that have shut the lights out on boxers countless times in ring history. One of the best times to unleash a left hook is as a counterpunch at an opponent who throws a right, because the opponent's extended right arm exposes a roundhouse path to the chin.

In the first round against Gordon, Taylor saw Gordon's right hand coming, and tried to dodge the punch and start his own left hook. But he misjudged the speed of Gordon's oncoming punch. Gordon's right met Taylor's mouth with such force as to ram his teeth through his lower lip and send a chunk of flesh flying. Taylor fell back into the ropes, semiconscious.

"I thought the roof caved in," Taylor said in one of the many times he recalled the fight. "I should've gone down, and as I came off the ropes, he nailed me with the right again, on the kisser. And it was like a hot shot in the arm, and brought me to my senses again."

Taylor fought on for two rounds in a fog until his head finally cleared in the fourth. By then, Taylor's left hook began to work for him, he picked up momentum and ultimately, he won the newspapers' decisions. He left the ring a bloody mess, with a badly cut lip and a gash under an eye.

"I won the fight, but Lon Chaney had nothing on me for makeup after that one," Taylor said, referring to the Hollywood horror-film star of the 1920s. "You should have seen my face."

Taylor would call the Gordon fight the closest he ever came to being knocked out. Twenty years later, the white scars on his lower lip showed where he had been cut by his own teeth from Gordon's blow.[3]

On Saturday, Aug. 11, 1923, 20-year-old Taylor and 16-year-old Iris Ward drove to Indianapolis, where they acquired a marriage license in the morning, and exchanged vows in the afternoon.

"The marriage of the pride of Terre Haute glove fans was intended to be kept secret," Ralph White wrote afterward, without elaborating. Bud and Iris invited only one couple, friends Carl and Florence Pfeifer of Terre Haute, as witnesses to the ceremony.[4] An explanation for the secretiveness of the ceremony never surfaced publicly; the couple simply may have wanted privacy that would have been impossible to achieve if they had wed in Terre Haute.

Ward had grown up poor, in a crowded house about a mile from the Taylors' neighborhood.[5] She was a looker, a petite girl with gorgeous eyes and an engaging smile.[5] She befit the image of the flapper of the times: giddy, attractive and slightly unconventional.[7]

The newlyweds moved into the house that Taylor had built for his parents at 2011 Third Ave. The couple planned to have their own home built while they stayed with Sam and Tillie Taylor.[8]

It was a rocky marriage, and not a good time in either of their lives to foster a mature relationship with a mate. In the press, it appeared all was well between them, but in reality, Iris would file for divorce twice over the next four years. Restless and extroverted, Iris liked to go out during evenings and drink and mingle. Although he liked to dance, Bud's strict training regimen did not allow for too many evenings out, and he preferred privacy—particularly as his ring successes propelled him more and more into the public spotlight. Iris may have needed more attention than her husband could supply in his suitcase career as a professional athlete. Despite the marriage vows, Bud's real commitment remained to boxing. He hardly missed a skip of the rope in training for his next bout, a victory over Hilly Levine in Aurora on Aug. 24.[9]

Taylor returned to Terre Haute from Aurora and immediately began preparing for a rematch with Gordon, set for Sept. 3 at the 3-I park.[10] Taylor had won all six of his outings since the April loss to Genaro, and he trained hard, wanting to ensure that another pulverizing right hand by Gordon didn't interrupt his momentum. The second Gordon fight took on even more significance when Taylor learned that Kane and Long had signed Bud to fight Villa on Sept. 8 in Chicago. The fight with Villa stayed on the schedule only if Taylor did not lose decisively to Gordon.[11]

Villa, by this time, had ascended to *world's* flyweight champion by having knocked out Jimmy Wilde in June before 40,000 fans in New York.[12]

The Villa-Taylor bout, however, would not be for the title, because the fighters agreed to set the limit at the "catchweight" of 116 pounds, four pounds above the flyweight maximum.

The tendency of champions to box nonchampionship bouts warrants an explanation here. The rules governing defenses of boxing titles were not as strict in the 1920s as later, when boxing commissions exerted greater control over the game. The fighters who held titles commonly fought nontitle bouts at weights set above the limit for their division. In fact, they preferred such fights, because they could make big money off their names, avoid risking their titles and not have the inconvenience of trimming down to a weight they may have outgrown. Their managers bided their time and picked bouts to put the title on the line only when the money was right. Boxing print columnists often blasted the champions who they perceived as exploiting the system for the money. "Champs prefer chumps," Chicago sportswriter Ed Smith titled one of his columns, in which he criticized champions for fighting inferior opponents at catchweights while ducking the quality challengers.13 Villa was not considered one of the worst violators, simply because few in his weight class rivaled his talent. Nonetheless, his reign as world flyweight champion 1923-25 proved typical for the times: it consisted of three title defenses and 23 nontitle bouts.14

    Taylor encountered little difficulty with Gordon in their rematch, winning unanimously in the press. Taylor threw more punches than in their first bout, rat-tat-tatting Gordon out of any chance to measure Bud with the dangerous right. Taylor's own right opened a serious gash above Gordon's left eye in the fifth round, and when Bud's jabs continued to find the eye, it forced Harry continually to cover.15

    The win pushed Taylor's pro record to 49-5-9, and he had become an established star in professional boxing. He did not have to look far for a reminder of how fast it had all happened. The first preliminary of the Taylor-Gordon card featured Davy Templeton, still fighting openers nearly four years since he provided the opposition in Bud's first pro fight.16

    In Chicago, meanwhile, the $5 ringside seats to Taylor-Villa were selling fast.17

Chapter 15

Christening a Terror

Francisco Guilledo of the island of Panay, Philippines, was a veteran of the ring before he ever entered America to earn big money from boxing. The sport was huge in the Philippines, and he fought about 50 times from 1919 to 1922 before coming stateside.[1]

That Guilledo would adopt the same name as an infamous Mexican revolutionary, Pancho Villa, resulted purely from coincidence. "Pancho" had been Guilledo's nickname, and "Villa" his foster father's surname.[2]

Villa had KO'd Johnny Buff in September 1922 to gain recognition as the American flyweight titleholder, soon lost that designation to Frankie Genaro, but then became world titleholder by knocking out Jimmy Wilde.[3] While promoters worked on rematching him with Genaro, Villa and his entourage flitted around the United States taking lucrative nontitle bouts, such as one with Bud Taylor in the fall of 1922.

As a fighter, Villa was a bundle of continuous movement. His legs and hands were extremely quick, which made him a hard target. He stood only 5 feet 1 inch tall, a height that positioned him ideally for his favorite ring endeavor—beating on his opponent's midsection. He also owned a hallmark of Filipino boxers: the ability to take massive amounts of punishment yet keep fighting.

Proud and self-assured, Villa also practiced model sportsmanship. He would hold the ropes apart to help his opponent climb into the ring, "and then shake his hand as if they were the best of friends."[4]

Outside the ring, Villa went wild over American fashion. His trainer said that on one trip across the nation, Pancho and his wife carried 22 trunks loaded with clothes. "Pancho would buy three suits, two perfect fits and one a bit loose. He would wear the loose ones after he had gained three or four pounds before resuming training," said the trainer, Whitey Eckwart.[5]

As fight day neared, Taylor worked out in Chicago's Arcade gym. "I was never in better shape," he told the press, "and I am going to try and stop Villa." The writers found the irrepressible Long much more quotable. "Bud is just as good as Villa and don't be surprised if he knocks that chink out of the arena," one newspaper quoted him.[6] The word "chink" appeared in print commonly at a time before intolerance for such slurs commanded otherwise.

Long summoned Blackburn to run the workouts, and the scar-faced one climbed through the ropes and into the canvas classroom to instruct his pupil. "When he tells me to do something, I do it," Taylor said about Blackburn, "for I know he knows what he is having me do. It's not try-this-or-try-that with him, but *do* this, and I find I can do it. He's the best I ever met."[7]

Matchmaker Joe Coffey had secured the Hawthorne Park racetrack to stage the show. Early reports forecasted a 20,000-fan turnout.[8] On the big day, however, the bout fell to the bane of outdoor sporting events: rain. Close to the start of the preliminaries, the weather improved, and 12,000 showed up on the gamble the rain clouds would stay away.[9] About 200 Taylor fans took a train from Terre Haute to watch the fight.[10] Iris Taylor also attended, still accustoming herself to the pulse-pounding duty of watching her husband make his living punching other men and getting smacked in return. Long planned to give Taylor a month off after the fight, and Bud planned to take his wife on a fishing trip.[11]

As the semifinal bout neared its conclusion, Long handed Taylor a telegram in the dressing room. It read, "I am pulling hard for you and hope you bring home the bacon." Printed as the sender's name: "Ora D. Davis." The mayor's well-wishes pleased Taylor.[12]

The fighters set a fast pace, and both landed blows in the early rounds that scored points. Bob Nesbit of the Terre Haute Star noticed splotches of red on the fair skin of Taylor's midsection, artwork from

Villa's body blows.13 Taylor tossed a right in the fifth round intended for Villa's jaw, but it landed high on his skull and fractured the bone between Bud's hand and forefinger. Taylor fought through the pain, not knowing the extent of the injury.14 Despite many flurries of punches, neither fighter had the other in peril throughout the contest.15 Taylor occasionally fell into his habit of wildness, even falling to the canvass after one swing in the eighth round.16 Most of the Chicago sportswriters cited Villa as the winner, with the difference in opinion ranging from 8-2 for Pancho by rounds, to a narrow victory for Taylor.17 The *Chicago Daily Tribune*, for example, scored it 5-2-3, Villa, who showed "classy footwork" and "telling blows while in the clinches."18

Promoters lost $7,000 on the fight because of the inclement weather.19 Taylor had worked on a guarantee, and collected his $5,000 with no trouble.20

Back in Terre Haute, X-ray images assured Taylor he would need that vacation Long had promised. The images showed the hand had been fractured, and the wrist bone shattered, as well.21

The fight game always has boasted its share of nicknames, from the bland "Boston Strongboy" for John L. Sullivan in the 1890s to the ominous James "Bonecrusher" Smith a hundred years later.

In a 1934 obituary for sportswriter Ralph White, White is credited as the originator of "The Terre Haute Terror," nickname for Bud Taylor, and the tag appears in print as early as November 1922.22

White tossed various nicknames for Taylor into his stories more often than the *terror*, among them the "Terre Haute Tornado" and "Hoosier Hellcat."23 Taylor also heard various takeoffs on his name based on the whims of ring announcers, who introduced him as "The Hoosier Hurricane" and the "Terre Haute Troublemaker," and surely others.24 The most common nickname in print, The Terre Haute *Terrier*, looked like the one that might stick until Ring magazine pictured Bud on the cover of its October 1923 issue and called Taylor the "Terre Haute Terror" in the text of the story inside.

New York sportswriter Nat Fleischer had started the monthly *Ring* magazine in 1922, priced it at 15 cents and it quickly became established as the No. 1 source of reading entertainment for boxing fans across the nation. Taylor's photograph appeared on the cover of the October 1923 issue, in which he was billed as "the most sensational flyweight in the West."

"Several leading bantamweights in the east have been offered lucrative matches with the Terre Haute Terror, but they refused to consider a match with him," the article reads. The article also identifies Taylor as "the biggest drawing card in the west among small men." The article also mentions that although Kane and Long have tried unsuccessfully to land a fight for Taylor in Madison Square Garden, Bud's recent success ensured a fight in the Garden soon.[25]

Time magazine also spread the popularity of the nickname "Terre Haute Terror" by using it in reference to Taylor in 1924 in a brief account of one of Taylor's fights.[26] The "terror" nickname would become as closely associated to Taylor as the "Manassa Mauler" is to Jack Dempsey. "Blond Terror of Terre Haute" is the nickname in Taylor's accompanying information in the International Boxing Hall of Fame in Canastota, New York.

Bud Taylor Jr. remembered his father being both flattered and amused by the "terror" reference. "He got a big kick out of it," Taylor Jr. said.[27]

By the second week of October, Taylor's management team had him booked for Madison Square Garden for a fight Oct. 19, 1923. He would debut in the Garden in the semifinal match of a card promoted by Tex Rickard.[28]

Charles "Tex" Rickard stands as one of the most influential figures in popularizing professional boxing. His previous occupations sounded as though they had been culled from the pages of a Wild West adventure novel: gold prospector in Alaska, town marshal in Texas, saloon owner in Nevada.[29] As for the fight game, Rickard's first big splash came in promoting the Jack Johnson-Jim Jeffries heavyweight title fight in Reno, Nevada in 1910. Later, he promoted many of Dempsey's fights. When New York legalized boxing in 1920, Rickard helped turn Madison Square Garden into the premier boxing palace in the nation. Marquee matchups such as Dempsey-Carpentier (80,000 fans, $1.8 million gate) and Dempsey-Tunney (120,000 fans, $1.9 million gate) helped propel boxing's heavyweight title fights into the financial stratosphere.[30] Rickard's customers had so much confidence in his integrity that they would send him signed, blank checks for seats to big bouts for which ticket prices had not yet been set, and Tex would fill in the amount.31

The condition of Taylor's right hand worried Eddie Long, causing deep concern about Taylor's first appearance in the Garden. The cracked bone suffered in a punch to Villa's head had not healed sufficiently, and forced Long to yank Taylor out of an Oct. 12 bout with Harold Smith.32 Long phoned Frank Flournoy, the Garden's matchmaker, and advised him that if the hand did not heal to Long's satisfaction, he would cancel. It didn't matter if Taylor was scheduled to appear in Madison Square Garden or the garden in his back yard, Long would not risk a permanent injury or extended layoff by aggravating the injury. Flournoy responded not to worry, that he would sign an opponent that Taylor could beat with one hand. Long's firm reply: the opponent does not matter, I will not unnecessarily risk my fighter's well-being.33

Flournoy scraped the bottom of the fistic barrel for an opponent and dug out Charley Phil Rosenberg, 22, a Harlem palooka who had won, according to contemporary boxing records, seven of his roughly 25 pro fights.

As fight day neared, Long gave Taylor the green light to go through with the bout despite Bud's tender hand. Taylor breezed through the 10-rounder, winning by unanimous decision of the two judges and referee. According to the *New York Journal*, Taylor "made a monkey out of the Harlemite, raining in punches from every imaginable angle to the amusement of the spectators." The *Journal*'s Sid Mercer leveled only one criticism at Taylor: he swings wildly at times.34

Promoters at Madison Square Garden wanted Taylor to reappear there Oct. 26, but both hands were too sore, and he took a train home.35

Tommy Gibbons, touring the nation putting on boxing demonstrations after going the distance with Dempsey on July 4, appeared in Terre Haute's Indiana Theatre on Nov. 28, 1923.36 When Gibbons arrived in the city three days earlier, Taylor stood as one of the first to greet his friend and boxing stablemate.37 In the show, Gibbons demonstrated his favorite punches and sparred three rounds with Taylor before a capacity crowd of about 1,600.38

As the days passed, Taylor believed his right hand had healed sufficiently to headline a boxing card Dec. 5 that would serve as a fundraiser for the Knights of Pythias lodge in Terre Haute.[39] For his main-event opponent, promoter George Grammell brought in Roy Moore of St. Paul, Minnesota, a veteran of more than 200 pro fights, according to one estimate.[40] Moore had beaten Frankie Mason and Pal Moore—but that had been four years earlier, ancient history in the fight game.[41] Moore had been an easy target for years; at age 34 he defended little better than a heavy workout bag. In the fight, Taylor floored Moore in the third and pummeled him from ring post to ring post for 10 rounds, using only his left hand so he could rest the tender right. Poignantly, the beat-up old-timer's first postfight question to a reporter was "Did the fans like the bout?"[42]

Taylor had planned to travel to Chicago to box in a benefit Christmas show on Dec. 9, but the Moore fight compelled him to take the rest of the year off. He had bounced so many punches off old Roy's head that now Taylor's left hand was swollen, too.[43]

1923 had been a springboard year for Taylor's career. The bouts with Villa and Genaro, his only two losses in 15 engagements, had earned him five grand apiece and given him national exposure on the cover of boxing's foremost monthly magazine. Fight promoters all over the nation wanted him.[44] He was by no means satisfied. He had defeated the pretenders and the mediocres in his weight classes and some better-than-average fighters, but his losses to champions Villa and Genaro and the draws with Pal Moore tugged at him. It was only a short distance to the top, and Taylor did not want to stall at the level just below.[45]

Chapter 16

Frankie Jerome

Bud Taylor opened 1924 swinging, with two bouts in New York sandwiched around a fight in Indianapolis, all within 11 days. Pulling it off required the fastest travel possible, and that meant riding "The Century." From 1902 to 1967, the New York Central Railroad operated a popular passenger train from Chicago to New York: the 20th Century Limited. The Century rambled across the prairies at up to 60 miles per hour, at least 20 mph faster than automobile speed limits.[1] Taylor rode to the East Coast for a New Year's Day bout with New Yorker Sammy Nable, back to Indiana to fight Johnny Brown in Indianapolis, then off to New York for the third bout.

Taylor's fragile hands felt strong, and he found good whip in his punches. He floored Nable three times in a 12-round win and sent Brown downward six times before the KO.[2] For the third bout, in Madison Square Garden, he faced a more formidable opponent: Frankie Jerome.

Taylor rented a flat on West 72nd Street, New York, and brought along Iris with plans to stay on the East Coast for as long as two months. He planned to schedule additional fights in New York City as well as Pennsylvania and New Jersey.[3]

Jerome stood taller, had a longer reach than Taylor, and moved just as quickly. He had been described as a tireless, springy-stepped boxer who threw accurate, if not felling, punches.[4] One particular trait made him extremely popular with fans: a granite jaw. In fights, Jerome had never been down for the count. He had taken single blasts and wicked combinations, but always managed to keep his feet riveted to the canvas.

Jerome, whose real name was Frank Dougherty, had grown up in the Bronx, where a priest trying to keep wayward youths out of trouble taught him how to box. He took the name "Jerome" from a church, St. Jerome's, and at 15 entered his first boxing match. He fought his early bouts in a crude, free-for-all style, and he once said that other boxers would tell him to quit trying to spar like an electric fan.[5] When World War I broke out with Germany, Frankie shipped off to France to fight the bigger fight, and stayed as a soldier for 11 months.[6]

Stateside, he returned to boxing, and after a gym mate taught him how to punch straight, he began to show some success.[7] He turned pro at 19 and built a local, then regional, following. Outside the ring, his counterparts considered him a likable fellow. His narrow eyes, set close together, could look menacing but his face was softened by thin, slight brows and wavy hair.[8] Abe Goldstein, a Hall-of-Fame bantamweight from the era who would later fight two bouts with Taylor, spoke publicly of his affection for Jerome.[9]

Promoters loved Jerome, too, because he put fans in the seats. His bouts in November and December 1923 drew 9,912 (against Carl Duane) and 8,270 (against Johnny Curtin) to Madison Square Garden.[10] Duane also hailed from the Bronx and his two fights with Jerome had become violently partisan affairs. Their respective followers stormed down the streets in tallyhoes, trucks and wagons with banners on their vehicles dedicated to their heroes.[11]

Jerome entered the Taylor fight having lost his past three bouts, and there were signs that the cumulative effects of 98 career bouts had slowed him. Duane had outweighed Jerome by a whopping eight pounds and battered Frankie through nine of the first 10 rounds, but Frankie, in character, survived the 12-round main event on his feet.[12] Curtin knocked Jerome down three times in the first five rounds before Frankie recovered and nearly came back to win in 10.[13] Now, in Taylor, Jerome faced an even greater puncher than Duane or Curtin.

When Taylor and Jerome entered the ring for their 12-rounder on Jan. 11, 1924, "Taylor weighed two pounds less than Jerome and appeared so slight of build that the force of his punches surprised those at ringside," according to the *New York Times*.[14]

The 8,554 people in the seats witnessed a lopsided contest all the way from the opening bell.[15] The *New York Tribune* had Taylor winning every round except the fourth and the 10th and opined that Jerome "managed to stay as long as he did by sheer, unadulterated courage."[16] Jerome nearly fell in the sixth, and again in the seventh.[17] In an account of the fight that hit the newsstands before Jerome's post-fight fate was known, the *Tribune* reported, prophetically, that Jerome put on "an exhibition of gameness that will never be forgotten by those who saw it."[18] Jerome took dozens of hits, perhaps hundreds, yet kept coming.

In the 11th round, Taylor struck a blow that ordinarily would finish an opponent. When two automobiles crash head-on, the force is far greater than when a car slams into a stationary object. The principle of linear momentum is the same in the ring. Jerome, a wounded man lunging forward head-on in desperate attempts to hit Taylor, took a punch to the chin with all Bud's weight behind it.

"We both started right-hand punches for the jaw," Taylor recalled, four days later. "My blow got just inside of Frankie's try, and the first thing I knew he was on the floor." [19]

At the count of 8 or 9, Jerome rose, miraculously, as if ordered by some inner voice to press on despite no hope of lasting. He staggered about the ring in the remaining seconds of the round, with his blond attacker in pursuit.[20]

Between rounds, Jerome's trainer, Lou Brix, wanted to toss in the towel but Frankie wouldn't allow it. "I'm all right. I can stand it," the fighter said. "I'll get by this round OK."[21]

When the 12th began, Taylor muscled his still-groggy opponent into the ropes and hit him with body blows until Jerome went down. Jerome used the ropes to pull himself to his feet before the count of 9, and tried feebly to attack. Instead, he wobbled into the arms of Referee Jack O'Sullivan, who stopped the fight at 43 seconds.[22]

Jerome passed out while being assisted to his corner and had to be carried to his dressing room.[23] His helpers revived him, but state boxing commissioner William McCormack insisted he be taken to the hospital.[24] Taylor, unaware of his opponent's perilous condition, left the Garden and joined his wife and friends on Broadway for an evening of dancing.25 At Bellevue Hospital, Tex Rickard and Jerome's former manager Billy Gibson and dozens of other well-wishers visited Jerome. The day after the fight, Taylor himself visited Jerome bedside and they chatted, according to one report. Later, doctors who examined Jerome suspected a cerebral hemorrhage and wanted to drill into the skull to relieve pressure on the brain from bleeding. Jerome was still conscious when told of the surgery, two days after the bout. "Well, boys, I guess this is my last fight," he told his friends from his bed.26 He never awoke from surgery. On Sunday, about 50 hours after the fight, and with his wife, Louise, by his bedside, Jerome died.27 "He died right in my arms, slipping punches," said his trainer, Whitey Bimstein.28

Eddie Long broke the news to Taylor, who "broke down and wept like a child."

"No one knows how I feel. I'd give anything to have Frankie alive tonight," Taylor said, between sobs.29

A spate of false rumors circulated after the fight and made their way into news accounts in the days that followed: that Jerome had died from a skull fracture when he hit his head on the ring canvass; that Jerome was out of shape and shouldn't have been allowed to fight; that the referee should have stopped the fight sooner ... 30 The *New York Times* tried to interview Taylor, but "he was grief-stricken and refused even to discuss the matter."31 Long expressed his surprise at the death, saying that Taylor had hit many opponents more frequently and as hard as he hit Jerome, without any serious consequences.32

A district attorney's office in New York began a homicide investigation into the death.33 On Jan. 15, Terre Haute's Fort Harrison Post No. 40 of the American Legion wired Taylor a message of support: "We want you to feel that you have many friends here who stand back of you at all times," wrote the Post commander.34 The American Legion and Elks lodges of Sullivan, Indiana, also wired telegrams to Taylor expressing sympathy and support.35

Dr. Charles Norris, medical examiner, determined Jerome's death was caused by a ruptured blood vessel between the skull and the base of the brain from a blow that landed to the right temple. He found no fracture. Specifically, Norris explained that one of the veins that travel from the surface of the brain to the skull had been damaged by the blow, causing a slow leakage of blood.

"I recall only two similar cases in the past five years," he said, "which is a remarkable record when the number of bouts conducted in New York is considered."36

Strictly interpreted, the ruling indicates the death blow could have been inflicted in the first, 11th or any round between, when Taylor struck Jerome on the temple and caused the vessel to leak.

As part of the investigation into the death, District Attorney Morgan A. Jones interviewed Taylor.37 Earlier, in a postfight interview, Taylor had told the press that as Jerome struggled through the 12th round, "I realized something was wrong and refused to hit the game fellow about the head."38 Taylor told the district attorney that between the 11th and 12th rounds, Long instructed him to stop aiming his punches at his helpless opponent's head and instead work over the body.39 Ordinarily, such an assertion might invite doubt. Since when does a manager tell his fighter not to go for the KO, in an important bout, at an easy target? In professional boxing, demonstrations of concern for the well-being of an opponent usually are withheld until *after* the fight. Written accounts in New York newspapers of the 12th round do, indeed, indicate Taylor threw only body punches at Jerome during the final round's 43 seconds.40

About 2,000 people crowded into the St. Jerome's church for the funeral, including columnist Westbrook Pegler of the *United News*. Pegler noted Taylor's presence: "A yellow-haired kid with a mashed nose and scalloped lips, dipped his fingers in the holy water fount of St. Jerome's church, crossed himself with the fist that killed Frankie Jerome and went to his knees on the cold marble to pray, when all that was left of the little fellow was wheeled up the aisle to the altar yesterday for the funeral mass that preceded the journey to the grave," he wrote.41 Taylor sat silently during Mass, nagged by the self-posed question, "Is boxing worth taking a life?" He leaned over to Long and whispered something about not boxing anymore. Long responded by saying they should discuss it later, perhaps on the train back to Chicago.42

Taylor visited the home of Jerome's mother, sending word ahead to ask if he could pay his respects.

"Frankie fought just one fight too many," she said. "There's no one to blame, and tell him to come up."43

Everybody in the house was crying, which made Taylor cry, too, but the grieving family treated visiting Bud and his manager kindly. The family attributed Frankie's death to fate.44

New York authorities ruled the death as accidental, deciding not to prosecute and clearing Taylor of any wrongdoing.45

The death provided fuel for opponents of boxing already clamoring for its abolishment for other reasons. Bert Lord of Chenango, N.Y., was one of two legislators who by Jan. 16 had introduced bills into the New York state assembly to repeal the Walker boxing law. Lawmakers also were upset with what some thought were boxing's unconscionable purses (including half a million dollars to Dempsey recently); exorbitant admission prices; that Rickard's grip on the game amounted to a "trust"; and questionable judges' decisions.46

In a ridiculous analogy, made during a speech before a state assembly on Feb. 20, Lord likened boxing to murder, saying: "The Diamond brothers killed a bank messenger for money; Bud Taylor killed Frankie Jerome in a prize ring for money. What is the difference?"47 The more popular notion, purveyed by the sports columnists of the nation, was that boxing was less dangerous than other sports and its benefits justified its continuance.48 "The law of averages holds that every now and again some unfortunate kid must be killed in the fight ring," one columnist wrote. "After 4,000 rounds of fighting in Madison Square Garden during the last four indoor seasons, it was time for someone to go."49 The bills designed to end boxing in the state of New York failed to muster enough support.

Boxing's defenders needed only to point to football, whose fatalities far outnumbered any sport. Interest in American football had skyrocketed in the late 19-teens, spawning teams at the levels of high school, college, semi-pro—and with the forerunner to the National Football League in 1920—pro. As examples, a game between the University of California and Stanford drew 100,000 fans in 1924, and Army versus Yale, 80,000.50 A football game in Terre Haute between Wiley and Garfield high schools in 1924 attracted 11,500 fans to Memorial Stadium.51 The sport's popularity came at a hefty price for many families. The young men of the gridirons who banged heads at full speed in the primitively equipped uniforms of the times suffered devastating injuries. Deaths were common, and in one particularly lethal period of Oct. 2 to Dec. 9, 1923, 19 players, including nine high-schoolers, died on the football fields across the nation. They died mostly from fractured skulls and backs, but also from neck and spinal injuries, blood poisoning from broken bones, and in one instance, from choking to death on a wad of chewing tobacco.[52]

Taylor returned to Terre Haute on Jan. 18, where Ralph White could elicit only a brief comment about the Jerome tragedy. "The very thought of the fight sickens me," Bud said, then describing the 11th and 12th rounds as he had to New York writers. "The whole affair has just got me and I'd rather not talk about it just now." Taylor finished the interview by pointing out that a Princeton University hockey player died from injuries suffered in a game on the same day as the Jerome bout (he had been hit in the head by a hockey stick), but that no one had called for hockey's demise. "But somehow or other they are only too quick to slam my profession. Few deaths occur in regulated boxing and I am sure the unfortunate death of Frankie will not stop the game in New York."[53] In his public statements, Taylor seemed to embrace the logical perspective that he was no more responsible for Jerome's death than the driver of an automobile who kills a pedestrian who has run out into traffic. Taylor continued his boxing career 10 days later by re-entering the ring to fight in his home state.

Chapter 17

Punching with Pancho

Amid the thud of gloves and the rattle of speed bags among the sounds of the Chicago boxing gyms, the hang-arounders could be heard muttering in disagreement. A boxer is never the same once he kills a man, one side insisted. Bud Taylor will become trigger-shy, lose his aggressiveness, and ease up on the force of his punches out of fear it will happen again. Hadn't Jess Willard turned soft after killing "Bull" Young in the ring back in '13?[1]

Taylor answered such speculation on Jan. 28, 1924, when he fought Herbie Schaeffer in East Chicago. The 2,300 fans in George Oswego's auditorium amounted to the biggest turnout of the season for the venue. From the opening bell, Taylor showed no signs of timidity, winning every round and having Schaeffer on the verge of a knockdown in the sixth and eighth rounds en route to a 10-round decision.[2]

And, Taylor was as popular as ever. By Jan. 22, Eddie Long had signed him for two bouts in Indianapolis, and Milwaukee promoters were inquiring about a rematch with Villa.[3] Two days later, Long had committed his fighter to bouts in the Ohio cities of Cleveland, Youngstown and Columbus.[4]

Long, however, had been unable to reel in world bantamweight champ Joe Lynch; he was not among Taylor's anticipated opponents. Villa remained the world flyweight champion, but the task of reducing to 112 pounds put the flyweight title out of Taylor's reach. Taylor's days of fighting in the tiniest division were past. "Bud simply can't reduce way down and be himself," Ralph White wrote.5 Trimming to 112, even to 116, drained too much of his strength. Any fight with Villa would have to go at catchweights.

Taylor wanted to leave the Jerome tragedy far, far behind, but the death had become a part of his boxing resume'. Sportswriters would mention it in their stories in advance of Taylor's bouts, as if to remind readers that the violence of the sport is authentic and its participants at risk to lose far more than just a contest. The publicity about the fatality also served to, whether intentionally or not, hype his fights. In a sport in which violence is so integral, Taylor was known for having achieved the ultimate. Fight fans may not have wanted to see a boxer actually beat another boxer to death, but they certainly wanted to watch a man whose punches were so capable.

Sometimes, fans would forget themselves and spew out heartless comments. In the Schaeffer bout, after Schaeffer landed a punch to Taylor's head during a spirited exchange of blows, an overzealous Schaeffer supporter yelled, "Hey, Bud, you're not fighting Jerome now," to which Taylor fans reacted by loudly admonishing the spectator.6

In Columbus, Ohio for a Feb. 7 bout with Phil O'Dowd, fans tried to question Taylor about the Jerome fight while he worked out in O'Rourke's Gym, but found Bud unwilling to discuss the tragedy. "Jerome was a great fighter and a mighty fine chap," is all he said.7

O'Dowd outpointed Taylor over 10 rounds, flooring Bud with a left hook in the sixth. Taylor and Eddie Kane offered no excuses for the loss, saying O'Dowd simply was the better man on that night.8 Taylor seemed stale from overwork, one sportswriter wrote.9 The fight was his fifth in six weeks.

At least one Ohio writer, however, also noted a flaw in Taylor's game: a tendency to swing and miss with the right.10 Sportswriters in Terre Haute, New York, Chicago and St. Louis had noticed these careless overthrows, too.11

A fundamental difference exists between a *swing*, which is a no-no in boxing, and a *punch*, which travels a shorter distance. Swings fit the arsenal of saloon brawlers and street fighters and have little use in the ring. A swing saps energy and is easily evaded, and worse, it fails to land even if aimed correctly because the targeted boxer sees it coming and beats the swinger to the punch.12 A swinging fighter is like the baseball pitcher with a fastball he can't control.

On Feb. 18, Taylor fought a rematch with journeyman New Yorker Sammy Nable in Tomlinson Hall in Indianapolis, flooring him in the first round and winning all 10 rounds. Nable realized early he was outclassed and tried to clinch throughout.13 Taylor earned $1,200 for the punch practice and dance lesson.14 The fight served its purpose as a tuneup for Villa, planned for March 6 in Milwaukee.

Back in Terre Haute, a week after the Nable drubbing and a month after the Jerome fatality, Taylor, surprise of all surprises, encountered difficulty finding a sparring partner. Regular partner Jackie Barnhart was out of town and Taylor could find no backup. He offered an ex-boxer, Paul Brown, $5 a round for three rounds, but "Brownie" said he wouldn't do it even if Taylor wore handcuffs.15 Bud Perrill finally agreed to help Taylor by filling in for Barnhart.16

Long, anticipating a blockbuster turnout for the Villa bout, agreed to a contract without a cash guarantee and to accept as payment only a percentage of the gate. Villa, the bigger name among the two fighters, negotiated a guarantee of $6,200 and could expect to earn as much as 10 grand if tickets ($1 to $5) sold well.17

The press liked to quote Villa in his broken English. A few days before the fight, a Milwaukee scribe asked him about Taylor's size advantage—5 inches in height and an anticipated 4 pounds. "Me bring him down to my size when me punch him hard," Villa replied.18 But on fight night, he did something rare for Villa: He lost.

Eight thousand fans in the Cream City Athletic Club watched Taylor win the 10-rounder easily.19 Some writers hailed the punching performance by Taylor while others thought Villa looked lethargic. "Bud forced the milling and took all the chances. The blows Villa managed to land did not slow Taylor," Walter Eckersall wrote in the *Chicago Daily Tribune*.20 Villa seemed baffled by Taylor's left, then in the seventh round, Bud sneaked in a terrific right cross that sent Villa clear across the ring.21 One writer thought Villa showed little fight until the last two rounds, and his paper's story ran under the pointed headline: "Ruler of midgets loafs through eight sessions."22 Villa blamed his shoddy performance on illness, and the *Wisconsin News* couldn't resist printing the Filipino's precious postfight lament: "My nose was stuffed and I had a bad colt on my chest."23

The $25,000-plus gate produced about $4,700 for Taylor and entourage.24 Two days later, the newspapers reported great news for

Taylor's side: the victory had clinched a match with bantamweight champion Joe Lynch in May.[25]

Indianapolis promoter Steve Harter wanted the Lynch-Taylor fight for May 29, the evening before the 1924 Indy 500.[26] A title fight in Taylor's home state, with attendance bolstered by the crowds in town for the race, looked like a promoter's dream. In Long Island, New York, matchmaker Lew Raymond also wanted the bout for an outdoor venue in early May.[27] Before Taylor began serious preparations for a bout with Lynch anywhere, he needed surgery on his lip, and several weeks to heal. His lip had been cut and re-cut without time to heal properly, so that blood sprung whenever he took a punch there. Dr. F.H. Jett removed the scar during surgery in Terre Haute.[28] Taylor used the off-time to enjoy the local boxing scene. He boxed a light exhibition with Eddie Dyer in Terre Haute's Pennsylvania Railroad gym and attended a fight card at the K of C.[29] After watching the fights, Taylor and Eddie Long took The Century to New York to sit ringside in Madison Square Garden for Lynch's title defense March 21 against Abe Goldstein.[30]

The ring announcer introduced Taylor to the crowd, and his presence drew huge applause. He took his seat and watched Goldstein win the world bantamweight championship, outboxing Lynch in virtually every round.[31]

In a sport in which rags-to-riches stories are common, Goldstein's life's journey emerges as especially compelling. Left parentless at age 2, he grew up in the slums of New York's lower east side raised first by a sister and then in a Jewish orphanage.[32] He began boxing in his mid-teens and soon met renown middleweight Willie Lewis, who took Abe under his wing and taught him Lewis' signature left-hook, right-cross combo. By the late 19-teens, Goldstein had climbed into the upper echelon of the bantamweight ranks. His career had stalled in 1919-20 when Lynch KO'd him in 11 rounds and Johnny Buff in 2. In re-establishing himself, he had assembled a four-match win streak going into the rematch with Lynch that brought Goldstein the title.[33]

The New York writers considered Bud Taylor the No. 1 contender for Goldstein's title.[34] Bud's pressing concern, however, was his third fight with Villa, scheduled for June 10, 1924, in Brooklyn.35 Villa had outgrown the flyweights, too, and the bout would signify Pancho's initiation into the bantamweight division.36 The outcome of Taylor-Villa would position the winner as Goldstein's top challenger.

Taylor fought twice in April and twice in May to prepare for Villa, with two wins and two draws. In the first one, he used body blows to KO Al Pettingill in Indianapolis before a crowd that included 200 Hauteans.37 Taylor kept his weight at near the bantamweight limit of 118, just so he'd be ready for any call to fight Goldstein. "I'm going to stick right at that weight until I have accomplished what I have started out for—the championship ...," Taylor told a reporter.38 Ten days before his third fight with Taylor, Villa successfully defended his world flyweight crown against Frankie Ash. Now, Pancho wanted the bantamweight title.

On the morning of the fight, Villa toyed with his press agent, Bill Miller. The bout worried Miller, and he asked, "How do you feel this morning, Pancho?"

Villa: "Like always, good."

"You going to win tonight?"

Villa grinned. "Maybe I no win," the champ responded.

Miller felt his heartbeat skip before Pancho added, "But you don't bet I lose."39

Standing in the ring before the fight that evening, however, Villa looked out of character. A reporter noticed that he wasn't smiling.40

The crowd in Brooklyn's Henderson's Bowl numbered between 8,000 and 12,000, about the same size as in the two fighters' previous bouts.41 Taylor held a four-pound weight advantage (117 to 113), as he had in their previous meetings.42 The outcome, however, proved far different than three months earlier. Villa baffled Taylor with his punching speed and a crouching defense that left his 5-inches-taller opponent with only the occasional top of the Filipino's head as a target. Some members of the pro-Taylor crowd heckled Villa by shouting "Stand up!" but Villa stuck to his game plan.43 Frustrated, Taylor let careless swinging infect his game. White reported that Taylor was "ineffective because of his wildness, which enabled Pancho to peck away at the body for the victory."44

Villa made Taylor "miss and miss and then lashed him to the face and body with salvo after salvo of rights and lefts that moved so fast it was hard for the eye to follow them." The *New York Times* scored it 8-3-1.[45]

Taylor's train ride back to the Midwest must have seemed to last forever. He had seen another chance for a title bout get away, and this time because he lost a fight.

Chapter 18

The Shoulder

Al Ziemer had won nine straight bouts over a 21-month period to rise to the top of the list of Ohio bantamweights.1 The streak seemed over in the second round of a bout on June 27, 1924, in Cleveland, when Taylor buried a right hand into his jaw and Ziemer dropped to the canvas. But the dazed fighter, egged on by 9,000 hometown fans, picked himself up and finished the round. At some point during the next few rounds, Taylor unleashed a right and felt a wave of pain from his shoulder. The pain proved too much to bear and forced Bud to complete the battle one-armed. Fortunately for Taylor, he found Ziemer's mug an easy target. He stuck lefts into Al's face all evening, like tossing darts into the point-value circles of a cork board. The *Cleveland Plain Dealer* scored it 8-2 by rounds, Taylor.2

The injury forced Taylor to cancel a bout in July, and when daily treatments of the shoulder didn't help, Long suggested he see a specialist in Chicago.3 About the same time, Long signed Taylor to fight on Aug. 1 in Terre Haute's 3-I League baseball park. Taylor put off consulting the specialist, and for a while, at least, the shoulder seemed to improve.

Taylor's popularity in Terre Haute created a demand for his presence by the organizers of various community functions, which he obliged. The Sullivan, Indiana Rotary welcomed him as guest of honor at a luncheon and he twice boxed exhibitions with Eddie Dyer for the circus visiting Terre Haute in July.4 As an antidote to all the attention and the increasing demands on his time, Taylor escaped to the countryside to go fishing.5

Taylor's fight with Tommy Ryan on Aug. 1 almost began at the morning weigh-in. Media accounts of personal disputes between opposing boxers always are suspicious given the principals' tendency to hype. In this case, however, the report appeared in the Terre Haute paper *after* the fight, giving it more validity. The trouble started when Ryan weighed under the 120-pound limit set for the bout, but Taylor, in a rare instance, tipped the scales at over the limit. Ryan wanted to see what Taylor weighed and demanded that he return to the scales. Long would later explain that at the weigh-in of the Taylor-Ryan fight two months earlier in Indianapolis, Ryan showed two pounds overweight, but Long generously overlooked the fact and Ryan didn't lose his forfeit money. Long thought Ryan should extend the same courtesy to Taylor in Terre Haute. Instead, the two fighters broke into argument, and when Long joined the exchange of words, Ryan threatened to "sock" the manager. Later, after Ryan had dressed, he walked past Long, saw him smiling, and took a swing at Eddie. News of the scuffle reached Taylor, who had been inside his dressing room, and he rushed outside, ready to nail Ryan. A police officer at the weigh-in separated the men, while Taylor yelled. Long held Taylor back. "Wait until tonight, kid," Long advised Taylor. "Why waste a fight in the street when you can get paid good money for it tonight?"[6]

In an interview years later, Taylor related what happened in the ring that night.

"... He was ready to kill me that night, but he was too peeved to use his head and I won," Taylor said about Ryan. "A fighter who loses his temper is half beaten. He forgets all his knowledge, let's go with both hands and wades in wide open—an easy target."[7]

Taylor found that wide opening in the third round, and filled the gap with a right to the jaw that spilled Ryan for a 9 count.[8]

In the fourth round, Taylor cut loose with another huge right but missed, and his shoulder dislodged—again to extreme pain. Between rounds, Dr. John Hewitt of Terre Haute's boxing commission snapped it back in place, but "the arm was just as useless as if it had been broken," according to a newspaper account. Taylor finished the fight left-handed, except for once or twice in the ninth round when pushed. By all newspaper accounts, he still won the fight easily.[9]

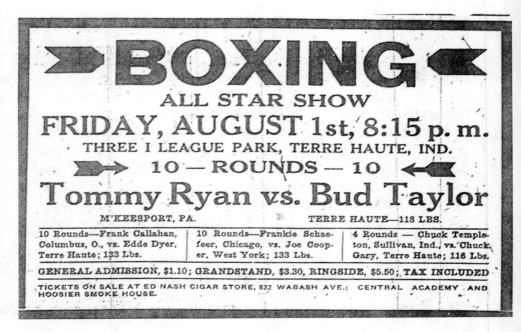

Newspaper ad promoting fight, 1924.

The $5,000 gate was respectable by Terre Haute standards, although the paid admissions didn't fill all seats. Shortly before the opening bell, Long had opened the gates to about 500 fans who had gathered there to watch the fight from a distance. Long said he didn't want any of Taylor's fans to miss the bout just because they didn't have the money.10

Since his lackluster showing against Villa, Taylor had won three straight. He had won his past two mostly left-handed, but he and his manager must have wondered: How long could he continue to fight the top-level pros *one-handed* and win?

Taylor's next challenge was Pete Sarmiento, a Filipino import who had won 14 of his past 15 bouts. Sarmiento's manager, Frank Churchill, brought his fighter to Chicago to train for the contest, slated for nearby Aurora, Illinois. Churchill drummed up publicity with a doomsday prediction for Taylor. "You can tell Terre Haute fans to bring along a group of pallbearers," he said four days before the bout.11

Taylor entered the Aug. 11 fight a 7-5 favorite despite admitting to Chicago sportswriters that he planned to use his right hand only sparingly.12 In truth, Bud's right was completely useless, and Long asked promoters to find a substitute for Taylor, but was told none were available for the contest.13

Since boxing still was illegal in Illinois, Taylor did not have to pass a physical. He entered the ring by all practical purposes a one-armed fighter before 2,200 spectators in Nobles Acres.14 The fight officially is recorded as a "no decision," but the winner was obvious to anyone in the arena. Taylor's left, sharpened by Jack Blackburn and honed by its repetitious use, opened a cut under Sarmiento's eye in the second round and Taylor speared him with the single member all evening.15 Chicago sportswriter Walter Eckersall, while serving as timekeeper for the bout, amused himself by counting the lefts thrown by Taylor. Eckersall lost track at 300 in the seventh round.16

"He doesn't need a right hand," Sarmiento later told a reporter. "I saw three left hands all night."17

In Taylor's "dressing room," a crude enclosure under the wooden stands, Bud stretched out on a splintery table. His long left arm dangled over the side, dead from overuse, but he managed a big grin. "Gene," he said to sportswriter Gene Coughlin, "if somebody laid a ten thousand dollar bank note on that stool right there and said, 'Bud, pick it up with your left hand,' I would have to pass. That's how I feel. Was it a good bout?"18

Clueless about how to treat his injury, and having exhausted all remedies suggested by others, Taylor decided to take Long's advice and seek medical help in Chicago. After five days of unspecified treatment there in mid-August, he returned to Terre Haute and declared the shoulder "improved."19 He began training for a bout with Carl Tremaine in Cleveland on Aug. 28.20

Tremaine, a 27-year-old Canadian-born Clevelander, carried a reputation as one of the hardest hitters in the bantamweight ranks, especially with the right hand. He had flattened Pal Moore and Phil O'Dowd, two fighters who had given Taylor trouble. But Tremaine's inconsistent results included losses to Taylor victims Frankie Genaro and Harry Gordon. One sportswriter predicted a Taylor victory, but only if Bud could land his right in the early rounds, before Tremaine struck with his own right.21

Taylor would take home a hefty $6,000, a factor that may have offset any notions Bud entertained of canceling the fight over doubts about his shoulder.22 In addition, Taylor craved a title fight with Goldstein, and needed to eliminate as many of the contenders as possible, including Tremaine. Tommy Gibbons made the trip to Cleveland to serve in Taylor's corner as his chief second.23

On fight night, 10,000 spectators attended, and the fighters could hear every one of them.24 The Olympic Arena, in the burgh of Brooklyn, Ohio, just outside Cleveland, had been designed so that the farthest seat from the ring was a mere 80 feet.25 Taylor seldom used his right throughout the fight and although his left hook found flesh, it couldn't score enough points for him to win. Tremaine, who scored a knockdown in the fifth when Taylor briefly went to his knees, took the newspapers' decision. In the final round, the adversaries stood toe to toe and exchanged an avalanche of blows. "Had Taylor used his right hand more, the result might have been different ...," a Cleveland sportswriter wrote.26

Ray Campbell of the *Cleveland News,* who interviewed Taylor afterward, credited him with good sportsmanship for not blaming the loss on the aching right shoulder.27

Back in Terre Haute, Long signed Taylor for his Los Angeles debut, scheduled for Sept. 23, 1924.28 Taylor traveled to Youngstown, Ohio to consult with a specialist about treating his ailing shoulder. He returned home elated.

"I was only in his office a few minutes and he worked on my shoulder only a few moments, but he is one of the most remarkable men I have ever met," Taylor told the *Terre Haute Star,* excitedly. The specialist had taken X-rays, put his hands on the shoulder and made one twist, Bud said. He told the fighter to take some more time off and he'd be fine.29

While Taylor rested, boxing shows sold out all over the Midwest; including ones in the Indiana cities of Marion, Evansville, Covington and East Chicago.30 In downtown Terre Haute, hundreds gathered on Sept. 11 between Seventh and Eighth streets on Wabash Avenue to hear a blow-by-blow account of the Louis Firpo-Harry Wills fight, announced by megaphone from the Tribune Building as the results came in by telegraph from New Jersey.31 No better evidence exists to demonstrate the sport's allure in 1924 than the interest generated in Terre Haute over a nontitle bout between two heavyweights with no direct connection to the city. In the midst of boxing's boom, Taylor leased the old K of C gym with a plan to put on amateur boxing matches. He hired three helpers to tend to the place while he traveled, and immediately put those helpers to use while he headed west for his California debut.32

    Bud and Iris Taylor departed on Sept. 16 for Los Angeles, giving themselves a week for the drive in an era of two-lane highways and speed limits of 35 miles per hour.33 The Los Angeles sportswriters ensured that Taylor's reputation preceded his arrival. Their sports pages showed photos of "The Terror" in fighting pose, squinting ominously. They compared his aggressive fighting style to Dempsey's. One newspaper article mentioned Terre Haute's famous sons Daniel Voorhees (1827-1897, U.S. senator) and Paul Dresser (1859-1906, song writer) and declared that Bud Taylor had in three years time popularized Terre Haute more than either.34

    In 1924, Los Angeles was a city whose residents were the children and grandchildren not of native Californians, but of all of America. The city's population had swelled to 1 million from just 100,000 20 years earlier, with many coming west for jobs as dockworkers, homebuilders and oil laborers. These coastal transplants once had cheered their heroes in the Friday night boxing cards from Dover to Denver, and were more than willing to plunk down a few bucks for the fights, just as they had back home. In California fight audiences, these working-class boxing buffs blended with aviation executives and movie industry people seeking their own forms of excitement and beckoned to the arena by the novelty of the game.35

    During Los Angeles' population boom, cattle rancher and oil man Jack Doyle financed the erection of an 8,000-seat stadium. The arena, in the suburb of Vernon, became by the mid-1920s the most popular boxing venue in the state.36 Boxing had been illegal in California since a decade earlier, when 20-round fights were outlawed.

By the end of 1924, boxing had regained its legal status, with 10-round pro bouts authorized in the state.[37]

Taylor was paid $2,000 for his California debut, a four-round main event Sept. 23, 1924, in the Vernon Coliseum against California's best bantamweight, Georgie Rivers.[38]

Taylor started fast, sticking the jab, rushing and darting and almost instantly winning over the crowd. About 25 seconds into the third round, he uncorked a right that swept over the top of Rivers' head. The right shoulder flew out with the punch, and, according to one report, stunned ringsiders saw the bone appear to stick up grotesquely. Taylor put his hand between his knees and tried to pull the shoulder back in place, then tried again, unsuccessfully. In the bizarre minutes that followed, he tried more than a dozen more times to restore the shoulder, pushing his right hand between his knees and tugging with all his might, at the same time firing left jabs to hold off Rivers, who was rushing him like a madman. Iris Taylor, sitting at ringside, panicked. She leapt to her feet and screamed "Stop the fight!" The referee asked Taylor if he wanted to quit, and Bud said "no." The action resumed, with Taylor machine-gunning lefts in a desperate measure to keep Rivers at bay. Taylor grinned as his lefts opened a big cut on Rivers' mouth. "For blood-tingling drama, that bout will never be surpassed," according to one account. "The spectacle of the cripple fighting at such odds and laughing at the furious fighter who kept charging, was hair-raising." At the bell, Taylor's seconds jumped into the ring and tried frantically to jerk the shoulder back in. Lloyd Mace, the Coliseum's physician, was summoned, examined the affected shoulder and said it could not be reset without anesthetic. Determined to finish despite the pain, Taylor sprung back into the middle of the ring at the bell. He alternatingly jabbed with his left and danced away from Rivers in the final round. Rivers landed some punches, but Taylor won the round, and the fight. At the final bell, the gallery responded to Taylor's grit with the greatest ovation theretofore given a fighter in Los Angeles.[39]

For years afterward, sportswriters would recap the details of the fight and the crowd's reaction. Taylor's willingness to withstand agonizing pain to win a garden-variety four-rounder endeared him to California fight fans, and built for him a loyal following. Their dedication would help inspire him to some of his greatest victories in the years thence. As for Iris Taylor, the experience unnerved her so much that she never attended another of her husband's fights.40

It was learned later that Taylor had fought most of the battle also with a sprained left thumb.41 In the aftermath, the digit needed a rest, and his wandering shoulder needed an accurate diagnosis and treatment. After returning to the Midwest, Long consulted with physicians, then told reporters he would shelve his fighter for at least two months.42 Long declined an offer by Cleveland promoters who wanted Taylor for a Tremaine rematch they anticipated would yield a $30,000 gate.43 Long had figured on shoulder surgery for his fighter, but their plans changed after Taylor drove to Chicago on Oct. 29.44 While in the Windy City, Taylor visited another "specialist." The nature of the treatment never was disclosed, but Taylor returned to Terre Haute beaming and saying again that he had been pronounced "fit."45

About this time, Eddie Kane and Eddie Long broke up their partnership, dividing their stable of fighters between them. Kane acquired Sammy Mandell and Tommy Gibbons while Long took Taylor, Eddie Anderson and Frankie Garcia.46

An article in the *Milwaukee Journal* 18 months later attributes the Long-Kane split to differences between Taylor and Mandell, two intensely competitive men between whom "professional jealousy" arose.47 Taylor and Mandell were only one weight division apart throughout their careers, and shared many common opponents. In an interview in 1939, Jack Blackburn spoke about the Mandell-Taylor intra-camp rivalry. "… Both of them wanted to be the top man and they used to like to kill each other when they was working out, so I finally had to separate 'em and not leave them work out anymore."48

Any hard feelings between Taylor and Mandell proved temporary; they would surface later to support each other in both their efforts to win a world boxing title–Taylor as a bantamweight and Mandell as a lightweight.

In Terre Haute, Taylor began staging amateur boxing shows on Tuesday evenings in the gym he had leased. He charged 50 cents for admission. The shows played to crowds in the hundreds.49

By December 1924, Taylor believed he had healed well enough to test the shoulder. He signed for a New Year's Day rematch with Ziemer in Indianapolis' Tomlinson Hall. Both were considered in the running for a crack at Eddie "Cannonball" Martin, who had won the bantamweight title from Goldstein on Dec. 19.[50] A newspaper report out of New York suggested Martin would defend his title in February 1925 and named Taylor as being considered as the opponent.[51]

Taylor closed 1925 as one of the top attractions among non-heavyweights in all of pro boxing. He owned his own home, and had recently built one for his parents in Terre Haute.[52] He was married, 21 years old, had plenty of money and many friends, and the gym he operated as a side business in his home city showed signs of becoming a successful enterprise. By fighting with one arm, he had demonstrated to the world just how much he wanted to win boxing matches. While Taylor stalked his adversaries inside the ring, Eddie Long chased after a contract for a bout that would satisfy his client's singular ambition: winning the world bantamweight championship.

Chapter 19

Boxing's Dr. Frankenstein

Indianapolis promoter Steve Harter put on 10 boxing cards from 1922 to 1927 that featured Taylor, including five outdoor shows in the city's Washington Park.

In 15 years in the boxing business, handling fighters in bouts all across the nation, Eddie Long never met a promoter he believed had more integrity than Harter.

"His word is as good as his bond," Long said in 1925. "In these days of double dealing and technicalities and general voodooism, he stands out like a lighthouse …"

"On one show which Harter promoted, he ran into bad weather," Long said. "He drew $5,700 and I knew his expenses would exceed $10,000. We had no understanding of what Bud was to receive and I will confess I had some misgivings. I thought Harter would probably give me about $250, and Bud would have a perfect right to give me Hail Columbia …," (a period slang term for "hell").

In Harter's office, Long said he asked for $750. "No," Harter said, "the loss is my misfortune, not yours. I'll make it back some other time." Harter gave him $1,500.

"We wanted to give the check back or split it with him," Long said. "He wouldn't talk about it."[1]

On Jan. 1, 1925, Harter promoted the 10-round rematch between Taylor and Al Ziemer. For eight rounds, the spirited contest delighted the Indianapolis crowd. In the ninth, Taylor nailed Ziemer with a left hook and he thought Al was going down, so he fired his right to finish him. The punch landed, and Taylor's shoulder popped loose. He twisted in pain and grabbed his arm, and the pro-Taylor crowd in Tomlinson Hall tensed. Ziemer, meanwhile, managed to stay on his feet and assessed the situation as Taylor flicked a few left jabs. It was still early in the round, and Taylor wanted to sink to a knee and use the ropes to force his shoulder back in. But he had a problem. Under the rules, a fighter could not go down unless struck by a punch.

"Ziemer knew the shoulder had gone out," Taylor recalled, years later. "Sportingly, he stepped back and didn't want to hit me. But I had other ideas. I figured that if I could get to the floor I could work my shoulder back into the socket ... I stuck my chin out, daring Ziemer to hit it ..." Ziemer tossed a light punch. Taylor deflected the punch against the side of his head, went down and the referee started his count.

"When I came up, I came up on the ropes, shoved the arm out over the top rope and with the left arm, pulled the shoulder back in place." The suspense from the injury and Taylor's improvisational fix had the fans screaming by the time Bud rose at the count of 9. Taylor finished the battle one-armed although he fought Ziemer even in the 10th. The next day's *Indianapolis Star* called it a draw.[2]

The recurring injury had stretched Taylor to the edge of exasperation. Tired of treatments that didn't work and wary of suspect physicians who were experts more at manipulating patients' wallets than body parts, he searched desperately for a solution. The simple truth was that in 1924, those practicing in the medical profession had not fully advanced from being merely purveyors of comfort into their modern role as that of dispensers of scientific-based treatment. This was an era when the family doctor still recommended whiskey to treat the flu and pneumonia.[3] Many serious injuries lingered without an accurate diagnosis, such as Taylor's—a tendon stretched way out of place by wild swings.

Necessity forced Taylor to continue to seek help, and in this period of great need he picked up a tip about a New York physician named Dr. William Fralick, who had experience treating boxers. Fralick told Taylor he could fix the shoulder, but Taylor must submit to two months' regimented care.4 Taylor canceled two bouts in January and headed east with Iris and Eddie Long.5 Taylor's hopes rose after he learned about Fralick's reputation for repairing boxers' body parts as somewhat of a pugilistic Dr. Frankenstein. "He made Jack Delaney a brand new knuckle, Jack Zivic a good shoulder, Mickey Brown a new ear, Paul Berlenbach a couple of good hands, Tony Vaccarillo a new elbow, and a hundred other things," Taylor wrote to Ralph White.6

On Jan. 26, Fralick cut through Taylor's flesh from the right armpit to the top of the shoulder. He snipped out a piece of the big tendon that controls the shoulder muscle, then sewed the ends together. He used 200 stitches to close the wound.7

Taylor recovered for eight days in the hospital before his release to a nearby hotel. Fralick instructed him to return to his office every day at 1 p.m. If Taylor was late a few minutes, Fralick scolded him. Other patients who were late 15 minutes were sent home like naughty children. Taylor learned that the eccentric man treated all his patients that way, but overall, he served them well, like a benign dictator.8

"Young fellow, I've seen you fight, and you don't hit correctly with your right," he told Taylor. "I'm going to make a puncher out of you." Fralick taught Taylor to carry his right elbow next to the ribs and punch from there. For weeks, Taylor shadow-boxed in the doctor's suite as his shoulder healed.9

"He came back often to see how I was working , and if he caught me with my elbow getting away from the side of my body, he lit all over me," Taylor recalled, months later. Taylor listened and learned from the odd fellow who seemed like a combination of a surgeon/drill sergeant/fight trainer.10

Taylor figured he owed Fralick thousands of dollars, but when it came time for the patient to ask about the bill, Fralick said, "Young man, do you ever gamble?" Taylor, surprised by the question, stammered out a "no."

"Well," the doctor said. "I'm going to gamble with you. I believe you can win the bantamweight championship of the world. When you do, pay me five thousand dollars. Goodbye, my boy."11

Chapter 20

The Prime

In the spring of 1925, Bud Taylor, 21, entered the prime of his career, the period of time when an athlete's youth blends with experience, his desire with opportunity and his skill with fate.

Five years and 85 professional bouts carried him to the verge of his prime. Surgery provided the missing element, perfect health, to reach it.

His left punch, developed during the injury to his right shoulder, had evolved into his signature blow. He snapped it forward or around with power, speed and accuracy. As for his renovated right, the shortened tendon in the shoulder kept him from taking big, looping swings that seldom landed and left him open and off balance. It helped change Taylor from a brawler to a measured puncher.

"From a wild swinger he has been changed to a sharp, accurate hitter and he seems to carry more power behind the punch than before, although it travels only a short distance and always straight from the shoulder," sportswriter Bob Nesbit wrote.[1]

"Although I am holding back with my right more than before, I really believe I am hitting harder with it than ever before," Taylor said.[2]

The time off from boxing, too, had revitalized his game. His hands and thumbs, repeatedly cracked, wrenched and reddened off the heads and jawbones of his opponents, had healed over a seven-month period in which he fought only one bout.

On April 20, Taylor returned to the ring in East Chicago to fight William J. Smith, a 5-foot-tall New York fighter known by his nickname, "Midget." Smith also was known for the oddity of employing his sister, Vera Smith, as his manager/trainer.[3]

Bud Taylor, the "bionic battler from Terre Haute" won the fight 7-2-1 by rounds, according to the *Chicago Daily Tribune*. Taylor "punched straight, mixed jabs and right crosses, and his shoulder showed no ill effects."[4]

"I feel I'm going to win the championship this summer," Taylor said. "I feel my arm is fixed for good and there's nothing holding me back in my chase for that title …" Taylor had reason for optimism beyond his good health. A month earlier, Phil Rosenberg outpointed Eddie Martin for the bantamweight title—the same Rosenberg that Taylor had thrashed the past October in New York. "I can whip Rosenberg and will, if I get the chance this season, and my manager, Eddie Long, says it's a sure shot," Taylor said.[5]

Taylor's confidence had soared, thanks to the return of his right-hand punch, his "sweetheart." In a few days, another sweetheart would enter his life. In the spring of 1925, the toughest man in Terre Haute and parts far beyond could be seen wearing a goofy smile and wiggling his fingers into a lumpy blanket, from which peered out a tiny face.[6]

Every day in 1925, thousands of motorists on the National Road (later known as U.S. 40) entered Terre Haute from the east. As they came upon the city limits near Fruitridge Avenue, they might have noticed through their glass windshields a handsome, three-story structure of carved stone, just southwest of the intersection. The Edgewood Grove Apartments housed 15 spacious units with such amenities as hardwood floors, mahogany and ivory trim, sun parlors, and fully equipped hookups for phone and radio.[7] Bud and Iris Taylor had moved into the complex shortly after the place opened in summer 1924, and their home would be the first for their daughter.[8]

Barbara Jean Taylor, born April 22, 1925, moved the needle to 6 pounds, 10 ounces at her first official weigh-in.[9]

"I'll admit I was strong for a boy," Taylor told a newspaperman, "but my daughter is just as sweet as her mother, and that's enough for me." Bud called her "Bobbie," as he would have if a son had been born.[10]

Taylor's former manager, Eddie Kane, had named the baby. "Here's a funny thing about babies," Taylor told a reporter. "Tommy

Gibbons wanted a girl. Mrs. Gibbons presented him with twin boys. We wanted a boy. But ... well ... here she is, and we love her more than all the boys in the country."11

The apartment provided first-rate comfort. The view out the French windows on the building's west side overlooked Edgewood Grove subdivision, a 150-home, tree-lined sector considered one of the city's exclusive neighborhoods.12 The apartment building sat only two miles east of the gritty, Liberty Avenue area where Taylor was raised, but the neighborhoods were as different as honey and tequila.

Little Barbara Jean developed a disposition that matched the serenity of her cozy surroundings. She never cried unless she wanted her bottle.13

Taylor would not travel far from home for his bout with Mike Moran on May 18. Terre Haute's Hippodrome Theater, or the "Hippo," as it was known, stood only a block west of Taylor's downtown gym. It was a sign of the times that in less than a year, the Hippo's owners would veer from its regular fare of vaudeville acts and devote its entertainment almost exclusively to the growing medium of the motion picture.14

Long had planned the Moran bout as Taylor's tuneup for two bouts of tremendous importance, on May 26 and June 2. The first was with former bantamweight champ Abe Goldstein in New York, the second with an undefeated fellow making headlines in Los Angeles: Jimmy McLarnin. Taylor, of course, hungered most for a bout with champion Rosenberg, a contest that promoter Jim Mullen hoped to stage in Chicago.15

Moran arrived in Terre Haute a few days before the fight, played golf in the city-run Rea Park and declared to a local reporter, "I'm going to whip your pride and joy."16 About 2,000 people jammed the Hippo at $3, $2 and $1 a seat, and standing. A fire marshal eventually cut off sales, leaving 200 people outside without chance of admittance. Taylor knocked down Moran three times in winning the 10-rounder.17 Before he left for Long Island, New York, for the Goldstein bout, Taylor packed one of baby Barbara Jean's dirty socks for good luck.18

Since being dethroned as bantamweight champ, Goldstein had put himself back in contention by winning four straight. As Taylor exited the door of the dressing room of New York's 20,000-seat

Queensboro Athletic Club and started down the aisle, he carried Barbara Jean's sock stuffed into the waist of his trunks.[19] Then he proceeded to sock his opponent.

From the opening bell, every facet of Taylor's game clicked. By the middle rounds, the bout had turned into a Bud Taylor showcase of expert jabs, hooks and crosses. "Bud fought the most wonderful fight of his career," Long said afterward. Taylor won the first round, staggered Goldstein in the third and fourth and owned an edge in the middle rounds. Goldstein thudded a powerful right off Taylor's face in the ninth and took that round. "In the 10th, a volley of rights and lefts had Abe Goldstein groggy and Bud Taylor was measuring him for a KO when the bell sounded."[20] Taylor won the decision. He decided to put one of his daughter's socks in his trunks every time he fought.[21]

Iris Taylor, Barbara Jean and Bud, 1925.

Terre Haute fans toasted the victory—and not just from afar. E.Z. Hanks, a Terre Haute businessman and Taylor super-fan, had traveled the 700 miles from home to watch the fight.[22] The Terre Haute City Council, upon hearing of the victory over Goldstein, wired Taylor a congratulatory telegram signed by its president.[23]

Between the Goldstein and McLarnin bouts, Taylor had just seven days to travel 2,000 miles to the opposite coast. Transcontinental commercial air service still was five years away, which meant he had to ride a train.[24]

The long trip would not be of the nap-and-magazine variety common to the ordinary rail passenger. When Taylor boarded, he found that his resourceful manager had equipped a baggage car with the elements of a makeshift gym.[25] Taylor worked out onboard in transit, and slipped in a few miles of outside running when he and Long changed trains in Chicago and other stops.[26] Iris Taylor did not make either the trip to New York or Los Angeles. She brought the baby to Chicago for the threesome to unite during the train's layover there.[27]

The 123-pound weight limit for the McLarnin fight was heavier than usual for Taylor, who had been scaling 118 to 120 over his past dozen or so bouts.

McLarnin stands as the only boxer to bring an undefeated pro record into a bout with Bud Taylor. The exact number of McLarnin's victories at that time varies depending on the source; assuredly it was more than 20, and probably less than 40. McLarnin, whose good looks and perfect record ensured a strong fan turnout, would get $8,000 for the bout, Taylor $3,500.[28] Despite McLarnin's perfect record, the Los Angeles Times recognized the boxing establishment's high regard for The Terre Haute Terror, and called the bout a toss-up.[29]

McLarnin had been born in Ireland in 1907 and reared in Vancouver, one of 12 children in his family. After he left high school, he occupied his only "job" of the traditional kind when he ran an elevator for a paper company. (McLarnin used to joke it made him a natural hitter.) He began boxing in his youth and had the good fortune of coming under the tutelage of an experienced boxing man, Charles "Pop" Foster. Foster refined the skills of the rangy lad and by 1923, flyweight McLarnin had turned pro. At 16, he and Foster moved to California. The youngster lied that he was 18, but found it difficult to get fights because he looked so young. With the pair nearly destitute after three months, Foster finally secured McLarnin a fight in San Francisco's Dreamland Arena for $50. The victories piled up in subsequent months as McLarnin matured from a flyweight into a bantamweight.30

The press liked to refer to McLarnin as "baby-faced," for his school-boy looks that over the years Jimmy had managed to maintain despite the disfiguring effects of his chosen profession. McLarnin stayed handsome because his stance and quick feet made him extremely difficult to punch in the head. He stood erect, kept his gloves high and used his quick feet to bounce in and out of the mix.31 Foster taught him to raise his *shoulders*, not just arms, to protect his chin, a posture they theorized also helped his offense. His high carriage meant his arms twisted as he punched, in a corkscrew effect they believed inflicted more punishment.32

A student of the science of boxing, McLarnin squeezed rubber balls and performed balancing maneuvers and other nontraditional routines in his training regimen, to which he adhered strictly.33

On the evening of the fight, Taylor lay in bed restlessly, so he decided to go out to a night spot with some friends. He ordered an orange juice, and left the drink unattended briefly while he danced. After he returned to finish the drink, he felt sick.34

"I was sick as a dog and my manager, Eddie Long, was in favor of calling the fight off ..." Taylor said.35 Taylor felt better the next day after eggs and beef tea, and insisted on fighting.36 For many years, Taylor believed that someone, perhaps a gambler betting heavily on McLarnin, doctored his orange juice.37

When the bell sounded in the Vernon Coliseum, McLarnin's performance proceeded to completely befuddle Taylor. "Thinking I'd be weak, I tried desperately to stop McLarnin in the early rounds, but he was such a fine boxer that I couldn't hit him with a broomstick," Taylor said later.38

But Taylor's left hook began to find its mark underneath McLarnin's high defense. Invigorated by the pace, Taylor began to feel stronger and mounted a comeback. The fight went the distance, and Taylor took the decision.[39]

The *Los Angeles Times* praised Taylor for winning under such difficult circumstances. He "virtually hopped off the train to fight McLarnin after traveling 4,000 miles, and doing all of his training in baggage cars en route. Bud fought McLarnin after having only twenty-four hours in which to shake his train legs …"[40]

Hindsight casts an even brighter glow on the feat. In a span of six days, Taylor defeated two Hall-of-Famers on opposite coasts in fights separated by a five-day train ride.

Taylor's defeat of undefeated McLarnin launched Eddie Long into a full-fledged campaign to line up a bout with world bantamweight champ Charley Phil Rosenberg.

Los Angeles sportswriters, impressed with the McLarnin conquest and aware that Taylor had handed Rosenberg a lacing in October 1923, tapped Bud as a championship certainty.

"Taylor will be the bantamweight champion of the world just as soon as the boxing commissions force the present titleholder to meet him," wrote a Los Angeles *Record* journalist, a day after the McLarnin fight.

Long wanted to capitalize on Taylor's popularity in California and steer the title fight there rather than New York. He figured Taylor a lock to win the fight, and didn't want his client restricted by New York's rules governing champions.[41] Champions in New York at that time had to defend their titles inside the state within six months, regardless of where the good offers lay. If they didn't, they faced suspension in New York, their title confiscated and the state would ask other states to ban them.[42]

Los Angeles promoter Jack Doyle shared Long's quest for a title bout in California. Taylor's high-flying popularity had Doyle visualizing a show that would attract the biggest fan turnout in the history of California boxing.[43] By June 24, 1926, Doyle had Taylor's signature and Rosenberg's manager Harry Segal's assurance for a bout Labor Day Weekend in Maler Ball Park. Doyle planned to reconfigure the ballpark for 35,000 seats, prompting one estimate of a $145,000 gate, if all seats were filled. The champ would be guaranteed $25,000, with a privilege of 40 percent, while Long achieved for Taylor a payday of straight 15 percent of the gate.44

Long, always astute on the financial aspects of the game, knew that even a $50,000 gate served his client well at 15 percent. "If we get $7,500 for our end, we will get three times as much as the last three contenders have received," he told a reporter. "Abe Goldstein got $2,500 for beating Joe Lynch; Cannonball Martin got the same for beating Goldstein; and Rosenberg got slightly over $2,400 for beating Martin." Champions routinely made significantly more money than challengers in title fights; Martin reportedly had received $24,000 against Rosenberg.45

With the date of the bout set, Long arranged his fighter's schedule for the next few months. It called for Taylor to fight twice on the West Coast before a homecoming bout in Terre Haute on the Fourth of July.46

On June 16 in Vernon, Taylor came off as a 5-1 betting favorite against San Diegoan Ernie Goozeman. Goozeman lasted until the seventh round before his seconds tossed in a white towel. "The punch that ended the fight was a fierce right thrust that caught Goozeman right between the eyes. Goozeman "reached up with a wet glove to rub away the mist and the tigerish Taylor numbed him with a shower of head punches."47

"Who taught you how to box?" inquired Paul Lowry of the Los Angeles Times, in a postfight interview with Taylor.

"Why, none other than Jack Blackburn, colored lightweight of Chicago, the greatest boxer of all times—a man who took on all comers from lightweights to heavyweights and beat them," came Taylor's reply.48

As he dressed before the Goozeman fight, Taylor had received a telegram from Terre Haute Mayor Davis.

"Good luck to you. You are doing more to advertise Terre Haute than the Chamber of Commerce. Hurry home," the mayor wrote.49

Terre Haute always was a willing topic of chatter for Taylor, who occasionally mispronounced it playfully as "Terry Hut."50

"Boy, she's some town, that old baby," Taylor told a reporter. "All my pals are there, and buddy wherever your pals are is where you should be. A chap in this racket meets many people, and when he's up and going, they're all for him. When he's down and slipping, he's got to go back to the old home town where the understanding folks are. Los Angeles may be all you say it is, and I have nothing against it, but boy, Terre Haute, Indiana is mine and shoot the piece on that one."51

Taylor finished his West Coast stay with a 10-round victory over "Dynamite" Joe Murphy in Oakland before heading home.

Chapter 21

A Hero's Welcome

The 1920s was a decade of pleasure, an oasis wedged between two periods of discontent. Scarred by the war in the 19-teens, it was as if Americans were determined to cram in as much fun as they could before the Great Depression drained their spirit in the 1930s.

The festive spirit never was more evident than in the summer of 1925. Terre Hauteans reveled in afternoons strolling Deming Park, or cheering at motor-boat races on the Wabash River.[1] They passed their evenings dancing the Charleston in the Trianon nightclub, or humming along to Paul Whiteman's band blaring out from their Brunswick radios. It was a time for diversions, of weekend afternoons trying to mimic the technique of Bobby Jones' chip shot or Bill Tilden's forehand, or for piling in for a leisurely ride in the family "machine." The national press, with no pending wars or world disasters to mine, turned its attention to a small town in Tennessee where attorneys debated in a trial the possibility that man evolved from lower primates: the John Scopes "monkey trial."

In the delightful breeziness of the era, it seemed as if anything was possible. On June 17, Terre Haute Mayor Davis, caught up in the roar of the 1920s, gave it a defining moment. During a bicycle parade downtown, he climbed atop a bike with an elevated seat stretched high into the air, and rode at the head of the pack. Citizens who had lined Wabash Avenue stared in amazement at the circus act by their civic leader, impressed as much by his unabashed enjoyment of the ride as his gift of balance and agility.[2]

Within this atmosphere of merriment, the citizens welcomed home the boxing hero whose victories they had followed by reading their newspapers.

The city's affiliate of the Zorah Shrine, a national organization that does work on behalf of handicapped children, secured the Memorial Stadium to stage Taylor's homecoming bout against Bobby Wolgast on July 4. The Shriners also brought to town a touring troupe, "India," which featured music, dancing and animals from the Middle East, to play nightly performances Thursday through Saturday the Fourth.[3]

Shrine commander Jay Short and fight promoter George Grammell hatched a plan to surprise Taylor, then enlisted the help of the press and Bud's family. As Taylor's rail car rolled into Union Depot near Sycamore and Spruce streets, the Shrine band played, and Short and Grammell stood waiting along with hundreds of fans. When Taylor emerged from the train, they sprung the surprise. Taylor had just enough time to kiss Iris before being hoisted onto one of the touring troupe's Asian elephants to ride in a parade into downtown.[4]

The band's brass players led the way as the pachyderm ambled down North Ninth Street. Taylor tipped his hat to thousands of cheering people lining the streets, who had turned out in even bigger numbers than when the circuses came to town and staged parades. Sportswriter Ralph White jogged alongside the elephant, fumbling to jot down comments from the object of affection.

"I can't get it," Taylor told White, "but I'm proud that I stand so well in my hometown ... Gee but I'm glad to be back and see the old town. And I'll whip Mr. Rosenberg and bring the world championship back to the town I'm for, when we meet at Vernon. As for Mr. Wolgast, he's tough, yes, indeed, but I'm not going to let any guy stop me now. Just tell 'em I'm the happiest kid in the world and that I hope I won't disappoint them in my effort to win the championship."[5]

The editor of the *Terre Haute Star* chose Taylor as the focus of its July 2 editorial. "Everywhere he fights he wins the admiration of the fans, for he plays the game according to the rules, and in his work in the ring he is a gentleman." The piece also praised Taylor for his effort and aggressiveness in the ring and his exemplary physical con-

Taylor rides elephant in Terre Haute parade, 1925.

ditioning, including the fact he does not smoke or drink.6

That evening, a standing-room-only crowd turned out to watch Taylor work out in the ring at the conclusion of his weekly amateur show in the K of C gym.7

Wolgast of New Jersey carried a fight record no better than mediocre, but it did hold one shocker: a 10-round win over Pancho Villa in Philadelphia a year earlier.

A sweltering heat crept into Memorial Stadium on July 4 as

4,100 fans watched three preliminaries precede the Taylor-Wolgast bout. Women in the crowd pushed open umbrellas for relief from the sun. Taylor's loyal supporters dotted the crowd, among them E.Z. Hanks in a $3 ringside seat. As Taylor climbed through the ropes, the Shrine band struck up "On the Banks of the Wabash," a song written by Terre Haute's own Paul Dresser that had become the Indiana state song in 1913.8

For the hardcore fight fan, the preliminary bouts and musical entertainment unfortunately provided the highlight of the afternoon's entertainment. The main event was a bore, and disgruntled fans enduring the July heat booed their disapproval. It wasn't Taylor's fault. He bloodied Wolgast's nose with a left hook in the first round, then reopened the gash with a hook in the second. Wolgast thereafter hunched into a shell and showed little interest in the bout beyond clinching and blocking punches. At one point, "After trying every other way to give the fans a fight, Bud left himself open on the ropes but even then Wolgast absolutely refused to take even the semblance of a chance." The *Terre Haute Star* gave Taylor every round.9

A week later, Long traveled to Cleveland to talk with Charley Phil Rosenberg's manager, Harry Segal. Jack Doyle, the West Coast promoter, had told Long that Doyle had never received Segal's signature. The needed signature contracted the champion for the Labor Day title bout with Taylor in Vernon, California. An additional development worried Long: Pete Sarmiento had decisioned Rosenberg in a nontitle fight July 8. Long feared the loss might have scared Rosenberg's people from risking the title against Taylor, who had beaten Sarmiento one-handed. The two managers met in Cleveland and Long found out that indeed, Segal had no intention of risking the title against Taylor. "We have the title, and we're going to keep it a while," Long quoted Segal as telling him.10

Chapter 22

Bushy, and the Timber Wolf

On July 15, Taylor was training in his gym when he heard the news that Pancho Villa had died.[1] The death of the great fighter was attributed to an infection in Villa's neck, related to teeth that he neglected to have extracted.[2] Villa had died as the reigning world flyweight champion, with a 24-2 record over the previous 21 months, having lost during that stretch only to Taylor and Jimmy McLarnin. Eighty years after his death, the Filipino Hall-of-Famer still is considered by some as the greatest Asian fighter of all time.[3]

With the Rosenberg match off the schedule, Taylor focused on training for a fight July 31, 1925, with Bushy Graham in Aurora, Ill. Graham of Utica, New York, had forged a name for himself on the East Coast by winning his past 10 fights. An Italian-American whose real name was Angelo Geraci, he also fought under the name "Mickey Garcia." Graham liked to outsmart his opponents, and relied on quick feet and finesse to outbox them.[4] The nickname "Bushy" came from his "wearing a bundle of kinky hair on his head, and when he is engaged in prize fighting it jounces about and flops down over his eyes like some deep-tangled shrub nodding in the zephyrs."[5] Along with his evasiveness, Graham confounded his opponents with unorthodox maneuvers. Sports columnist Westbrook Pegler characterized Graham's fighting style as "frolicsome, leaping and whirling from rope to rope and throwing punches in sprays, few of which land and none of which do any damage."[6] These kinds of reports didn't scare too many of Graham's prospective opponents. But when news arrived that Graham had landed enough leather to outpoint Abe Goldstein on July 23, the Taylor camp figured on a tough contest from the bushy one.

In Aurora, Taylor executed his typical fast start, landing two quick jabs and a left uppercut that knocked Graham down in the first round. Graham started to rise, then fell again, before struggling to his feet at the count of 9 to finish the round. Graham survived a bloody cut under his eye to last the 10-round distance, evading Taylor with his quick feet, and slipping in his own jabs. The *Chicago Daily Tribune* scored the fight 4-2-4, Taylor. A hundred Terre Haute supporters made the 200-mile trip.[7]

Taylor had little interest in a rematch with Graham, telling the press, "He simply won't stand up and fight and I'm tired of chasing those kind of birds all over the ring. It was an easy scrap for me. Yes, lots softer than I had anticipated."[8]

Unable to corral Rosenberg, Long eventually signed Taylor for a second go with Graham on Aug. 25 in the Queensboro Stadium in Long Island, New York. Long took the fight under the rationale that victory over Graham was a certainty, and by getting the endorsement of a referee's decision over Graham in New York instead of the newspaper decision gained in Aurora, Rosenberg's camp would not have an "out" to deny Taylor a title match.[9] To solidify Taylor's status as the No. 1 contender, Long also was negotiating for a rematch with Pete Sarmiento.[10]

The crowd of 6,267 at the second Taylor-Graham fight witnessed a classic fox-hare chase of the same type as a Dempsey-Tunney, Louis-Conn or Frazier-Ali. Graham, playing the rabbit, of course, jigged and wheeled around his attacker from the opening bell, avoiding a repeat of his first-round mistake in Aurora. Graham grew so confident on this evening that at times, he danced about with his hands down. Both men landed stinging punches and drew the other's blood in 12 rounds of fast action. Graham planted his feet long enough to knock the bridge out of Taylor's mouth; Taylor broke a bone in his left hand off Graham's forehead.[11] Graham won the judges' decision, but Taylor may have been sleighted by Graham's home-state panel of judges. The *Los Angeles Record* later reported that among the 14 major newspapers in New York, seven gave Taylor the decision, five called it a draw and two gave it to Graham.[12] Nonetheless, Taylor left New York saddled with the loss, and having to eat his comment after the first bout about Graham being an "easy scrap."

Before he left New York, Taylor visited his career-saving surgeon, Dr. William Fralick, who set the fractured hand in a cast.[13] Taylor told the press that the blow that injured the hand had been thrown in the second round; a chilling inference that he fought eight rounds with the fracture.[14]

The loss kept Taylor from finishing the calendar year undefeated. Still, he could look back on a 9-0-1 record for 1925, compiled against most of the best bantamweights in boxing.

The fracture suffered in the Graham fight sidelined Taylor for two months in the fall of 1925. He used the unscheduled vacation for a two-week hunting trip to North Dakota, returning with tales of his conquests that apparently carried the ring of exaggeration. Sportswriter Ralph White joked that the beasts he bagged included "badger, wildcat, elephant, lions and tigers."[15]

Terre Hauteans immersed themselves in the World Series, watching hometown hero Max Carey at age 35 bat 4 for 5 as the Pittsburgh Pirates won the seventh game over the Washington Senators.

In October, Taylor returned to Los Angeles for a 10-rounder against Doc Snell. He brought Iris and Barbara Jean, and a newspaper photo shows Bud smiling while feeding a bottle to the infant in his arms. "Bud knows just how to mix the milk for Barbara Jean's bottle—the proper temperature and all about it ..." the story reads.[16]

Snell, 22, whose real name was Bill McEachern, had been working as a drug-store clerk in Peshastin, Washington, just three years earlier. A promoter recruited him into the fight business by assuring Snell that he could make enough money to buy an entire chain of drug stores.[17]

Sportswriters billed Snell as the "Tacoma Timber Wolf," or "Timber Wolf of the Northwest" and even sillier, the "rugged lumberjack from the wilds of Washington."[18] A more accurate tag, which never saw print, would have been "The Peshastin pill pusher."

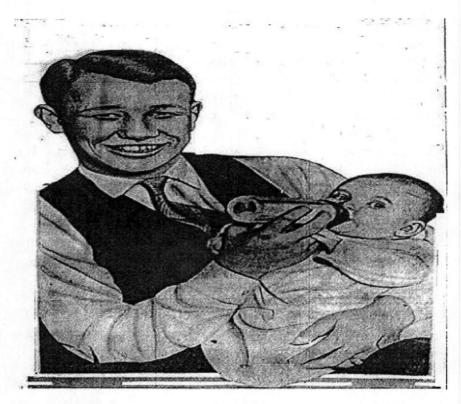

Bud and Barbara Jean Taylor, 1925.

For the fight, promoter Jack Doyle ordered Taylor and Snell to wear different-colored trunks to help the referee tell them apart. The fighters had the same height, reach and color and length of hair, and reportedly looked like twins.19

The press tabbed Taylor as the big favorite to win, but claimed that Snell had a prized punch in his repertoire. They called it the "Ketchel Shift," a left-feint, then intentional miss with a right, followed by the finisher, a left to the jaw. "A fighter who can use it successfully may be hopelessly beaten and then upset the cards," the *Los Angeles Times* reported.20

Of course, by publicizing Snell's so-called secret weapon, the weapon ceased to be secret.

If Snell had such a trick, either he didn't use it or it didn't work. He barely lasted all 10 rounds. When the fighters left the ring, it was easy to tell the "twins" apart—Snell was the one with one eye closed and his other eye bloodied from a cut just above.[21] Taylor won the referee's decision and earned $4,000.[22]

At that time, bantamweight champ Rosenberg and former champ Abe Goldstein also were staying in Los Angeles, looking for fights. Belittling Rosenberg soon became what seemed like a national pastime for sportswriters–and one in which the L.A. press eagerly participated.[23] Ed Frayne of the *Los Angeles Record* ridiculed the champ for demanding $5,000 guarantees to fight lesser talents when promoters on the West Coast would pay him $20,000 to fight Taylor.

"By every law of business, sportsmanship and common sense, you should fight Taylor," Frayne wrote in his column, directly addressing Rosenberg. "If you beat him, you are $25,000 ahead. If you don't you will probably make more money in a year fighting every two weeks than you will trying to plow the soft sofa, as you are now. What do you say, Charley? Are you going to make that title work for you, or are you going to starve to death for it?"[24] *Los Angeles Times* writer Paul Lowry wasn't quite as harsh, criticizing Rosenberg for "gracefully ducking" Taylor.[25] Syndicated columnist Bob Edgren described Rosenberg as the poorest example of a titleholder he had seen in many years.[26]

Ed Smith of the *Chicago American*, always high on praise for Taylor, harpooned Rosenberg mercilessly. Smith described the champ as the "laughing stock of the world," a "coward" and wrote that the mention of the name "Bud Taylor" causes Rosenberg's "hair to turn prematurely gray and his teeth to chatter when there is a sudden commotion at the door."[27]

While in Los Angeles, Rosenberg told the *Record* that he accepted Taylor's challenge. "Taylor has been saying a lot of things about me. I am going to make him eat them when he gets in a ring. I think I can knock him out and when I do, I'm going to try and dump him in Eddie Long's lap," he said.[28] But when the fight failed to materialize after additional attempts by promoters, the press continued to blame the champ.

Long told reporters he planned to complain about the champion to the California Boxing Commission. He would tell the commission that since Rosenberg agreed verbally to fight Taylor in California the previous summer, then backed out, the champ should be forced to fight Taylor or not allowed to box in the state.[29] Whether or not Long actually filed a complaint is not known.

In Rosenberg's defense, he, like most fighters, left the business of selecting opponents to his manager. A boxing manager's decisions on who, when and where to fight are based mostly on financial reasons. Segal knew, of course, he could get a huge payday out of a bout with Taylor. If his fighter lost badly, however, which Segal had to know was the likely outcome, then Rosenberg's boxing market value would drop considerably and the money train would slow. Common sense dictates that staying at or near the top of the ladder in boxing necessitates avoiding one's biggest threat.

Taylor, who avoided no one, signed for a rematch with Pete Sarmiento, the former world flyweight champion then navigating through the bantamweight division. The date was set for Nov. 18, 1925, in Los Angeles, with the weight at 122 pounds.

Because Sarmiento had defeated Rosenberg in July, the fight was billed as one for "the right to face the champ."[30] The promoters need not have hyped the fight. Taylor and Sarmiento were the two best bantamweights in the game, rivaled by no one, and Taylor was the top draw for boxing in California at the time.[31]

When he boxed, Sarmiento kept both hands in front of him, like someone huddled under a narrow umbrella. He blocked left hooks to the body with his right elbow.[32] A punch off an opponent's elbow can break a hand, so Taylor knew he would need a true aim. Sarmiento's fighting style, like Taylor's, did not include clinching or evading. The anticipation of a brawl turns fight fans ravenous, and 14,000 would pack the Olympic Auditorium, 4,000 over seating capacity.[33]

After their 2 p.m. weigh-in, Taylor retreated to his Los Angeles apartment and put on his pajamas for a nap of several hours. Barbara Jean, however, had other ideas. "She came into my room and was so darn cute that I started to play with her," Taylor said. "I forgot all about having a fight on and didn't get any sleep at all."[34]

Taylor would be glad that he didn't get the nap, for he would enter the ring that evening with all the tools of his prime at his command. He pecked Sarmiento over 10 rounds with pinpoint lefts, and he rocketed rights that nearly buckled Sarmiento's legs.35 "Three or four times he had the Filipino out on his feet," read one report.36 Two ringside spectators counting Taylor's punches said that he started 96 of them in the ninth round, and landed 95—an astounding display of accuracy if even close to correct numbers.37

The Taylor love-fest continued from the typewriters of the Los Angeles press. He was the puncher-with-personality:

"No one can meet Bud Taylor without liking him. He's a Hoosier through and through and ever loyal to Terre Haute despite the allurements of Los Angeles. He's a quiet-mannered, soft-spoken youngster who without mentioning any names manages to convey the impression that Bud Taylor will be the champion of the world some day."38

Chapter 23

The Dirty Sock

In the fall of 1925, Bud Taylor remained the only person in the world who had beaten Jimmy McLarnin. McLarnin had posted three victories since the June defeat, and his manager, "Pop" Foster, wanted nothing more than to exorcise the Taylor loss from the fight public's memory by winning a rematch. Taylor had nothing to gain careerwise from a second bout with McLarnin, but the money looked good, and since he couldn't get to Rosenberg ... Thus, when Jack Doyle waved a $10,000 guarantee at Eddie Long, Long showed his palms.[1] Ten grand was more money than Taylor had ever earned for one bout. Ten grand in 1925 could buy outright among other things, a nine-room, two-story house in a well-to-do section of Terre Haute.[2]

Rosenberg also had shown an interest in a bout with McLarnin and the match almost went to him instead of Taylor when Long and Foster began haggling over the weight limit for the rematch. McLarnin had been fighting about four pounds heavier than Taylor, and Foster wanted the limit set at 126. Foster didn't want McLarnin to lose strength trying to reduce. Long countered with 124. Long complained that at 126, he would have to build up Taylor to at least 121 1/2 to be competitive, and that would make his fighter slow and sluggish. Foster retorted that 121 1/2 was exactly Taylor's weight when he fought McLarnin in June.

"I didn't see anything about Taylor that made me think he was slow and sluggish when he fought my Jimmy," Foster said during negotiations. "He looked like a machine gun to me for 10 rounds."[3]

On Nov. 17, the two managers compromised at 125 pounds and Doyle set the fight for Dec. 8.[4]

Four days before the fight, a painful boil developed on Taylor's left arm. "Now I feel natural again," he told the *Los Angeles Times* with a smile. "I'm lonesome when there isn't something the matter with me. In the last 18 months, I have fought with broken hands, arms out of sockets, sprained ankles, a lame back and most everything that classifies as a physical ailment."[5]

Taylor planned to end his nearly two-month stay on the coast by leaving right after the bout. "I can't spend Christmas out here where there is no winter time," he said. "I'm used to snow and overcoats for Christmas."[6] He also wanted to participate in a benefit at his gym Dec. 18 in Terre Haute for the Poor Kids Christmas Fund, an annual communitywide effort.[7]

McLarnin-Taylor II sold out the Los Angeles Coliseum, with 10,000 fans paying $2 to $5 a ticket.[8] Unlike their first encounter, however, the rematch left most of the spectators unfulfilled—and many in an uproar. Referee Benny Whitman ended the fight in the second round after calling a foul.

Taylor won the first round, but in doing so he appeared to hit McLarnin low, twice, unintentionally. McLarnin protested to the referee. Whitman did not act on the supposed fouls, and Foster protested vehemently between rounds about the blows and lambasted Whitman for his inattention. Whitman walked to Taylor's corner and warned him to keep his blows higher.[9]

About a minute into the second round, Taylor landed a low left punch, and Whitman stopped the fight and lifted McLarnin's hand in victory. A stunned crowd watched McLarnin shake hands with Taylor before heading for the dressing room. Long pleaded with Whitman to allow the fight to continue, to no avail. Taylor waved his right arm in a gesture of disgust, then stayed in his corner for several minutes, so discouraged that he cried. He broke out into tears again in his dressing room.[10]

The Los Angeles newspapers denounced the stoppage, with one writer calling the decision "one of the most weird and putrid decisions ever rendered in this part of the country."[11] The writers reported that McLarnin had said immediately after the fight that the punch did not hurt him and he could have continued. "I wasn't hurt at all. I didn't think I was fouled," McLarnin said.[12]

Taylor claimed that he hit McLarnin low once in the first round, but it was a glancing blow that did not hurt Jimmy. In his defense, Whitman declared he had seen several low blows by Taylor and had warned him. Dozens of ringsiders saw the warnings.[13]

Boxing writer Paul Lowry of the *Times* concluded that Foster had rattled the referee with his between-rounds tirade, to which Whitman overreacted with the make-up call that ended the fight.[14]

In the midst of 10,000 agitated boxing fans, Whitman fled the Coliseum. "He left coatless, hatless, with a face white as grandmother's sheet, eyes popping out of his head and calling lustily for a cab," the *Times* reported.[15] The decision stood.

In a postfight interview, Taylor explained why he attacked McLarnin's body. "Jimmy's right-hand crazy since he knocked out Jackie Fields, and he had his right corked up around his ear to swing at me. I was trying to get [McLarnin's right] down in order to land myself."[16] In attacking low to set up a high assault, Bud had used a centuries-old fighting tactic in reverse. Warriors on ancient battlefields who raised their shields to block arrows raining down from their enemies did so at the risk that those archers might follow with volleys into their opponents' exposed bodies.[17]

Twelve days after the fight, Taylor spoke about the McLarnin bout while at home in Terre Haute.

"I don't yelp, never did in my life, but there was something funny that night. Either the referee lost his head completely or the money bet on the outcome had something to do with the decision. I have my own opinion, but I am not in a spot to declare myself ..." he said.[18]

Ultimately, the fight was never proven to have been influenced by gambling. A fix seems illogical given the circumstances, which includes Whitman's upstanding reputation. Syndicated columnist Bob Edgren praised Whitman for having the courage to enforce the disqualification rule while knowing the decision would incite the crowd.[19]

Taylor's statement suggesting a fix may have resulted from sheer frustration over the loss. He knew that one of his friends in Los Angeles had bet $15,000 on him to win. Unfazed by the outcome, the friend told Taylor just before Bud left for Terre Haute that he would wager another $15,000 if he ever fought McLarnin again.[20]

At 8 months, Barbara Jean Taylor would propel her little arms up and down excitedly, like a tiny drummer, and she called her dad "Pop." Home in time for Christmas 1925, Taylor made his debut as Santa Claus for the bouncing, 22-pounder. Taylor also brought generous gifts for the adults in his life—a Ford sedan for his dad and a squirrel coat for his wife.[21]

Eddie Long, who wanted to present Taylor the gift of a scheduled date with world champion Rosenberg, headed to New York City with $2,500 to post with the New York State Athletic Commission for a bout with the champion. The posting of "challenge money," a common practice then, served as a kind of formal request to fight a champion and represented the challenger's forfeit money, refundable if the match didn't happen. Long hoped that with the cash posted upfront, Tex Rickard would take notice.[22]

A published report out of New York indicated that Rosenberg was considering any one of four fighters for a title shot in late February or early March 1926, one of them being Bud Taylor. Taylor felt deserving; he had traveled more miles, fought more fights and made more money than the other three—Bushy Graham, Chick Suggs and Eddie Anderson.[23]

In Los Angeles, promoter Jack Doyle knew he could sell out the Coliseum again with a third Taylor-McLarnin match. McLarnin's manager again wanted the heavier weight limit, 126. This time, Long accepted without quarrel. Taylor had told Long he felt like he owed the customers a fight because of the premature ending to the last bout. Bud said he didn't care if they paid him nothing.[24]

When Taylor returned to the coast, he discovered an important item missing from his luggage. He had forgotten to pack one of his infant's dirty booties. He had not carried the charm for the first time in a year on the evening he lost to McLarnin on a foul. He didn't want to tempt bad luck again. Immediately, he wired Iris, "send on Barbara's dirtiest white sock," with hopes it would arrive in time for the fight.[25]

Taylor told the *Times* that he would not shy from body-punching his foe just because of last month's outcome. "I'll be careful all my punches are above the beltline for I'm terribly sorry for what happened in the first rematch," he said.[26] A vindicated Benny Whitman was again named to referee, to no one's objection.

On the afternoon of the fight, Jan. 12, 1926, oddsmakers made McLarnin a 10-7 favorite.27 They also reported brisk betting on both fighters. Taylor weighed 121, McLarnin 125. The difference didn't worry Taylor, who believed a four-pound difference mattered most in the clinches, and neither he nor McLarnin held much.28 Of bigger concern to The Terror of Terre Haute was that by time for the weigh-in, his little girl's sock had not arrived.29

Two hours later, the little piece of clothing was delivered to Taylor at his hotel, which boosted his confidence.30 A few hours later, Taylor laced up his size 7 sneakers, tucked the sock into the lining of his trunks and emerged from a dressing room before an audience of 10,000 in the Vernon Coliseum.31

Taylor pressed the action with his usual, fast start, and won the first round. The left landed, a good sign for him. McLarnin won the second round, showing a decent 1-2 and bloodying Taylor's mouth with a right. Then Taylor's left took over, and he put on a jab-and-hook clinic, landing three punches to McLarnin's one. "He threw them in droves, in armies and in gross lots," wrote one journalist. McLarnin wouldn't lead, but laid back and tried to launch his right hand. The right kept missing, and McLarnin took a left-handed beating. Taylor had McLarnin "completely mystified," according to one writer. The assault swelled McLarnin's face so high that it closed both his eyes. McLarnin managed a minor rally in the final two rounds, but failed in desperate attempts to land his specialty punch. *The Times* scored it 6-2-2, the *Los Angeles Examiner*, 7-2-1.32

Afterward, reporters found Taylor attributing his victory to his daughter's good-luck sock. Long was looking ahead. "Now we're out gunning for Rosenberg," he declared. "Bud beat the champion once, but that was before [Rosenberg] won the title. Since then, Rosenberg has been running out on us."33

As for McLarnin, good fortune lay ahead. He grew heavier and won the welterweight championship of the world. He retired in 1936, became wealthy from his investments and lived to be 96 years old. In interviews over the years, his opinion of Bud Taylor seemed to vary depending on his mood, from praising Taylor as the best fighter he ever fought, to complaining he was the dirtiest.34

Chapter 24

The Chase Continues

Bud Taylor had plenty of company chasing Charley Phil Rosenberg for the bantamweight championship of the world. As 1926 began, the challenges to Rosenberg's title numbered so many that the New York Boxing Commission was considering its own elimination tourney to determine the opponent. In January, Tex Rickard ranked the pro boxers in each division for *Ring* magazine, and the lists made the daily papers across the nation. Basing his ratings solely on the boxers' performances in the previous year, Rickard rated Taylor third among the bantamweights, behind No. 1 Bushy Graham and No. 2, a Massachusetts boxer, Chick Suggs. Rickard listed champion Rosenberg as fourth-best.[1] Like Bud, both Graham and Suggs had filed money with the state of New York as a challenge to Rosenberg.[2] The state of New York operated unattached in its oversight of professional boxing, because it did not belong to the national governing body for the sport, the National Boxing Association.

Long before the National Basketball Association, the familiar acronym "NBA" referred to the National Boxing Association. It formed in 1921 and was comprised of boxing commissioners from the states in which boxing was legal.[3] By 1927, the NBA's membership consisted of 25 states; four nations affiliated with the International Boxing Union of European nations; and Australia, South Africa and Argentina.[4]

Becoming the "world champion" of a weight division in 1926 generally meant the endorsement as titleholder by the NBA. The organization recognized champions for each of boxing's eight weight divisions, and among its functions had the power to administer suspensions. Any state that wanted to stage a title defense first needed NBA approval, which the NBA usually granted without difficulty.

In 1926, three boxing states did not belong to the NBA: New York, California and Pennsylvania.[5] These maverick states operated under their own commissions' guidelines, which at times conflicted with the NBA's rules. New York, whose commission consisted of a three-man board, seemed particularly insistent on maintaining its autonomy. Although the NBA and New York Athletic Commission usually operated compatibly, honoring each other's suspensions and recognizing the same champions, differences arose. For example, New York staged a "world championship" bantamweight bout between Abe Goldstein and Eddie Martin in 1924. The NBA refused to recognize the winner, Martin, as champion because it had not approved the bout.[6] Similarly, when the NBA states banned boxer Johnny Dundee in 1925 for failing to go through with a bout, Dundee still could fight in New York.[7] (New York eventually suspended Dundee, too. He was later reinstated.)

The differences among the NBA states and the independent states in the 1920s created plenty of confusion for the journalists, fans and even the boxers themselves. The NBA maintained its status as the predominant body controlling boxing until 1962, when it became the World Boxing Association. The competing World Boxing Council also formed in the 1960s, and additional competing agencies later would further convolute the situation.[8]

Taylor followed the McLarnin victory with a 10-rounder against Joey Sangor of Milwaukee on Feb. 3, 1926. The two fighters, Midwesterners born in the same month, also shared a mindset within the ropes: they seldom backed up. Sangor stood 5 feet, 5 inches tall, and his freckles and bony build made him look deceivingly fragile. Like Taylor, he compensated for his lack of brawn with impeccable technique and timing. He owned a terrific punch with either hand and had proven he could take a hefty punch by never having been knocked out.

Also like Taylor, Sangor had suffered nagging problems with his hands. His right hand, broken twice over the previous 18 months, had healed and he had gladly pronounced it healthy for the Taylor bout.9 Oddsmakers installed Taylor as an 8-5 favorite.10

The crowd in a sold-out Olympic Auditorium witnessed an entertaining 10-rounder, slowed by only three clinches that all came in the first round. Taylor pumped Sangor full of lefts, and won the decision by taking eight rounds. It was no foxtrot for Taylor; a Sangor right hand knocked out two of his teeth, and Bud left the ring with a gash in his lip and a swollen face.11

Taylor and company had planned to return east after the fight, but promoter Doyle induced him to stay in California for an additional bout. The opponent, Johnny Brown, was being billed as the bantamweight champion of England. Taylor canceled his train tickets, and wired for Iris and Barbara Jean to join him for a month of sunshine. Iris and a friend, Mary Gerhardt, made the trip from Terre Haute with the baby, and upon their arrival, Taylor moved the entire party into an apartment.12

The newspapers hailed Brown as a knockout expert in his home country, and the master of other English fighters of his weight class, but untested in America. "Being the champion of England might mean something over there, but I live in Indiana," Taylor said.13 The Los Angeles sportswriters were unable to assess Brown's chances against Taylor because Brown trained in private while stateside.14 Fight fans smelled a mismatch and "the smallest house Vernon has had in a long time" turned out March 9, 1926.15 Brown wore into the ring a belt given to him by the British aristocrat Lord Lonsdale, emblematic of the status of champion in England. The belt glittered with diamonds, but his game had no such shine against Taylor.16 He took a tremendous beating, and Taylor won all 10 rounds. "It was unfortunate for Bud that he can be given credit for a single victory," mused the *Los Angeles Times'* writer, "for he piled up enough points against the game Englishman to win six or seven fights."17

Chapter 25

Accused of Fix

Jim Mullen, whose successes at promoting boxing had earned him the nickname of the "Tex Rickard of Chicago" in the press, believed boxing on the verge of legalization in Illinois and stood ready to capitalize on the resulting explosion in customers.[1] Around early March 1926, Mullen scrawled "35,000" next to a dollar sign and sent the promise off to bantamweight champion Charley Phil Rosenberg if he would fight Bud Taylor, an eye-popping figure for a bantamweight title defense. There were no immediate reports from the Rosenberg camp of a response to the offer.[2]

In Cleveland, 8,000 jammed into Public Hall on March 26, 1926, to watch Taylor in a rematch with "Doc" Snell. Since his bad beating by Taylor four months earlier in Vernon, Snell had gone 5-1, with wins over Sangor and Rosenberg (in a nontitle fight). The Snell-Taylor rematch played out like the first fight, with Bud's left hand dominating throughout. By the fifth round, one scribe counted that Taylor had landed 74 punches to Snell's 27, and Bud won most of the remaining rounds to take the 12-round referee's decision.[3]

Taylor had been drawing 8,000 to 15,000 fans in his bouts around the nation, but Terre Haute did not have a venue to seat anywhere near that number. Promoters George Grammell and Tommy Moore wanted to bring Taylor back to his home city for a rematch with Abe Goldstein. The promoters chose the downtown Hippodrome Theater, which, if packed, could hold 2,000.[4] Counting on a huge demand for tickets from locals who had not seen Taylor fight in 11 months, Grammell and Moore jacked up ringside-seat prices to

Bud Taylor fought many of his 166 bouts in a black jumpsuit, as pictured.

$5.50, a then-record high for an indoor fight in the city. Still, ticket orders kept Grammell's head pressed to the phone receiver so often it left him rubbing his ear.5

Goldstein's manager, Willie Lewis, spoke to the press about the importance of the bout. "You see, it's our shortest cut back to a championship shot by defeating Taylor, and that's what we're after," he said. Goldstein had won only two of six fights since Taylor defeated him a year earlier.6

While Goldstein needed a victory just to inject some life into his career, Bud had won 14 of his past 16, and he wanted a victory to stay the course.

The fight April 8 sold out the theater, and hundreds who had failed to buy tickets in advance were turned away at the door. Taylor fought cautiously, relying on his left to score, while Goldstein won points with his right. The *Terre Haute Star's* opinion was that Taylor won. The fight is best recorded as a draw, the outcome reported by the city's *Tribune* and the *Indianapolis Star*.7

Word reached Taylor that in Cleveland, his named had surfaced in a controversy. Cleveland's boxing commissioner, Edwin Barry, had refused to sanction a bout between Doc Snell and Eddie Shea, and suspended Snell, claiming Snell's fight a few weeks earlier with Bud Taylor had been a "fake" and a "money bout." Barry indicated that he thought Taylor, after piling up a big lead in the early rounds, "carried" Snell through the rest of the contest.8

Snell promptly hired an attorney and announced he would sue Barry for $50,000.9 Taylor seemed bemused by Barry's actions. He said he remembered the sting of Snell's punches well, since the fight had been a much tougher one than their first encounter, five months earlier in Vernon.10 "If my fight with Snell was a fake, I would hate to engage in a real one," he said.11 Long, furious, sent Barry a letter demanding a retraction or he would sue for $100,000. "Bud Taylor," Long wrote, "… has taken part in 105 contests and has boxed before half a million people. This is the first time any individual has raised a voice against his integrity. He always has given his best efforts to the boxing public and he never has and never will take part in a match that is not waged strictly on its merits."12

Boxing columnist James E. Doyle of the *Cleveland Plain Dealer* wrote that the fans who saw the Snell-Taylor bout seemed pleased at the action. Doyle opined that Taylor eased up a bit after the early rounds so as not to tire himself or leave himself open to one fight-changing punch, as Snell had a reputation for throwing.[13]

The controversy died when Barry backed down, saying he never made such a statement about Taylor and that he simply was not impressed with Snell's effort.[14]

Taylor never again was accused publicly of engaging in a "fixed" fight. Certainly, bouts with predetermined outcomes existed in the 1920s, and even more so in the 1930s during organized crime's well-documented influence on the sport. If anyone ever approached Taylor about the prospect of fixing a fight, he never said so.

Chapter 26

Clever

Pancho Villa's success in boxing made him a hero in his impoverished home country of the Philippines, inspiring legions of children to take up boxing to escape the islands.

Sencio Moldez was one of them. Moldez had been born into a large family on the island of Leyte, and was hired out to the fields as a child. In his mid-teens, he developed a passion for the sport of Villa's mastery.

To practice boxing, Sencio worked overtime three days a week just to earn enough pesos to rent gloves for one hour. When Villa left for the states in 1922 to seek fame as a boxer, Moldez, dressed in rags, joined thousands at dockside to say farewell to their idol.

In more than 40 fights in his home country, young Moldez compiled a record impressive enough that when Villa returned to the islands in May 1925 as world champion, he gave the boy a title shot. Villa won the 15-rounder.[1]

When Villa died in July 1925, Filipino sportsmen in Manila called the late champion's manager, Frank Churchill, in the states, and asked him to manage Moldez's affairs.[2] Moldez made his U.S. debut that summer under the name "Clever Sencio."

Despite the nickname, Moldez boxed with a no-frills, mechanical style. Villa had been the clever one, mixing and moving, sometimes erect and other times crouched, baffling opponents with his finesse. Sencio showed little flair, moving forward and throwing punches relentlessly. He got hit a lot in return fire.

Sencio's fearless style nonetheless satisfied the bloodlust of boxing fans. By the spring of 1926, he had banked $15,000 in U.S. ring earnings, money he planned to send home to help with his siblings' education.[3] New York and Cleveland promoters were negotiating for his services against Taylor when Milwaukee matchmaker Frank Mulkern slipped quietly into the bidding in early March and signed the fighters for April 19.[4]

Sencio's seven months in America almost seemed to be guided by some mysterious force, as if his sudden presence on U.S. soil upset the pro boxing circuit from its natural order. In his U.S. debut, he pounded Mickey Gill of San Francisco until the referee stopped the bout in the second round. Gill then turned on the referee and landed several blows to the ref's face before Gill's manager ended the bizarre incident by carrying his fighter from the ring.[5] After a bout in New York, angry patrons threw seat cushions at referee Leo O'Shea after he proclaimed Sencio the winner over Izzy Schwartz.[6]

At 17, Sencio should not even have been boxing in the United States, where the minimum age in many jurisdictions was 18. Either Sencio or his handlers had listed his age as 21 when he entered the country, and boxing officials didn't question otherwise.[7] He had arrived having lost his previous two fights in the Philippines, and virtually no one in the states gave him serious recognition as a fighter.[8]

Yet Sencio dug in and won his first eight U.S. contests, displaying what seemed like a robotic resistance to punishment. In September 1925, Teddy Silva had Sencio on the verge of a knockout until the Filipino was saved by the bell.[9] The following January, Fidel LaBarba had the Filipino out on his feet, but he didn't fall, as Sencio seemed "possessed of unlimited powers of endurance."[10] The Milwaukee boxing writers seized on this theme to justify colorful prose that suggested that the Filipino boxers were a mere generation away from swinging in banana trees. They wrote, "It is more or less jungle fighting with these brown boys—ring fists being an outlet for their wildcatty nature," and, "The sun of the jungles seems to burn courage and animal stamina ..." in them, and other such nonsense.[11] In reality, Sencio and Villa came from a community of peaceful farming families.[12]

Taylor considered Sencio a friend.[13] Sencio had fought several bouts on the West Coast in the fall of 1925 during Taylor's last trip there, and the two likely became acquainted while frequenting the same gymnasiums for training. They shared a workmanlike attitude toward their profession, investing long hours in the gym and adhering to strict diets. Sencio while stateside even refused to eat the familiar Filipino dishes his girlfriend prepared for him.[14] In the ring, their charging styles were similar—relentless hounds, willing to take a punch–or eight or 10—to land one.

Eddie Long planned no special fight strategy. He told reporters to look for what his fellow did best: to throw the double hook (a left to the body followed with the same punch to the head), while looking for an opening with the right cross.[15] The betting odds veered to as lopsided as 10-4 in Taylor's favor.[16]

Boxing was legal in Wisconsin. A week earlier, a bill had passed in Illinois legalizing the sport, and many of that state's boxing officials planned to attend the fight to view how the sport functioned in their neighboring state.[17]

Seven thousand fans filled the Cream City Athletic Club for the bout.[18] As Sencio squatted in his corner before the opening bell, a Milwaukee boxing columnist noticed how relaxed he appeared, "prepared for battle with the nonchalance of a flapper biting a fresh stick of gum."[19]

At the gong, Sencio snapped into action, proving all that had been written about his brawling style. He bore in and tossed arms from all angles, like some angry octopus. For six rounds, he kept up a tireless pace, throwing more punches than Taylor, and landing enough of them to keep the fight close.[20] Sencio appeared so superbly conditioned that he did not seem to breathe hard between rounds. Ringsiders shouted for Taylor to throw his right, but Bud couldn't find an opening.[21] In the fifth, Taylor found that seam and landed a right that dislodged Sencio's mouthpiece and brought first blood. By the eighth, Taylor's blows were landing with regularity. In the ninth, Taylor jolted Sencio flush on the chin with a forceful right, the kind of punch that whips the head and shakes the brain. Sencio did not fall, but looked unconscious on his feet for about half the round, while Taylor pummeled him.[22]

At the start of the 10th round, Sencio looked rejuvenated and wanted to mix it up until Taylor stunned him with two left hooks. Sencio staggered out of the way of Taylor's six follow-up leads before

Bud found Sencio's chin again with a left hook.[23] Taylor hooked to the body and the crowd screamed for a knockout.[24] Sencio "reeled about the ring on the verge of collapse, with hardly enough strength to deliver a blow."[25]

At the last bell, a groggy Sencio flopped onto his stool, with his arms dangling at his sides. Taylor shook hands with him before leaving the ring, and a reporter noticed the red marks on Bud's body from the effects of Sencio's left-hand punches.[26]

To bring Sencio out of his haze, his corner men waved smelling salts beneath his nose and splashed his face with water. He appeared to gasp for breath, and minutes passed before he tried to rise. When he did, he found his legs would not respond, and he slumped back into his chair. When he rose again, he wobbled until he fell into the arms of his trainer, Whitey Eckwart. Eventually, Sencio's seconds lifted him between the ropes and guided him to the stairs leading to his dressing room. While ascending, he fell again and had to be carried the rest of the way.[27]

Taylor telephoned Terre Haute to tell Iris that her husband felt well and came out of the fray without a scratch.[28]

Two physicians from the Wisconsin Boxing Commission examined Sencio in his dressing room. He showed no marks from the fight, except for a small cut inside his mouth. The physicians later reported that they checked Sencio's heart, looked for fractures and other routine injuries, and found nothing. They told him to rest.[29] Arthur J. Schinner, chairman of the commission, also visited. He talked with Sencio, observed Eckwart doing the same, and found the boxer "… in the same condition as any boxer would or should be after engaging in a hard contest."[30]

Later, in the Plankington Hotel, Sencio lay undressed on the bed in his room. "I kept asking him how he felt and he said, 'all right, Whitey, only a little headache'," Eckwart recalled.

"We bathed him and kept putting cold packs on his forehead. It seemed to relieve him and he said he wanted to go to sleep. For more than two hours, I was beside him, putting packs on his head," the trainer said. Eckwart left the room, and returned about 4:30 a.m. to ask Sencio how he felt.[31] "I'm all right, I just want to sleep," he said, expressing difficulty at dozing off.[32] Eckwart left the room for the morning.

About 8 a.m., window washer Frank Wallace glanced into the hotel room and saw a body lying on a floor. Blood trickled from the nose and mouth, forming a puddle. Wallace called hotel management. When Eckwart heard from management, he rushed to Sencio's room. He thought he felt a faint pulse, but by the time an ambulance arrived, Sencio had died.33

Dr. Edward L. Miloslavich performed the post-mortem exam. A brain hemorrhage caused Sencio's death, he concluded.34 The fighter's fate had been determined before he left the ring.

Taylor and his manager were given little time to mull the tragedy. They were summoned from their hotel to Milwaukee police headquarters, then asked to visit District Attorney Eugene Wengert. A newspaperman seeking Taylor at Wengert's office found Bud waiting for the D.A. with his head buried in his hands.

"I don't worry as much over the legal processes involved in the death of Sencio one hundredth as much as I do about the thinking I'm going to do about it," Taylor said. "I feel terrible over it. I can't believe the little Filipino is dead." Taylor raised his head to show his face to the reporter only a few times. It looked shattered by grief and worry.

" … We were friends when we went into the ring and friends when we left it," Taylor said about Sencio. "… I won't quit the fight game, but I know I won't be able to fight for a while."35

The police investigation into the death merely satisfied a formality, and Wengert on April 21 announced that no crime had been committed.

"Boxing is legalized in Wisconsin, and the Boxing Commission passed on Sencio's physical condition before the bout and found him perfectly fit," Wengert said. "The law and rules were observed in every way. It was just one of those unfortunate things that happen in any sport," he told the press.36 Boxing officials did not learn Sencio's true age of 18 until days later.37

No American boxer of prominence had ever killed two opponents until Sencio's death branded Taylor with that macabre distinction.38 Discussing Sencio's death with Ralph White of the *Terre Haute Tribune*, Taylor said he had never felt so sorry over anything in his entire life.39

Unlike the aftermath of the Jerome death in New York, boxing's opponents did not rush to outlaw the sport in Wisconsin. A *Chicago Daily Tribune* editorialist put the tragedy into perspective by noting that all sports carry a certain element of risk. "Do not put the blame on boxing but instead on the universal frailty of human life," the columnist wrote.40

St. John's Catholic Church in Milwaukee conducted a service for Sencio before his body was sent to Vancouver, then shipped to Manila. Taylor sent a wreath of flowers to the church.41

On April 23, four days after the fight, a Chicago paper reported that Taylor had agreed to fight Tommy Ryan on May 14 in Louisville, Kentucky. The same article stated that Taylor had not decided whether or not to go through with a bout against Harold Smith scheduled for April 30.42

Taylor's decision to carry on with his career within a matter of weeks of Sencio's death struck a Milwaukee sports columnist as calloused. The writer, Manning Vaughan of the *Milwaukee Journal*, hammered Taylor in a piece published April 23.

"Common decency and respect for the memory of a gallant foe should keep Taylor out of the ring for many months—if not always," Vaughan wrote. "But no, the lust for prize ring gold is so great that all the finer instincts of the real sportsmen are mere things to talk about. Get the money while the getting's good, seems to be the motto of the modern pug and the modern pug's manager." Vaughan also mentioned the Jerome tragedy and wrote that Taylor's tears were merely "crocodile tears" and his "hollow grief" ... "was that of a professional pallbearer."43

On the contrary, all that is known about Taylor indicates that his nature would have been not only to anguish over the death, but also to suffer from such stinging personal criticism.

Taylor rarely spoke publicly about the deaths of Jerome and Sencio. Privately, he stayed silent as well, leaving friends and family often to ponder the magnitude of his burden.

Chapter 27

Reeling in Rosenberg

Within a week after the Sencio bout, Eddie Long told the press that his boxer needed time to cope with the tragedy and he would cancel a bout scheduled for April 30 with Harold Smith. Taylor would, however, travel to Louisville to fight Tommy Ryan on May 14.[1]

Long accepted the Louisville fight because he wanted Taylor to remain match-sharp while negotiations continued with bantamweight champion Charley Phil Rosenberg. Long also wanted an excuse to attend the Kentucky Derby on May 15.[2]

First, Long headed to New York. There, during negotiations, Chicago promoter Jim Mullen offered Harry Segal $40,000 in guarantee money for Rosenberg to fight Taylor in Illinois—twice as much as Rosenberg could make if the fight were staged in New York. Rosenberg signed the contract. Taylor would receive $10,000 for the bout, which would be staged in June.

"When Eddie told me he had Rosenberg's contract in his pocket, I about fell over," Taylor said in Terre Haute. "All I hope is that the bout goes through, as I have no fear of the champion."[3]

At last, the bout looked imminent. Such plans had collapsed before, but never with Rosenberg's signature on a dotted line. The only possible hitch in the deal was that Mullen had to wait for the formation of the state of Illinois' boxing commission before he could set an exact date for the fight. The commission also would need Rosenberg's signature and the posting of a forfeit by both fighters.[4]

Aware that any loss beforehand could nix the opportunity he had long awaited, Taylor launched into serious training for the bout with Ryan. His opponent was the same Ryan that Taylor had outpointed two years earlier and with whom Bud and his manager had scuffled at the weigh-in.

The Louisville fight would prove a difficult one for Taylor, as he struggled with the nuances of Ryan's awkward style. Taylor hated to fight opponents who clinched and crouched, and Ryan did both, staying bent over like a cave explorer while trying to muscle Bud around the ring. A butt of heads carved a gash in Taylor's forehead in the first round. Taylor cut Ryan near the eye later with a hard right, and landed enough overall lefts to win the writers' decision. Eight thousand witnessed the bloody fight, while about 75,000 watched Bubbling Over win the Kentucky Derby.[5]

On June 2, 1926, Mullen signed an agreement with park owner Charles Comiskey to use the White Sox ball park for the Taylor-Rosenberg bout.[6] A week later, however, the new Illinois Boxing Commission announced it would issue no permits until at least late July.[7]

With the date of the fight pushed back, Long scheduled his top client for bouts on the West Coast. In three matches there in June, Taylor fans packed the arenas for The Terror. Five thousand people jammed San Francisco's Dreamland rink and at least 2,000 were turned away as Taylor won a 10-rounder easily over "California" Joe Lynch—not the former bantamweight champion Lynch of New York.[8] In Portland, Oregon, hometown scrapper Chuck Hellmann ground out a draw against Taylor, although at least two newspapermen had Bud winning by a substantial margin. One wrote that Taylor gave Hellmann "a terrific beating," and that the announcement of the judges' verdict drew laughter from the crowd.[9] Taylor closed out the West Coast jaunt with a six-round decision in Seattle over Filipino boxer Young Nationalista.[10]

Three weeks in California had left Taylor homesick, and he wanted to return to watch Sammy Mandell box in Chicago. His former stablemate's big night had arrived: a title fight with world lightweight champion Rocky Kansas. "Sammy will beat Kansas for the title," Taylor wrote in a letter, "and I'll do the same when I meet Rosenberg."[11]

The Mandell-Kansas fight in the White Sox ball park on July 3, 1926, marked the first legal boxing match in Illinois since 1901.[12] Similar to the Taylor-Rosenberg situation with the bantamweights, Kansas held the lightweight championship although the experts had long considered Mandell the superior fighter. Kansas would not take the fight for less than a $50,000 guarantee while Mandell had no guarantee, but agreed to accept half the gate.[13] Mandell and his manager, Eddie Kane, agreed to put up Kansas' 50 grand themselves, to which Paul Lowry of the *Los Angeles Times* responded by characterizing Kansas' title defense as "simply a case of selling the title."[14]

Mandell won the 10-round fight and became the champion. It rained, and the disastrous effect on the attendance meant Mandell failed to recoup the $50,000. Mandell lost money on the bout, but at least the title had moved justifiably to the best lightweight in all of boxing.[15]

A week later, Long and Mullen were back in New York negotiating with Rosenberg's manager. This time they agreed to stage the bout in the Chicago Cubs' ball park, and Long again felt assured the bout was "on." He sent a telegram to the *Terre Haute Tribune* with the news. Ralph White then informed Taylor. "Say, boy, I'm tickled pink," Taylor said.[16]

A sportswriter noted that the signing ended a 12,000-mile chase by Long to secure the title fight. Long had traveled to Los Angeles, Cleveland twice and New York three times trying to get Segal's signature.[17] The agreement called for Rosenberg to receive a guarantee of $45,000 and Taylor, 10 percent of the gate.[18] Mullen predicted a gate of $100,000 to $150,000.[19] Rosenberg's guarantee money seems to have been Mullen's responsibility; no mention is ever made of Long or Taylor putting up any of that cash themselves. A final adjustment on the date set the match firmly for Sept. 16.

Taylor kept his excitement in check. "He had been disappointed so often that he declared he would have to see the forfeit placed in the hands of the commission first before he would believe his great chance had come," a Chicago sportswriter wrote.[20]

Taylor's immediate concern was super-stooper Tommy Ryan, whom he was scheduled to fight for a fourth time on July 24, 1926. "All I ask of him is stand up and fight," Taylor told the press. "…

Before the last Kentucky Derby, he crouched with his head about two feet above the floor. I clubbed him on the back and the back of the head to *make him* stand up, but he refused. I wasn't going to take chances of breaking my hands by hitting him on top of the head or on the elbows."[21] Taylor had won their three prior matches, but Ryan kept surfacing as a bantamweight contender by recording wins along his career over such first-raters as Carl Tremaine, Bushy Graham and Chick Suggs.

The fourth Ryan fight drew 7,500 spectators to White Sox ball park, with a gate of $26,685.[22] Ryan hit Taylor low four times and in the third round, the referee stopped the contest and raised Bud's hand. Taylor had wanted to continue, despite the fact that the fourth foul had reduced him to his knees.[23]

Taylor and Long took a train to Los Angeles in August for a final warmup for Rosenberg.[24] Dixie LaHood, a decent boxer with some big-name wins, was no match. He fell in the first round and Taylor hammered him into a wobbly state in every round until the eighth. By then, LaHood's face had been replaced by a bloody mass of flesh, and his seconds heaved in the towel.[25]

Rosenberg tuned up for the Taylor fight with a nontitle bout against Pete Sarmiento. Taylor watched from ringside as Sarmiento, whom Bud had beaten twice, fought the champion to a 10-round draw.[26]

Chapter 28

Champion by Appointment

Terre Haute businesses sold tickets by the stack for the Bud Taylor-Charley Phil Rosenberg fight, which prompted a contingent of fans to arrange with the C&E Railroad for a special train run to carry supporters from Bud's home city to Chicago. It would make stops in Clinton, Indiana, Newport, Indiana and Danville, Illinois en route to the Dearborn Street station in the Windy City. The $5 round-trip price included the final leg of transportation to the Cubs ball park. About 350 Taylor fans planned to travel by this mode. It was anticipated that Mayor Davis would declare Sept. 16, a Thursday, a half-holiday in the city so fight fans could depart at 1 p.m. on the train to ensure they reached Chicago in time for the fights. The Monon Railroad also offered a special rail trip out of Indianapolis to carry Taylor's fans to the bout.[1]

Taylor arrived in Chicago on Sept. 8 and hit the road for a 5-mile run.[2] He had not fought at below 118 pounds since the Sencio bout five months earlier, and he knew that long jogs served as the best way to burn calories to keep below the required poundage.[3] Rosenberg had not defended his NBA title in 14 months. Over that stretch of time, he had fought eight nontitle contests, with a record of 4-2-2, while Taylor had gone 13-2-2 against tougher competition.[4] Rosenberg no longer was considered "world champion" by the state of New York, which had suspended him for refusing to fight Bushy Graham.[5]

Ralph White, in Chicago to cover the fight for the *Terre Haute Tribune*, reported that he saw a Chicago beer baron lay down $1,400 on Taylor to win $1,000.6

Despite his status as the underdog, the champion showed no signs of cowering. "I can lick Taylor every day in the week and don't forget it," Rosenberg told a reporter.7 "He may have outpointed me in New York, but I was indifferent that night and I am not counting that bout at all ... I can think of four or five boys in the division who can make it tougher for me than [Taylor] can."8

Taylor spoke of his desire to bring a world boxing title to Indiana. Such well-known Hoosier fighters of Taylor's past as Milburn Saylor and Ray Bronson (lightweights, Indianapolis), Jack Dillon (light-heavyweight, Indianapolis), and Jimmy Clabby (middleweight, Hammond), all top talents in their respective divisions, had never accomplished the feat, although Dillon's claim as champion in the pre-NBA years of 1912-16 held wide support.9

In 1926, the Illinois Boxing Commission required boxers to post their forfeit money (the guarantee of a fighter's appearance, and under the weight limit), eight days before a bout.10 Under ordinary circumstances, Rosenberg's skipper Harry Segal should have posted the required $12,500 (one-fourth of Rosenberg's purse) for the Taylor fight by Sept. 8. The Boxing Commission, however, had given Segal a four-day grace period to post.11

When Segal failed to put up the money by Sept. 14, the Illinois Boxing Commission called off the bout. In a formal announcement, the commission also suspended Rosenberg and Segal from fighting in Illinois for life and stated it would recognize Taylor as world champion.12

The ensuing weeks produced a flood of speculation over why Segal had not posted the money. One Chicago newspaper reported that Segal had been seen flashing the $12,500 check and that a bank had OK'd its sum.13 Many assumed that Rosenberg simply could not make the weight and didn't want to lose the forfeit money. Reports surfaced about gamblers trying unsuccessfully to control the outcome of the bout, and one report noted that a considerable amount of money had been bet on Rosenberg in the previous few days—so much so that he had gone from a 9-5 underdog to being the favorite.14

Along with the failure to post forfeit money, the commission suspended Rosenberg and Segal "because of the injection of political and other influence" in the matter of the commission's pending selection of the referee for the fight, according to the commission's statement.[15]

The statement read that "Segal and Rosenberg, in our estimation, are not the caliber of men who belong in boxing and their unsportsmanlike attitude, coupled with their disregard of our law and rules, compelled us to take this action." The commission further stated that "we believe that if boxing is to survive, it has to be kept clean."[16]

Segal told the press that he had planned to post the forfeit money the next day. He said he did not regard the timing of the posted forfeit as of any great importance, and reacted furiously to the suspension.[17] Rosenberg expressed disappointment at the cancelation.[18]

In 1940, a Chicago sports columnist reported that the reason the commission canceled the fight is that it had uncovered evidence of an attempt by a clique of New York gamblers to influence the outcome by either bribes or threat of violence.[19] Mullen, the promoter, also was reported to have been strong-armed with threats not to keep Rosenberg's $12,500 if the champion did not make the weight. But when the thugs leaned on Mullen, he reportedly told them: "Where the hell do you get the idea that you New York gunmen can scare a Chicagoan? Why, Chicago is the killers' capital city. Now get the hell out of here."[20]

Long told a Terre Haute newspaper he had been offered not less than 10 times his cut from the fight (10 times being probably $25,000) "to do business" with New York gamblers betting big on Rosenberg. "You would be surprised to know just what and how many propositions have been made me," Long told a newspaperman in September 1926. "I could get a chunk to toss Bud overboard, but I'm with him if we never get a shot at any champion. There isn't enough filthy money in the world for me to cross him."[21]

Taylor offered a simple explanation for the entire Rosenberg fiasco: "I could whip him and as he couldn't make the weight and be strong, he took the forfeit route as the means to ease out."[22]

Mullen, as with Taylor and Long, never was accused by the commission of any reprehensible conduct. Mullen was saddled with the task of refunding $50,000 to advance-sale ticketholders.23

In 1970, Rosenberg told an interviewer his side of the story: He said he failed to make the weight limit intentionally by drinking malted milk after his manager heard that the Taylor camp planned "to steal the title from us." In the interview, he did not clarify what he meant by "steal the title." Rosenberg indicated that in retrospect, he wished he had gone through with the bout—because of the guarantee money.24

The result of the bout's cancellation was that Taylor, at least in the view of the state of Illinois, officially became the world champion. But it would not have mattered to him if the world had named him champion of the universe, it meant little. "I wanted to *win* the championship, not get it as a gift," he said.25

The boxing world greeted the state of Illinois' declaration of Taylor as world bantamweight champion with mixed reactions. Illinois officials immediately notified all the states in the NBA about its proclamation of Taylor as champion, and its suspension of Rosenberg and his manager.26

On its face, Illinois' decision to install Taylor as champ carried no binding effect outside the state unless the move met NBA approval. The chairman of the commission in California, a non-NBA state, immediately endorsed the move, saying it would propose Taylor be named champion at its next meeting.27 In New York, where the bantamweight title had been vacant since the state suspended Rosenberg for refusing to fight Bushy Graham, the commission ignored Illinois' action.

While members of the press seemed united in the opinion that Taylor stood atop the bantamweights, they remained loyal to the principle that he must earn the title in the ring. "Though he is the best bantamweight in the world, he is as far away from the championship now as he ever was," wrote Warren Brown of the *Chicago Herald & Examiner*.28 Columnists such as Brown would get no argument from Taylor. "I'd rather win it in the ring," Taylor said.29

Who, then, deserved the title of world's bantamweight champion? Mullen began negotiating for a Taylor-Graham matchup that many believed would settle the matter.30 Meanwhile, Taylor underwent surgery in Chicago to correct the appearance of his ear.31 Dead cartilage had caused it to swell into an enlarged state, a deformity known as "cauliflower ear," and common in his line of work.

The Jack Dempsey-Gene Tunney fight for the heavyweight championship on Sept. 23, 1926, drew a crowd of 120,000 to Philadelphia, and the interest of millions across the nation. Taylor was so eager to learn its result that he planted himself in the newsroom of the *Terre Haute Star* and watched intently as the results came in by telegraph.32

In October, Taylor traveled to St. Paul, Minnesota, for a bout with Vic Burrone of New Jersey. While he trained in Minnesota, members of the National Boxing Association gathered in Detroit on Oct. 18 for their annual meeting. After review and some debate, the NBA settled the bantamweight muddle by endorsing Illinois' action and naming Bud Taylor the bantamweight champion of the world.33

The chase had ended. After 109 boxing matches, tens of thousands of miles of travel, hours of sweaty practice inside gyms that totaled to months, and broken bones and surgeries, Taylor had accomplished his goal. But he did not feel like celebrating. Taylor deserved to win the title inside the ring, to a roaring crowd, with a tired arm raised high in triumph. Ironically, the championship had been conveyed to him in a typed order by a panel of men in business suits, from a city where he had never stepped inside a ring. All his life, Taylor had achieved by proving himself, from asserting his superiority as a child in the roughneck neighborhoods of Terre Haute through the conquests of his chosen profession all the way to its highest level. Taylor needed to *seize* the title; a gift of it would not suffice.

Though he felt unfulfilled, he could not have helped but feel honored. In Terre Haute, the *Star* topped a page with the headline "Taylor recognized as bantamweight champion."34 In St. Paul, the auditorium provided the setting for the first opportunity for Taylor and Long to hear a ring announcer blare the words, "the bantamweight *champion of the world*, Bud Taylor," a pronouncement that is the dream of every young man who ever laced up a boxing mitt.

The 10-round bout Oct. 23 against Burrone had been planned

well in advance, and the title was not at stake. Taylor used his left hook effectively and won seven rounds, and the newspapers' decisions.35

Los Angelinos greeted Taylor with a reception befitting a dignitary when his train pulled into the Southern Pacific Station on Oct. 28, 1926. A motorcycle escort took Taylor and Long to City Hall, where they met with Mayor George Cryer.36

Taylor's bout in Vernon, California with Young Montreal had been set at the nontitle weight limit of 120 pounds.37 His opponent, 28, had grown up in Rhode Island, and had been fighting since 1916. Early in his boxing career, he changed his bookish-sounding given name of Maurice Billingkoff to the more palatable "Young Montreal." His most noticeable physical endowment—and a big boxing advantage—was a pair of abnormally long arms, which he used to fire-hose his way to a 38-3-3 start.38 That hot start didn't last, and Montreal began a four-year-long habit of finishing second in boxing matches.

Then, in September 1926, a single, jaw-dropping victory revived Montreal's career. Promoters had induced Bushy Graham into going to Rhode Island to fight Montreal, and the two fighters battled twice in one month. Graham won the first, but Montreal beat up Graham thoroughly in the second. Bushy left the ring with one eye closed, the other half-closed, and a bloody mouth.39 The victory emboldened Montreal's manager to trot before the New York Boxing Commission and ask that Montreal be allowed to fight Rosenberg for the title. The commission told him no, it preferred Graham.40

In Vernon, Montreal's manager, Charlie Rose, boasted to reporters that "if anyone is champion in New York, it's Young Montreal." He said he would lay a $30,000 side bet on his fighter against Rosenberg or Taylor in any title fight.41

The Montreal fight worried Eddie Long, according to the press. Anyone who could reel in the gazelle-like Graham enough times to make his face rise like baked dough deserved respect. "I'm not patting myself on the back for making this match," Long told a reporter. "I've made lots softer matches than this. I think Montreal is the most dangerous man I could ask Bud to fight. He's smart, he's game and he could punch."42 Taylor went from a 2-1 favorite two days before the fight to 10-9 by show time.43

Taylor owned the heart of the average West Coast boxing spectator.

"Taylor is the idol of idols in Los Angeles," it was written, and so adored that fans rearranged their daily schedules to attend his fights.44 Among his rabid boosters was Carlo Curtis, manager of the Main Street Athletic Club. Curtis canceled the weekly Monday night fight show at the club so that he and all the club regulars wouldn't have to miss the Taylor-Montreal fight.45

Taylor needed just one round to solve Montreal's awkward style. Taylor's left jabs and right cross landed almost at will in the second round, and he floored Montreal twice. Before Taylor could finish him off, with Montreal clinging helplessly to the ropes, the referee interceded and stopped the bout.46

The victory, Taylor's 13th straight, prompted syndicated sports columnist Bob Edgren to write that the bantamweights finally had an authentic champion, "the most aggressive and most dangerous fighter of his weight seen in recent years and nobody who ever sees him will think him a cheese champion, such as the class has been affiliated with recently."47 Well-known sportswriter Damon Runyan called Taylor "the outstanding bantam of the land."48

Taylor remained unsatisfied; he desired universal acceptance as the champ.49 New York, which never had joined the NBA, still considered the throne vacant. New York seemed to reserve its "world bantamweight title" for its natives—Rosenberg and the previous three holders, for example.50 On Nov. 18, the New York commission lifted Rosenberg's suspension after Rosenberg agreed to fight Graham (also a New Yorker) for that state's version of the "world" title.51 When Long heard about the impending Rosenberg-Graham match, he wired the New York commission. Why had it not honored two challenges to Rosenberg filed by Taylor with the commission? he asked.52 It is not known if he received a reply.

Taylor did enjoy the fruits of his notoriety. In Los Angeles, filmmakers working on the silent boxing movie "Is Zat So?" wanted to pay Taylor to help them shoot realistic fight scenes.53 In Terre Haute, Elks Lodge No. 86 initiated him as a member when the group met on Nov. 17. Taylor, who never felt comfortable speaking before crowds, briefly muttered that he was a better boxer than a speaker, then took a seat. Attorney John M. Fitzgerald presented him with a diamond-ruby Elks button, and Taylor stammered a few words of thanks. Not until after the meeting did Taylor recover from his shyness enough to express how much he appreciated the Elks' gift.[54]

The Dempsey-Tunney rematch in 1927 showed just how big a business boxing had become in America, when Tunney pocketed $990,000 and Dempsey $450,000. By comparison, Babe Ruth earned a salary of $70,000 in 1927, an income less than Taylor and dozens of other boxers.[55]

Gymnasiums all across America housed wannabe Dempseys, Tunneys and Taylors, pounding the heavy bag, perfecting their footwork. Every metro area in the nation had a fan favorite that an enterprising promoter longed to match with a big boxing name such as Bud Taylor's, for a guaranteed windfall. In Milwaukee, their boy had been Joey Sangor. Sangor had begun his pro fight career in 1921, winning and losing with no particular distinction for two years. In March 1923, his right hand knocked Sammy Mandell into dreamland and propelled Sangor into the top echelon of the featherweights (125-pound class). Sangor proceeded to fight the highly ranked bantams and feathers with mixed results; Taylor had decisioned him in February and McLarnin had knocked him out in March. Sangor had rebounded by winning six matches in a row, and Milwaukee promoters dialed Long's phone number to suggest a rematch.[56]

Sangor normally boxed around 125 pounds, too heavy for a bantamweight bout, so he and Taylor did not fight for the title in their rematch Nov. 29, 1926, in Milwaukee.[57] Taylor never faced a boxer with as similar a style as his own. Both pressed forward uncompromisingly, tossing left jabs and hooks and always looking to finish with the right.

Inspired by an audience of 7,500 in his home city, Sangor fought his greatest bout to date. Taylor won the first two rounds, and appeared to have matters under control. During the third, Taylor emerged from a furious exchange of blows with a severe cut over his left eye, either from a punch or butt. The area swelled and "in ten seconds was closed tighter than an Indiana Prohibition padlock," and Sangor set about banging away at the vulnerable area. In the ensuing rounds, Taylor couldn't see and he began swinging carelessly. Sangor landed at will, winning all the rounds and knocking Taylor down in the seventh.58

Taylor offered no excuses for the loss, admitting to the *Chicago Daily Tribune* that he had simply taken a bad beating.59

On Dec. 14, Bud had surgery to remove a lump above his left eye. The procedure meant canceling a Dec. 17 bout in Madison Square Garden with an up-and-comer named Tony Canzoneri.60 Graham accepted the fight as Taylor's substitute.61 Canzoneri outpointed Graham over 10 rounds, adding a new player to the throng of top bantamweights. Since Canzoneri had weighed in for the fight at over the bantamweight limit, the New York Boxing Commission decided that Graham retained his status as the man Rosenberg would fight for the New York version of the title.62 Canzoneri, however, would soon prove that he could fight—and fight well—at the bantamweight limit of 118 pounds.

Chapter 29

... For the Honor of Terre Haute ...

While recuperating from surgery, Taylor started a business venture in Terre Haute. He poured as much as $50,000 into an elaborate renovation of the gym that he leased on the second floor of the K of C building.[1] The money mostly went for gym equipment, including a boxing ring mounted on wheels, as well as weights, pulleys and punching bags. He installed a handball court, a putting area for golfers, steam baths and rubdown tables.[2]

Taylor sold monthly memberships and advertised the place as an excellent way for businessmen to lose weight or stay in shape. His initial plans included staging boxing matches twice monthly, amateur and pro, to a seating capacity of 1,600.[3] Taylor's fitness center arrived well ahead of its time—more than 50 years before the workout craze of the early 1980s ushered exercise into the retail market.[4]

The place opened Dec. 6, 1926, to an overflow crowd treated to seven boxing matches. Taylor's good friend Fred Bays, a Sullivan, Ind., attorney, served as master of ceremonies. The best of the Terre Haute boxers, among them "Farmer" Joe Cooper, Jackie Barnhart, Jimmy McDermott and Don "Kid" Porter, took part in exhibitions. When Bays turned the microphone over to Taylor, the champion thanked the crowd for attending.

"I think my hometown, Terre Haute, is the best town in the world and I think the best people are right here, so I have tried to give you a gym worthy of this city," he said. "... I want you to know that every time I fight, I think of you, and I feel like I am fighting for you and the honor of Terre Haute just the same as for myself ..."[5] Eddie Long also addressed the crowd, promising he would try to rematch Bud with Sangor to avenge the past month's loss.[6]

By early January 1927, Taylor's eye had healed well enough for him to resume training.[7] His training regimen at this time in his career consisted of three sessions daily. A typical day began at 7 a.m., with a five-mile run. He considered the run the most important part of a boxer's training, essential to strengthening legs and wind. Taylor had grown fond of running alongside "Pal," his Boston terrier, but the dog recently had been stolen, causing the jog to make him feel lonesome. When his run ended, he headed to the gym for a shower and a rubdown, and by 9:30, breakfast. A typical breakfast consisted of fruit, a soft-boiled egg, toast, tea and water. After a short break, he entered phase two of the routine, during which he employed full use of his specialty equipment. He hit the bags, jumped rope, worked with weight pulleys and caught an 18-pound medicine ball, the latter to harden the stomach and chest muscles so he could withstand body blows. A bath and rubdown followed. By 2 p.m., his sparring session began, usually four to six rounds with the best boxers available, preferably close to his weight. The evening meal followed. Taylor's last punch of the day went into the soft cushion of a pillow at 10 p.m., his bedtime.[8]

Chapter 30

Preparing for Tony

On Feb. 5, 1927, Charley Phil Rosenberg won a 15-round decision over Bushy Graham in a fight that had been billed as being for New York's version of the world bantamweight title. Rosenberg, however, weighed 4 1/2 pounds over the limit, so the New York boxing commission declared the title still vacant. NBA champ Bud Taylor thought the outcome strengthened his claim as the one and only world champion, an assertion he hoped to prove with a victory in his upcoming bout with Tony Canzoneri. "I guess Graham's defeat put [Graham] out of it and Rosenberg can't make the weight, so I think I have a right to the [New York] title," Taylor said. "I'll box anyone the New York commission wants me to in an effort to clear up the situation. If I beat Canzoneri at Chicago, I will be set as Tony already has a victory over [Graham]. Maybe right will crop out now."[1]

When the New York commission met on Feb. 8, 1927, both Eddie Long and Canzoneri's manager, Sammy Goldman, filed petitions seeking recognition as champion. New York's three-man commission granted neither request.[2] Four days later, the commission announced a suspension of Rosenberg and Graham for one year, alleging that their managers had secretly bet each other on the outcome of the fight.[3] As for the New York "world" title, the commission left it vacant.

A week later, Taylor returned to action after 2 1/2 months without a bout. Several hundred fans from Terre Haute drove to Indianapolis to watch him fight Midget Smith. By the newspapers' tally, Taylor won all 10 rounds.[4]

In the meantime, Canzoneri came down with an infected foot, forcing postponement of the bout with Taylor. In rescheduling the fight, promoter Jim Mullen in Chicago found he had competition from Rickard in New York, who wanted the marquee matchup for Madison Square Garden.5 Mullen's more pressing problem was finding a replacement for Canzoneri against Taylor on Feb. 24. The promoter signed Eddie Shea, a crowd-pleasing Italian-American from Chicago's west side.

With all the anticipation of Chicago's own, homegrown, 25-year-old Shea going against the city's adopted son, Taylor, 10,000 fans sold out the Chicago Coliseum. Gate security turned away an additional 5,000.6 Scalpers sold $3.30 tickets for $10. Mullen confronted a scalper outside the Coliseum and after an argument, whacked him over the head with a heavy cane, putting him in the hospital.7

Shea outweighed Taylor by 3 1/2 pounds, but the Chicago native left the ring that evening with one eye closed, the other half-closed, and lips cut and swollen. Taylor won the 10-round decision, a nontitle bout.8

Mullen won out over Rickard and secured the Taylor-Canzoneri fight for March 26 in the Chicago Coliseum—Taylor' first defense of his NBA world bantamweight title.

Long also signed Taylor for a tuneup March 15 against Sarmiento inside the Zorah Shrine Temple in Terre Haute. Taylor had won both their previous meetings, and this one would run as a nontitle bout at 121 pounds.

"I need one real battle before defending my title …," Taylor said. "Pete is a willing mixer and a stiff puncher, and I am sure to get what I need, a grueling, fast contest. The bout should make me fit for my championship match …"9

Sarmiento had proven himself a remarkably durable fighter over the years, engaging in 38 pro contests over 1925-26. The Filipino had fought nearly every ranking bantamweight and featherweight of lofty status on down to the mediocre ones as well, losing only about five bouts in those two years, including a 10-round decision to Taylor. He had beaten Shea, Rosenberg, Harold Smith and Pal Moore, and lost to Sangor and Chick Suggs.10

In 1927, however, he had lost his first four fights, and the signs pointed to flameout. The accumulation of punches to the head over a period of years inevitably slows a fighter's reaction time, with serious consequences. In boxing, the difference between getting hit and slipping a punch, and between firing a punch and waiting too long, hinges on decisions made in a fraction of a second.

During his training period for Sarmiento, Taylor traveled to St. Paul, Minnesota for the funeral for Jimmy Delaney, a light-heavyweight managed by Long who had died at age 24 from boxing-related blood poisoning. Taylor, along with Mike and Tommy Gibbons and other fighters, served as pallbearers.[11]

In Terre Haute, Taylor trained for the Sarmiento fight in his refurbished K of C gym, before crowds numbering in the hundreds.[12] The hometown fans also watched Taylor continue his mastery over Sarmiento, as Bud knocked him down in the first round on the way to winning the 10-round bout decisively.[13]

Bud departed for Chicago eight days before the Canzoneri bout, for final pre-fight training sessions under the supervision of Barney Furey.[14] Furey, 49, a short, balding ex-fighter, had boxing credentials similar to Jack Blackburn's: both had earned respect in the business from their own fight careers in boxing's difficult childhood a generation earlier, despite societal limitations of being black. After he discarded his gloves, Furey served as one of Jack Johnson's principal trainers while Johnson reigned as heavyweight champion.[15] Taylor had worked with Furey previously; Eddie Long had employed the trainer to work with Bud before the ill-fated Rosenberg match six months earlier and for the Sangor bout in November.[16]

Taylor needed a trainer with whom he felt comfortable, because the Canzoneri bout meant much more to him than just the first defense of his title. Canzoneri's defeat of Graham had thrust Tony to the forefront of bantamweight challengers, a young athlete on the verge of greatness at merely age 18. Moreover, Canzoneri lived in New York, the state whose three-man commission refused to recognize Taylor as champ despite Bud's NBA status. "[Bud] realizes he has the opportunity of his career to convince the pugilistic world he is the world's legitimate bantamweight champion, and he intends to take advantage of it," Ralph White wrote.[17]

Chapter 31

First Defense

Tony Canzoneri grew up in the New Orleans west-side burgh of Slidell, one of six children whose Sicilian father worked as a butcher. After learning how to fight on the city streets, he took up amateur boxing at 14. He already had dozens of fights by the time his family moved to Brooklyn in his early teens. He punched his way to a state amateur title in New York and turned pro at 16.1

Sports columnist Westbrook Pegler thought the prominent-cheeked Canzoneri resembled an Italian version of Babe Ruth.2 "Canzi," however, as he was called, was far more handsome with his swarthiness and his wide-set eyes set under arcing eyebrows. When he flashed his incredible smile, it reached across the entire width of his face. He stood 5 feet 4 inches tall and could expand his brawny chest to 34 1/2 inches—9 inches farther than Taylor.3 He was built like a caveman, but he could move like a cat.

Canzoneri had been an admirer of Pal Moore's dancing defense, and Tony crafted a style that used power and speed, either or both, depending on how he assessed his opponent.4 Canzoneri often fought in rushes, bouncing in and out, seldom staying within punching distance of his opponent unless himself throwing punches. He also liked to fight out of a half crouch and he could snap off punches powerfully off his solid frame. A single punch broke an opponent's collarbone in 1928.5

After his sterling career as an amateur, Tony began flattening professionals like a combine over stalks of corn. His mark had reached 19-1-3, with nine knockouts, and the victory over Bushy Graham verified he was of championship caliber.

Tony Canzoneri. *Winkler Collection, University of Notre Dame.*

Mullen decided to award the winner of the Taylor-Canzoneri fight a $4,000, diamond-studded championship belt. He displayed the prize in his gym, where both fellows trained before large crowds. Taylor was overheard commenting to Long that the belt would serve as a dandy item to take back to Terre Haute to show his friends.6

Hordes of reporters shadowed the boxers, trying to capture the title-bout atmosphere. The newsmen and their flashbulbs became a distraction for Taylor in his training, but did not affect him as much as what he heard had happened in Terre Haute.

He found out that Iris had been injured in a car accident. She had suffered bad cuts and bruises while riding in a car hit by a train.7 Initial reports called her condition "severe," and five days before the bout, Taylor considered breaking training and heading home.8

Taylor phoned home repeatedly over the next several days to ascertain her condition. He reached Iris on the line on March 24, two days before the contest. She reassured him that he need not return to Terre Haute. Her voice sounded weak and made Taylor cry, but she insisted he concentrate on his training.9 On March 21, her birthday, he had sent her a basket with roses, lilies and carnations, with the message "Birthday Greetings from Buddy." Iris Taylor showed the flowers to a reporter who visited her to check on her condition. Taylor's original idea for a gift had been much grander. He had called his sister, Edith, and asked her to send Iris an arrangement with "Happy Birthday to you, Dear Iris, from Buddy" *all spelled out in flowers.* "Edith would not do it and had quite an argument with him over it," Iris said. Edith was said to have told Bud, "It will look like a funeral and the piece would have to be large enough to cover a bed."

Bud, however, "... still insisted and said that would be OK; cover the bed with flowers, it would look pretty," Iris told the reporter. Edith eventually succeeded in persuading her brother to send the more modest gift.10

Interest in the Canzoneri bout prompted the *Terre Haute Tribune* to arrange to megaphone the results blow-by-blow out the front window of its downtown building. White, ringside in Chicago, would dictate the results to an operator by his side, who would telegraph a description of the action to the newsroom. As the results reached the newspaper's upstairs office, they would be relayed to folks waiting below on Wabash Avenue and within earshot beyond. The *Tribune* also would publish a special edition after the fight.11

As the fight neared, Taylor turned surly. "I was always irritable and said many things I did not mean before a fight, being on edge," he said in 1938. "Boxers differ, though. While Jack Dempsey was as nervous before a bout as a race horse at the post, I've seen some fighters sleep on a rub table in their dressing rooms—snooze right up until it came time to enter a ring."12

This time, when Taylor's pre-fight belligerence emerged, he snarled at friends and nitpicked over routine matters. His anxiety over his wife's condition along with the importance of the bout, his first title defense, did not help his mood. Three days before the bout, Taylor snapped at his handlers over minor dressing-room irregularities, then snubbed news photographers who wanted him to interrupt his training routine to pose. He pointedly refused to pose with Canzoneri, and seemed miffed at the mere suggestion.[13]

Taylor's sparring partners absorbed the worst of his ferocity on this day. As a general principle, boxers don't beat up their sparring partners too bad if they expect them to stay around—sparring partners seldom get paid enough to justify taking repeated bashings. Long had hired Chicago fighter Joey Medill and a flyweight named Brown to work with Taylor, temporary helpers who didn't know what they were in for. Bud flattened Medill with a left hook and later floored Brown with a right cross. Both rose only to take an additional pounding, and Brown would have fallen again if Taylor hadn't rushed in to hold him up.[14]

About 500 Taylor backers made the trip from Terre Haute for the fight. Among them was Mickey Meharry, who found himself in an argument in Mullen's gym over the predicted outcome of the fight. Meharry ended the verbal exchange by pulling out a $1,000 bill and offering to plunk it down on Taylor.[15] No one took the bet. Bettors elsewhere, however, laid enough down on both sides for the fight to go off at about even money.[16]

On fight night, the crowd primed itself for the title contest by watching Abe Goldstein win the semi-final over Pete Sarmiento. Among the throngs of spectators was Dr. William Fralick, who had performed Taylor's career-changing tendon operation.[17]

In the interval between the semi and main events, a band played "On the Banks of the Wabash," in honor of Taylor.[27] The tune, a huge national hit in its time, strokes a sentimental chord in the minds of people with ties to Terre Haute. Its native Paul Dresser wrote the song in 1897 based on his fond recollections of childhood times along the Wabash River.[19] The choice of songs demonstrates the partisanship of the band—there is no account of the musicians playing then-popular tunes "Way Down Yonder in New Orleans," or "Sidewalks of New York," for example, for Canzoneri.

In the introductions, the challenger's name triggered an eruption of cheering, much of it from a large bloc of Italian-Americans. Taylor responded to his own name with a bow and a smile, also met by a rousing ovation.[20]

At this moment in Taylor's home city, crowds of people jammed Wabash Avenue between Seventh and Eighth streets, in front of the Tribune Building. A thousand such souls had arrived even before the start of the semifinal, eager to follow their hero's progress via results announced through megaphone. When the masses of spectators grew so thick that they blocked passage of the street cars along the avenue, police arrived to clear the line.[21]

By all accounts, it was a thrilling fight. Neither Taylor nor Canzoneri scored a knockdown, but their blows landed with such authority that "their heads bobbed like punching bags" over the course of the fight. Taylor seemed bewildered at times by Canzoneri's here-then-gone style, by which Tony scored repeatedly with left jabs and hooks. Canzoneri alternatively used an erect stance and a crouch, and switched from a right-handed to a southpaw style at times. Taylor was at his best when leading, and connected on enough head-snappers to stay even on the scorecards. At ringside, raucous spectators crowded in against press row, pushing White against the ring, so crammed that he joked to his readers that he was forced to use his nose to strike the keys of his typewriter. Both fighters threw punches frantically in the 10th as if the decision hinged on that one round—and it could have if one had gained an edge then—but neither did.[22]

The crowd reacted to the official decision, a draw, with approval, or a chorus of boos, according to differing accounts. Most of the sportswriters viewed the decision as justified; among those who didn't agree with it, most believed Canzoneri had won. It was not revealed how the judges and referee scored the fight. The *Chicago Daily Tribune* scored it 3-2 Canzoneri, with five rounds debatable, but conceded, "Taylor's punches were more effective and he was more the aggressor than Canzoneri."[24] *The Milwaukee Journal's* Sam Levy gave the challenger the edge, 5-3-4: "The two judges and referee were mighty kind to the Terre Haute lad, an adopted son of Chicago."[25]

Taylor regretted not being more aggressive in the middle rounds, especially his weak fifth and sixth. "I was laying back, prepared to nail Canzoneri in these rounds, and he didn't do the things that I had figured he would," he said.[26]

Tony Canzoneri vs. Bud Taylor, March 26, 1927. *International Newsreel.*

The draw verdict meant Taylor retained his NBA world title. He earned his biggest payday yet: $13,500, while Canzoneri took in $10,000.[27] Canzoneri used the money to buy his parents a $25,000 farm in New York.[28] Promoter Mullen lost money on the card since the 7,000 attendance fell 3,000 short of expectations. Fans may have stayed away because of the pricey tickets—$16.50 ringside, $11, $7.50 and $3.30.[29]

Mullen immediately went to work on signing the pair for a rematch, this time outdoors and with a bigger seating capacity, and at lower ticket prices. Rickard wanted the bout, too, and instructed an associate to begin negotiations to bring the bout to Madison Square Garden.[30] On March 31, Mullen announced he had signed the pair for the rematch June 23, 1927, in the Chicago Cubs' baseball park.[31]

On that last day of March, Mullen traveled to Terre Haute from Chicago to present Taylor with the $4,000 diamond belt—the prize Mullen had held onto because of the draw outcome. The promoter had changed his mind and decided the belt belonged to the sitting NBA champion. Taylor's friend Fred Bays of Sullivan, Indiana, arranged to have Mullen present the belt to Bud at an annual Elks lodge party and boxing card in that town, at which Taylor served as honored guest. More than a thousand people enjoyed the buffet lunch, music and boxing. In the presentation, Taylor and Long were choreographed to walk under an arch of flowers along a path to the belt. The Elks group even managed to squeeze a few words of a speech out of timid-speaker Taylor, who said he felt honored.[32]

The next evening, Taylor helped stage a fundraiser in his gym for money to build a new gym for the Terre Haute Boys Club. The Lions Club sponsored the affair, selling $1 tickets weeks in advance and promising a four-round boxing exhibition by the world champion.[33] A series of preliminary bouts, a performance by the vocal group Harmony Four and Taylor's four-round exhibition bout with Jackie Barnhart helped raise $1,050. The larger fundraising drive for the new gym ultimately raised $11,000, which covered nearly the entire cost of the gym.[34] By the summer of 1927, workers began erecting the facility, and within months, the gym's fresh hardwood surface thudded and squeaked to the sneakers of youth.[35] Eighty-one years later, great-grandchildren of those youth are swishing jumpers in the same gym on North Third Street.

Long, in setting up Taylor's fight itinerary for the two months leading up to the Canzoneri rematch, did not skimp on the quality of the opposition, although all were nontitle bouts. First, Taylor TKO'd Young Nationalista in the sixth round in Chicago, thanks largely to Bud's combination of a left to the body instantly followed by a left to the head.[36] With this "double hook," the first left causes an opponent to drop his arm instinctively, leaving his jaw as exposed as a billboard.

Key to the effectiveness of the double hook is arm speed. "Taylor keeps his lightning-like left working like a machine gun. It is the fastest in the world," the *Los Angeles Times* reported.37

In May, Abe Goldstein came to Chicago for a rematch with Taylor. Sources differ on the reason the pair did not fight this bout with the title at stake. One newspaper reported that Taylor had been willing to risk the title in this bout, but Abe's weight was too high and Goldstein said he was not ready for a championship fight.38 Since the weight limit was set at 120, just two pounds above the limit, a second reason seems more plausible: that Canzoneri had first been promised a second bout with Taylor. Sammy Goldman, Canzoneri's manager, feared that if Goldstein won the title, than Goldstein and his manager Charley Cook would pass up Tony for a title fight.39

In the Taylor-Goldstein rematch, Abe boxed masterfully. Taylor fought hard and won the decision, but Goldstein controlled the fight from long range and many thought he deserved the nod. The crowd of 8,000 booed when announcer Al Smith raised Bud's hand in victory, although the decision favored their darling Midwesterner over the invading New Yorker.40 The reaction of the crowd in the Chicago Coliseum underscored a rule of principle among fight fans to desert fighters who don't produce, no matter how strong the bond.

On the same card, Canzoneri won by TKO over Ray Rychell. Canzoneri battered his bleeding victim all the way from the first round to the bout's merciful end in the seventh, when Tony finally turned to the referee and appealed to him to stop it, and the ref complied.41

Based on their respective showings on that May 3rd card, Taylor's June date with Canzoneri looked troublesome.

Chapter 32

A Taylor Toboggan?

Six days after his unimpressive performance against Abe Goldstein, Bud Taylor fought Pal Moore in the latter's home city of Memphis. The bout, for whatever reason, does not appear on most contemporary listings of either Taylor's or Moore's pro records. The choice of opponent suggests that Long believed that fighting Moore would help Taylor prepare for Canzoneri's in-and-out boxing style. Taylor is reported to have won the eight-rounder over Moore narrowly, with no official decision rendered.[1]

Chicago sportswriters, in their advance stories for the Taylor-Canzoneri rematch, declared that Taylor's consecutive lackluster showings pointed to a decline in his game. They wrote articles headlined "... Hoosier Hellcat on the Toboggan," and "Many fans say Bud has slipped."[2]

Taylor scoffed at the suggestion. "Here I've gone ahead for eight years winning and just because I make a poor bout and slip down against Goldstein and Moore they say I am going down the toboggan. I'll show 'em," he told a reporter.[3]

On May 20, 1927, while Charles Lindbergh took off from New York in the first, solo nonstop flight across the Atlantic Ocean, Taylor traveled in the opposite direction, aboard a train to the West Coast to fight Chick Suggs.[4]

Suggs owned victories over Sangor and Goldstein and had stayed among the top bantamweight talents for years before weight gain moved him into the featherweights. Suggs carried the informal title of "colored featherweight champion," a nice compliment to his talents but also indicative of the enduring difficulty of blacks in landing bouts with whites for sanctioned title fights. Before 7,500 fans in Los Angeles' Olympic Auditorium, Taylor dispelled notions of a decline in his own skills. He dropped Suggs three times in the second round and twice in the fourth. In the fifth, one punch severed an artery inside Suggs' mouth. By the end of the fifth, the referee waved off the fight after seeing blood spurting from the wound.5

Taylor returned to the Midwest just in time to box in a benefit to raise money for the widow of Jimmy Delaney, a fighter under Eddie Long's management who had died in March of blood poisoning.6 In Minnesota for the benefit, Bud boxed his final preparatory bout for Canzoneri—a second-round KO over Johnny Hughes in St. Paul.

To prepare Taylor for the most important fight of his career, Eddie Long sought sparring partners who could simulate the feel of boxing against Canzoneri. He hired Pal Moore to come up from Memphis to get Taylor used to hitting a moving target. Sammy Mandell joined the camp, and helped by throwing left hands at Taylor to prepare him for Canzoneri's jabs and hooks.7 The addition of two crack sparring partners boosted Taylor's confidence, and the *Chicago Herald-Examiner* found him uncharacteristically boastful.

"A lot of folks seem to think that Bud Taylor is all through ...," Taylor said. "Canzoneri's style puzzled me in our first bout, but I know his style now and if I don't stop him within five rounds I will be the most surprised fellow at Wrigley Field next Thursday night."

The newspaper stretched that comment into the headline "I'll Knock Out Canzoneri in Five Rounds, Taylor's Forecast." The provocative headline along with a comment by Taylor that Mandell's left-hand punch made Canzoneri's left look like "slow motion" triggered an exchange of trash talk between the two camps.8

Canzoneri countered by saying Taylor's enlistment of Moore and Mandell as sparring partners showed that Bud was worried about the fight. As for his "slow" left, Canzoneri said, "I intend to start jabbing him with my left in the first round and I'll keep it up until he is dizzy. Before the bout is over, he will think everybody at the ringside is jabbing him with a left."9

Canzoneri seemed to have more reasons than Taylor to feel confident about the fight. His boxing style had confounded Taylor in the first fight and some reporters thought the judges' decision should have gone to him. His results since then had been far more impressive than Taylor's. Canzoneri had knocked out Harold Smith and sailed through Ray Rychell, while Taylor hiccupped against Goldstein and Moore before rebounding against Suggs and Hughes. The betting odds on June 22 showed Canzoneri a 7-5 or 6-5 favorite.10 The odds presented the unusual situation in which a sitting champion rated as the underdog.

Jim Mullen charged $11 for a ringside seat—$5 less than the March bout—and sold some distant seats for the rematch as low as $2.20. The more affordable ticket prices coupled with the considerable publicity surrounding the fight accelerated ticket sales.11 Sportswriters looking for a story latched on to whatever angle they could exploit during the pre-fight hype: Canzoneri is struggling to make weight; Taylor is stale and past his prime; and so forth. Abe Goldstein, in Chicago to fight in the card's semifinal, contributed to the publicity with a quote reminiscent of John L. Sullivan: "I can lick both those boys in the same ring the same night …," Goldstein boasted to reporters about Canzoneri and Taylor.12

The popularity of the contest undoubtedly pleased organized crime. Gambling flourished in the city and suburbs of Chicago in the summer of 1927. Two factions of gangsters controlled the lucrative, illegal business. Money bet on the fight ended up in the pockets of either south-end crime czar Al Capone and his associates or rival gangsters on the metro north side.13

Taylor told the press about how he felt when Chicago fans booed the decision awarded him over Goldstein. "Sure it hurts me," Taylor said. "I don't want to be handed anything. That's why I've never called myself 'champion.' I want to win it in the ring …"14 To Taylor, "world champion" was a meaningless title if Joe Boxing Fan wasn't convinced.

Over the past months, Taylor had begun to realize how much of a struggle it had become to scale under 118 pounds for a bout. He had fought Suggs at 123, his heaviest weight ever. At one month shy of age 24, the weight didn't peel away as easily as at 18. His ring performance at 123 had assured him he could hurt the bigger men, and he told a reporter that the upcoming bout with Canzoneri signaled the end of his bantamweight days.[15]

For the task at hand, however, he plodded the necessary miles of roadwork in Chicago's Lincoln Park and felt reassured when the scales read at below 117, with days to spare.[16]

Chapter 33

The Big One

About noon on June 23, heavy rain and chilly air blew into Chicago. Promoter Jim Mullen, who had sold $50,000 worth of advance tickets, knew he risked losing an additional bundle on walk-up business if the bad weather persisted until the 8:30 p.m. start of the preliminaries. He called the fight off and rescheduled it for the next evening.[1] By midafternoon June 23, the clouds rolled out and the freakishly low summer temperatures rose in an extraordinary reversal to normal weather, but too late for Mullen to reinstate the bouts.[2] It was as if the gods of boxing could not decide the winner, and fouled the weather just long enough to ensure an extra day to deliberate the outcome. Mullen decided to proceed with the 3 p.m. weigh-in, and both fighters weighed 117 1/2. They would not have to weigh in again the next day, so they were free to eat whatever they wanted in the 28-hour interim to the fight.[3]

Sportswriters in Chicago, grasping for angles during the one-day delay, filed stories speculating who gained an advantage by the postponement. One wrote that Canzoneri, because he gains weight easier than Taylor, would benefit from the one or two extra pounds. The same writer countered that premise with a comment by Barney Furey that he believed Bud was in better physical condition than in the first Canzoneri fight.[4]

Normal weather greeted June 24, and by the bell for the first of five preliminaries, about 17,500 witnesses had gathered in the ball-park.[5] Hundreds from Terre Haute attended, including many who had been Taylor followers since The Terror was merely a scrawny teenager throwing roundhouses for five bucks a bout. They were the ones who were worried that Taylor had been thrown to a wolf when Tex Johnson matched him against Frankie Mason. They shifted in their chairs at the Mason fight, swigged from their flasks and proudly watched Bud outfight the veteran. They had followed their boy Taylor's progress loyally as he slashed his way up boxing's hamburger hill on his way to becoming the nation's best-known living person from their city.

Among those in Chicago for the fight were Taylor's friends Fred and Lee Bays, and Terre Haute supporters such as undertaker Arthur Gillis, musician Billy Joyce and clothing-store owner Phil Silver. Sam and Tillie Taylor had arrived, too, hoping to see the crowning achievement of their son's career.[6] Taylor could have scanned the ballpark and seen all the important people of his life, there in one place for him, just as they would gather for a man's wedding—or execution. In Terre Haute, his fans repeated their vigil of three months earlier, waiting outside the newspaper building for the megaphoned results.[7]

Taylor, introduced as "bantamweight champion of the world," stepped forward dressed in black tights to rousing cheers, but also boos, some of which could be attributed to those still offended by the decision in the Goldstein bout. Canzoneri, clad in purple trunks, heard a thunderous ovation follow his name.[8]

In Round One, both connected with stinging punches. Canzoneri's left jabs bloodied Taylor's nose and Bud landed a right that opened a flow from Tony's lips.[9] Taylor maneuvered close enough to Tony in the second round to score repeatedly, and landed a right that had Canzoneri spitting blood.[10]

Canzoneri's punches began to find their mark in the third.[11] He began to move his feet and use his left more in the fourth and fifth. He outboxed Taylor with the punch-and-move game.[12] One of Canzoneri's favorite ploys was to rush an opponent with a jab or combination, then backpedal before the other guy could counter. In Rounds Three through Five, Taylor could not position himself close enough to Canzoneri to outscore him.[13]

By the midpoint of the bout, Taylor had fallen behind on points, teetering on losing what he'd fought his entire life for.[14] He could no longer afford to wait for Canzoneri to lead before he looked for an opening—not even part of the time. He had to step up the pace, throw gloves over gloves. He wanted this bout more than any other and he would have to take it by force, just like when as a little boy he slugged his way onto the best-selling newspaper corners.

Pal Moore, serving as a second for Taylor, recognized Bud's emergency and exhorted him appropriately. "Take the lead away from him, Bud," Moore told Taylor in his corner between the fifth and sixth rounds. "Do all the leading. Be on top of him all the time—you'll win."[15]

In the sixth, Taylor took the offensive and pursued Canzoneri around the ring relentlessly. In the final 10 seconds of the round, they slugged it out at ring center to a roaring crowd, with Taylor landing the better shots. Taylor put a left-right to Canzoneri's face at the bell, then jogged to his corner.[16] The sixth was Taylor's round, and ultimately figured hugely in the outcome.

The breakneck pace of the round apparently sapped Canzoneri's strength.[17] He began to lead less, and the power in his punches seemed gone while Taylor quickened the pace and tore after him.[18] In the seventh, eighth and ninth, Taylor charged and Canzoneri fled, and Bud won the latter two rounds by wide margins.[19]

Canzoneri opened the 10th round with punches that closed Taylor's already swollen left eye.[20] Taylor fired lefts into Canzoneri's face, and brought more blood from Tony's busted lip.[21] The final minute of the bout found them popping each other in an all-out exchange at midring.[22]

Judges William Fetze and Earl L. Cook voted Taylor the winner, while Referee Joe Choynsky scored the fight a draw. The sportswriters agreed with the verdict; a sample of 10 accounts shows they all had Taylor winning: by as decisively as 6-1-3 by rounds to as close as 3-2-5.[23] Taylor had stolen the victory from Canzoneri with the sizzling pace of his performance in the final five rounds. For most of his career, the press had exalted Taylor for his punching prowess, but The Terror of Terre Haute owed his greatest triumph at least as much to physical fitness.

When the ring announcer announced the decision, wildly enthusiastic fans rushed toward Taylor while police struggled to keep them away.[24] As the fighters managed to snake their way through the mob to shake hands, one of Taylor's handlers celebrated by hoisting Bud high into the air. Taylor seemed to have regained the respect of his deserters, because the crowd erupted with cheers.[25]

Both fighters exited the ropes with blood-smeared faces, swollen almost beyond recognition.[26] To Taylor, who had become famous for taking a beating to give a worse one, the blood must have tasted like victory.

Chapter 34

Honored at Home

Bud Taylor arrived back in Terre Haute in the heart of the summer of 1927 with plans for a vacation. He had bought a new speed boat and intended to run it up and down the Wabash River and to camp, fish and swim.1

A *Terre Haute Tribune* newspaper editorial called him the city's "best press agent," and praised his work ethic and sportsmanship.2 The citizens of the community showed their affection, but not lavishly as they had two years earlier when he returned from California and they hoisted him onto an elephant in a parade. This time, their welcome of handshakes and smiles of acknowledgment befit the style of a man more comfortable with simpler courtesies than grand demonstrations. When Taylor refereed at the amateur bouts in his club on June 27, the crowd gave him a huge ovation, but he declined to give a speech.3

The Elks Lodge in Sullivan invited Taylor to attend a lodge meeting in Cincinnati on July 11-15. On their invitation, the lodge members wrote that they appreciated Taylor's charitable work for the miners, soldiers and other citizens, and they sought to entertain him as guest of honor.4 Fred Bays joined Taylor at the function and afterward the pair continued east to New York to attend the heavyweight championship fight between Jack Dempsey and Jack Sharkey on July 21, 1927.5

Before he left, though, Taylor took care of his face. A chipped frontal bone over his left eye had bothered him for months, and he drove to Chicago to have it removed by a surgeon.6

On Aug. 2, Taylor offered the newspaper boys of Terre Haute a free pass to his Tuesday amateur boxing show. Two hundred young sellers took in the show. Remembering his own childhood days hawking the *Terre Haute Post-Telegram*, Bud treated youth with these freebies several times through the years.[7]

Taylor served as an inspiration to boys of the Wabash Valley, typified in adulation shown by such youngsters as Tom Jennings.

Jennings grew up about 20 miles south of Terre Haute on a 300-acre farm. With its bins and fields and animals, the spread looked like thousands of other Midwest farms except for the oddity positioned in the middle of its apple orchard. Jennings and his brother had erected a makeshift boxing ring of 4-by-4 foot posts with rope stretched between, and a floor of sand. The brothers and their neighborhood friends battled there weekly, using a gourd-sized dinner bell for a gong. Bud Taylor's success fueled their own dreams of sports stardom, Jennings said in 2005, at age 90. "I wanted to be like Bud Taylor because he was champion, and he was from Terre Haute," he said.

Eventually, Jennings' passion for the sport drew him right into the ring in Taylor's gym. In his only professional fight, Tom wound up staring at ceiling lights from a punch he never saw coming, from an opponent long ago lost to obscurity. After the bout, Jennings ditched his plans for boxing and went off to embalming school. His brief ring career gave him an appreciation for the difficulty of the sport, and a great respect for Taylor's perseverance and commitment. Jennings became the best at his own chosen profession—embalming. Ultimately, he drew more blood over the course of his career than Taylor, Jack Dempsey and John Dillinger combined. Jennings embalmed, by his estimate, 60,000 people, four dogs and one goldfish.[8]

Careerwise, Taylor had reached the top, but matters at home had hit bottom. On Aug. 13, he filed to divorce Iris after four years of marriage. Public interest in the divorce illustrated the breadth of a champion boxer's celebrity: the Associated Press picked up the story of the filing and it made the papers in such places as Chicago and Washington, D.C.[9] The end of the marriage did not affect Bud Taylor's devotion to Barbara Jean, and he continued to see her on visits and to provide for her well-being.

Chapter 35

Sangor Gains Edge

Taylor resumed his fight career Sept. 1 in Culver City, California with a first-round TKO over Don Smith of Salt Lake City. The main reason for Taylor's trip west, however, was a lucrative bout with Joey Sangor on Sept. 20, 1927, in the Olympic Auditorium. Sangor preferred fighting at heavier weights than 118, so the bout would not be for the title. Eddie Long told a reporter he would work Taylor in the heavier, (featherweight) bouts until some promoter made it "worth his while" to drill Bud down to 118 to defend his title.[1] The bantamweight class lacked its quality fighters of two, three years earlier.[2] The better money lay with the feathers—Sangor, McLarnin, and a host of others including Canzoneri, who would never again try to trim to 118.[3]

Taylor's manager did have an intriguing offer from overseas: $30,000 to fight in London against Englishman Teddy Baldock. England was not affiliated with the NBA, and the English press considered Baldock the bantamweight champion of the world. Thirty grand sounded sweet, but figuring in the travel plans and the block of time necessary for travel, the take did not amount to much more than Taylor could make stateside now that his stock had increased with the victory over Canzoneri. Baldock showed a better won-loss record than Johnny Brown, the British champ that Taylor had annihilated 18 months earlier, but the quality of Baldock's opponents rated nowhere near that of Taylor's. "Bud Taylor has more of a legitimate claim to bantamweight champion of the world than Baldock, despite what the English press says," Nat Fleischer wrote in *Ring* magazine.[4]

The press hyped the Sangor-Taylor fight to the hilt, and in this case the combatants and their show-stopping reputations justified the exposure. Sangor had been a huge draw in Los Angeles, with all five of his fights there going off as sellouts, and Taylor himself had been a party to three sellouts there.[5] The two had split their two previous decisions. Since his win over Taylor on Nov. 29, 1926, Sangor had gone 3-2-0 against quality opposition, and he had not lost since a Jimmy McLarnin right hand KO'd him, 13 fights earlier. Likewise, Taylor had won 13 straight in California.

A mild controversy brewed between the two camps when a member of the Sangor entourage was spotted watching Taylor work out in Los Angeles' Manhattan gymnasium. Taylor gave the spy two choices: leave the building or enter the ring and become his sparring partner. Sangor's associate chose the door. Taylor also is reported to have been miffed about a publicity poster the Sangor people had published after their last fight, showing Bud on the canvas after the seventh-round knockdown.[6]

The sportswriters also ventured into story lines of a more personal nature. Sangor revealed to a reporter that he never fails to call his mother in Milwaukee after every fight. The woman did not exactly relish the thought of her Joey entering the ring against an opponent whose blows had killed two men. "My mother would rather I would fight anybody else than Taylor," Sangor said. "She has heard so much about him that she knows it is a hard fight. But all fights are hard. I'll be the happiest boy on earth if I can tell her that I beat Taylor."[7]

Rare for a boxer, Sangor knew the line of work he would enter after he retired from the ring: the drug business. He and his brother Lou were registered pharmacists and owned a chain of drug stores in Milwaukee.[8]

Taylor, meanwhile, spoke about possibly relocating to Los Angeles. He had developed an interest in investing in real estate there. "It will take Terre Haute a long, long time to grow," he said. "But Los Angeles will have two million people inside five years and property here will go out of sight."[9] History would prove him correct on both counts.

Taylor weighed in at 124 pounds on the afternoon of the fight, his heaviest ever for a bout.[10] Trying to return to the hotel, he found himself swallowed up in a tremendous mob of pedestrians. Sixty thousand people were on their way to swarm the Los Angeles Coliseum to see Charles Lindbergh, who had performed the miraculous feat of flying an airplane all the way from America across the ocean to France. Taylor, himself caught up in the spirit of the moment, strained for a glimpse of the Neil Armstrong of the times. By the time Taylor returned to the lobby, all disheveled and mussed from the jostling crowd, his mood had soured into its customary pre-fight state. An admirer made the mistake of asking him if he planned to nap before the fight.

"... If anybody can go through what I did just now, greeting Lindy, and all the rest of it, and then lie down and have a snooze, I'd like to meet the chap," Taylor roared. "That mob pretty near tore me to pieces and now you should ask me if I'm going to sleep. You're crazy."[11]

So, Taylor didn't sleep and he lost the fight, albeit by the slightest of margins. Slowed by the extra poundage, he played the target to Sangor's left hand all evening.

At least two Los Angeles newspapers scored the fight even going into the 10th. Taylor, trying to breathe through a broken nose, chased Sangor all around the ring, but couldn't catch him. Sangor fired enough left jabs into Taylor's mug in the final round to win the round and the decision.[12] The loss to his rival undoubtedly discomforted Taylor worse than the smashed nose.

Three days later, 100,000 fans went to Chicago's Soldier Field to witness the rematch between Gene Tunney and Jack Dempsey, a defining moment for the sport. Tens of thousands more across the nation tuned in by radio. In a train station in Los Angeles, Taylor and Long and pals lounged aboard their railroad coach in a farewell party before their return to the Midwest. Former heavyweight champion Jack Johnson was one of their guests.[13]

Chapter 36

Changing Times

On Oct. 14, 1927, the marriage between Bud and Iris Taylor officially ended in divorce. The next day, Taylor boarded a train to return to California to fight Johnny Farr on Nov. 8 in the Olympic. Farr was a bulky 22-year-old Clevelander with the same hit-or-be-hit style as Taylor's, and a deformed right ear that whispered of too many left hooks. His won-loss record failed to impress, but his ledger showed wins over Sangor, Suggs and Sarmiento, which commanded serious attention from any opponent.[1]

The weight limit was set at 125. Taylor, in an effort to regain the quickness he had lost fighting Sangor at 124 pounds, trained with a target weight of 120.[2]

Taylor rallied in the late rounds to win a close fight, criticized in the press as a "hugfest," for all its clinches.[3] He walked into his dressing room feeling upbeat about the victory until Long pulled him aside, draped a brotherly arm around his shoulder and slipped him a telegram from Terre Haute. The message read that Iris had undergone surgery for appendicitis, and peritonitis had followed, and that she is gravely ill.[4] Peritonitis, in which infection causes membranes in the abdomen to inflame, had a high mortality rate in the 1920s. Taylor made immediate plans to return to Terre Haute, and secured a Western Air Express flight for 7:35 a.m. the next day.[5]

Taylor's first ride in an airplane proved short-lived when he ran out of courage. Air turbulence over the mountains bucked the craft, and by Salt Lake City, the shaken passenger told pilot Jimmy Jones to return them to the ground. Taylor stayed within the familiar confines of a train car for the rest of the journey.6 To his relief, Iris' condition improved along the way.

While Iris recovered in St. Anthony's Hospital in Terre Haute, friends of the couple expressed hope for a reconciliation.7 Taylor visited her bedside while he resumed training.8

Taylor found that most of his onetime sparring partners, mainstays on the pro cards in Terre Haute four or five years earlier, were unavailable. Eddie Dyer had relocated to Toledo, Ohio; Jackie Barnhart was boxing sporadically, if at all; and Bud Perrill had quit the game and joined the Terre Haute Fire Department. "Tex" Johnson, Taylor's first manager and promoter, had moved to Detroit.9 The more successful of the local fighters, such as "Farmer" Joe Cooper, Jimmy McDermott and Ward "Kid" Sparks, had taken their gloves on the road seeking bigger purses. Sparks was fighting out of Detroit, while Cooper and McDermott still called the Wabash Valley their home.10

In Terre Haute, professional boxing had declined from its high point in the early 1920s, and Taylor's weekly amateur shows in the K of C gym furnished most of the action. When Taylor was out of the city, his helper Lee Sullivan ran the cards, assembling eight to 10 fights weekly from among the locals who fought merely for a few bucks and bragging rights around town.11

On Nov. 6, 1927, Taylor's amateur show featured a bout advertised as between "small but mighty" Robert Miller and Robert McFarlin, both age 4.12 Bouts featuring pre-schoolers were gimmicks thrown in for the fans' amusement and not part of the regular shows. These peewee boxing matches nonetheless existed on a semi-regular basis in a kind of informal boxing league, with shows inside Terre Haute's Labor Temple or the Moose Hall. Dick Brokaw (then known as "Ritchie") started his boxing career in these three-rounders—at age 7—when his older brother pushed him into the ring for the brother's amusement.13

Brokaw grew up even poorer than Taylor, crowded into a shanty with his parents and seven siblings on Terre Haute's south side, with no hot water, no flush toilet. The family scraped by on his father's earnings as a bartender. Brokaw spent his late-1920s childhood fighting kids on the street or joining with pals to jump onto passing freight trains to steal coal. One of his older brothers, Howard, was one of Taylor's best friends, and it was not uncommon for Bud to sleep over on a couch in the Brokaw house. Not surprisingly, Dick Brokaw grew up idolizing Taylor. Brokaw himself returned to the boxing ring to help support his family after he quit school as a young teen.

"Bud taught me how to box, the basics, things like 'hands up', 'punch straight', 'move to your right', or left," Brokaw said in 2005. "Bud would say, 'Rich, the closest thing to your opponent is your left hand. Use it. Use it to feel your way in, to jab and score points ...'"

In his eighties, Brokaw loved to reminisce about boxing, and had stored seemingly every bout of his career in his memory, available for instant recall. Though craggy-faced from scars and wrinkles and half-blind, he still flexed the steely biceps of his boxing years. Lost in the moment, he would spring to his feet in his Terre Haute apartment to hurl punches at imaginary targets, or to illustrate a maneuver he used 70 years ago.

Brokaw credits boxing for helping him grow into a responsible adult. In his teens, the sport provided him with much-needed discipline and direction, and kept him off the streets. As an adult, he fought several dozen pro fights, then refereed thousands of amateur bouts over a 46-year boxing career. As for Taylor, Brokaw admired him most for his compassion, shown in such acts as when Bud donated all the money from a K of C amateur show in 1924 so unemployed miners could enjoy a better Christmas.[14]

With so much time on the road fighting, Taylor may not have noticed the changing face of his home city in the fall of 1927. Big buildings were sprouting up with the prosperous times, concrete giants that nudged the sky. Most prominent of them was the frame of the downtown Terre Haute House hotel, reconstructed to 10 stories, awaiting interior work before its bellhops, clerks and cooks could return to serve its overnight guests.[15] Moreover, technological advancements were changing the daily routines of Americans. After Nov. 26, when Taylor picked up a telephone receiver to make a call in Terre Haute, he no longer heard the anonymous female operator utter the familiar "number please" and wait for an answer so she could connect him to the party he sought. Instead, the newer phones were equipped so that callers dialed the number *themselves*.16 Airplanes occasionally buzzed overhead, their passengers in the primitive vessels perhaps as terrified as Taylor on his first flight. There was talk about even using airplanes to carry college and pro athletes from one point of the nation to another for games.17 Electronic traffic signals, or "Stop Thru Street" signs, regulated street traffic in U.S. cities. It had been a quirk of history—with devastating results—that mixed autos, street cars, freight trains, horses-drawn buggies and pedestrians, with their variances in speed and mobility, all together in the urban traffic of America. The staggering consequences included 36 traffic deaths in Terre Haute in the first eight months of 1923. Four years later, the wonderful invention of the traffic light helped reduce the carnage.18 Radios were found in nearly every home. Taylor's fans who wanted a blow-by-blow account of his bouts no longer had to gather downtown to hear it by megaphone—they could find a boxing match broadcast into their homes if the signal was clear enough.19 In New York, inventors had demonstrated they could show moving pictures out of a portable console in a device called a "television," although more than a decade would pass before the device started appearing in homes.20

One element of Taylor's life had not changed—his hand problems. Sparring in Chicago for a Nov. 30 bout with Canzoneri planned for Madison Square Garden, Taylor caught Pal Moore squarely on the side of the head and felt the pain. Taylor feared a fracture, but X-rays showed only ligament damage. The fight was delayed a month.21

Taylor went home from Chicago lugging a big load of Christmas gifts, with one particular beneficiary in mind. Barbara Jean, age 2 years and 8 months, greeted dad with a hug, squeeze and a kiss. "When will Santa come, daddy?" the curly-haired one asked.22

About 2:30 p.m. Christmas day, 1927, Santa left the holiday cheer behind and headed to his Terre Haute gym for a workout. His right hand still felt gimpy and he favored it during the session, but he told the press he intended to use it Dec. 30 against Canzoneri.23

Jess McMahan, Tex Rickard's matchmaker, had anticipated a sellout, and guaranteed Taylor's side $25,000 for the third Canzoneri fight, the most money Taylor's camp would ever earn for one bout.24 The winner had been guaranteed a title shot with NBA world featherweight champ Benny Bass.

Taylor's main concern in going against Canzoneri was the 126-pound limit—heavy for Bud, suitable for Tony. Results at the weigh-in did nothing to ease that apprehension, when Taylor scaled 121 to Canzoneri's 125. With both at 117 in Chicago in June, Taylor had only eked out a victory, now he would have to give away four pounds to the Italian grizzly.25 Oddsmakers gave Canzoneri a 7-5 edge.26

Twelve thousand fans in the Garden saw a melee from the opening bell to the final one. Canzoneri fought in vintage form, with bursts of furious punching mixed with evasive footwork. The judges gave Canzoneri the decision, which most of the sportswriters supported; The *New York Times* scored it 4-3-3, *Chicago Daily Tribune* 3-2-5. Six weeks later, Canzoneri outpointed Bass to become featherweight champion of the world.

Taylor had fought gamely, but his punches did not seem to pack with their usual force. Columnist Westbrook Pegler also noticed a tendency by Taylor to smile when hit by a punch, and smile wider when punched harder.27

Chapter 37

A Straight-Punching Nemesis

A left hook put Phil Zwick on the canvas, but it was bad luck that counted him out on Jan. 24, 1928.

Taylor landed the hook in the second round in Milwaukee, then watched as the Clevelander capsized. Zwick maintained his senses, however, and kneeled as if ready to rise. While waiting, Zwick glanced over to his corner, and lost track of the referee's count. When the ref swung his arms to count him out, Zwick leapt to his feet, but it was too late. The bout was scored as a knockout. A heavy underdog, Zwick had come out swinging and battled Taylor on fairly even terms until the odd ending, which left the embittered loser and his fans forever to speculate, "What if?"[1]

The Zwick anomaly was one of two nontitle Taylor outings in January 1928, the other being a decision over Roy "Babe" Ruth in Chicago. Taylor fought both fights around 121-122 pounds, light for a featherweight. Fighting at this weight meant that if his featherweight opponents scaled at the limit, Taylor had to give up four to five pounds. But if Bud took on extra weight to even the poundage out, he sacrificed quickness, and the tradeoff wasn't worth it.

Taylor continued to fight the more numerous featherweights, while Long worked out a deal to defend Bud's bantamweight title. Two of those potential bantamweight title fights made it onto Taylor's schedule: Jan. 20 against Willie Smith, who had displaced Teddy Baldock as British "world" banty champ; and in mid-February against Kid Francis, French champion of the division. Those bouts fell through for reasons not apparent; neither gained further mention in the press as their dates neared.[2]

Instead, Taylor's attention shifted to his nemesis, Joey Sangor, for a meeting in the Chicago Coliseum on Feb. 9 with a 126-pound limit.

The Chicago sportswriters, well aware of the bad blood between the two fighters, exploited the rift to juice up their stories. They induced Sangor to talk at length about how he beat Taylor in their previous encounters. Taylor relies on his hook too much, Sangor said.

"You know that I punch straight with both hands," Sangor said. "By doing this, I beat Taylor to the punch consistently. I'll show you why. Put an object on a table in front of you. If you want to pick up the object, your natural impulse is to reach straight out for it. That is the way I punch … Now if you were to make a hook motion … I would be able to pick it up a second quicker than you would. That is how I beat Taylor. I punch straight. He hooks. Simple, isn't it?"[3]

Sangor's comments appeared in the next day's papers, and of course, the reporters beat a path to Taylor's feet for his retort. "Where does he get that stuff?" Taylor said. "I'll show him what a straight punch looks like Thursday night and when I connect, he'll think the building has fallen in on him."[4]

Taylor needed a victory over Sangor to mount any serious campaign for the featherweight title. His record against Sangor stood at 1-2, and to lose a third straight time to him would mean any legitimate route for Taylor to the title first would have to go through a fighter who obviously had his number.

Ten thousand customers filled the Chicago Coliseum, with the ringsiders paying $7 a ticket.[5] About a hundred Terre Hauteans filled the gas tanks of their Model A Fords and Durants at 15 cents a gallon and made the half day's drive north.[6] Taylor weighed 121, Sangor 126.[7]

The fighters went at it like two men with a grudge to settle. Neither gave ground through the first six punishing rounds, showering punches on each other. Early in the seventh, Sangor hit Taylor with a straight right that appeared low. Taylor dropped, twisting in pain. The referee and one judge ruled the blow landed on the belt line—a legal punch, while the second judge said he did not see it. As allowed by referee's discretion, Taylor was granted five minutes' rest. Instead of recovering, he grew worse, half falling off his stool in pain. His seconds cut his gloves off before the five minutes elapsed. Since the ending punch had been deemed a legal one, Sangor was awarded the fight by TKO.[8]

Not surprisingly, the outcome was hotly disputed and bantered about in the newspapers. All parties involved agreed that low blow or not, the punch had been delivered unintentionally. Taylor and Long argued that unintentional violation or not, Bud should have won by a foul. The Illinois Boxing Commission reviewed the fight, conducted a hearing on the matter, and let the outcome stand.[9]

For all his pleadings, Taylor was forced again to accept defeat by a fighter to whom he loathed to lose.[11] The *Chicago Daily Tribune's* scorecard legitimized Sangor's victory, showing him ahead 3-1-2 at the time of the foul.[10] The *Chicago American* had it 4-1-1.[12] The Tribune's reporter thought the aborted affair "showed that Sangor has something on Taylor and that Bud is not quite as good as he used to be."[13]

Chapter 38

Ellen's Choice

Ellen Grabski grabbed Bud Taylor's attention like a whiff of Hoosier honeysuckle, and soon he knew he wanted her forever.

They met when their paths crossed somewhere inside the circle of high-society Los Angeles, possibly through friends.[1] Taylor might have seen Grabski on stage, and asked to meet her.[2] She had appeared under the stage name "Ellen Allyn," on Feb. 25, 1928, in a variety show in the Ambassador Theater in Los Angeles, playing piano with the King Sisters, a novelty act.[2] She also could sing and play violin, and had appeared in movie parts as an extra.[3]

Grabski's looks brought to mind the Mexican screen actress Delores Del Rio, a slender, raven-haired woman with high cheekbones above a cursory mouth that gave her a look of intrigue.[4] An appealing beauty from her wiry hair down to ankles thin as a race horse's, Grabski attracted other male admirers.[5] Taylor's main competition for the woman was Walter Lance, a cartoonist for Universal Pictures who 12 years later would create an icon, Woody Woodpecker.

Both men wooed the woman until the day arrived when she knew she had to choose between the two suitors: Walter, the stable, sensitive, 9-to-5er with a promising future, or Bud, the handsome and charismatic boxer whose aftercareer held uncertain prospects.[6]

Grabski would have been drawn to Taylor by the contradiction: a champion fighter, the epitome of masculinity, yet a sentimental man who allowed himself to cry openly and liked to present women with flowers.

"They both wanted to marry her," Bud Taylor Jr. said. "My uncle told her, 'you better think about this. Walter Lance has talent that will go on and on while Bud Taylor, his will be limited.' But she followed her heart." Lance won on the scorecards of Ellen's advisers, but Taylor won the decision.7

Taylor left the chilly Midwest in mid-February for an eight-round bout on the coast against the latest Filipino sensation, Ignacio Fernandez. With lady friend Ellen to visit in California, Taylor extended his stay by two months, and boxed two additional bouts. Fernandez's manager, Frank Churchill, had offered to put up $15,000 in guaranteed cash for Taylor to fight Fernandez for the bantamweight title. For reasons not known, Long declined, and the bout went off at 124 1/2 pounds instead.8

Fernandez showed no fear of The Terror, moving right inside to slug with him and nearly pulling off an upset. Taylor usually clobbered guys who chose to mix with him, but this time The Terror took more punishment than ever in a Los Angeles ring.9

Sportswriters in Los Angeles and Chicago, mulling over Taylor's recent performances, reached the conclusion that Bud had become an easier target. Warren Brown, a Chicago sportswriter who had covered Taylor for years, provided this grim assessment: "The principal change that I have noted in two of Taylor's recent ring appearances have been his inability to get out of the way of punches to the head."10

Taylor had to contend with the reality of how 130 bouts—more than 1,000, three-minute rounds of being hit—affects a man's ability to perform inside a boxing ring. Moreover, the advantages Taylor had owned over his bantamweight opponents did not transfer to the heavier featherweights. He stood taller and reached farther than nearly all the 118-pounders, but he lost that edge against the featherweights, who were bigger without sacrificing any quickness. In his column, Brown suggested Taylor fight less and prepare for his inevitable bantamweight title defense.11 Taylor's two other nontitle bouts on the West Coast in the spring of 1928 did little to restore anyone's confidence in Bud's boxing future. He lost a 10-rounder to Vic Foley in Vancouver and narrowly won a bout over the same distance with Santiago Zorilla in Los Angeles. Zorilla, "the fastest human of the ring," nearly toppled Taylor in the fourth round with a barrage of left hooks.12

Chapter 39

Title Departs

In the American Midwest, the month of May revitalizes its residents after the bleakness of winter. Bare landscapes and cold, howling winds are replaced by the beauty of dense forests and yellow mustard fields, the warbles of migrant songbirds and the fresh scent of green plants and grass. Taylor took in the sunshine with a weeklong escape about 100 miles southeast of Terre Haute to French Lick, Indiana, accompanied by a friend, billiard-parlor owner C.V. McGregor. They played golf, hiked and swam. Taylor added jogging and rope jumping to keep fit for the ring.[1]

Eddie Long continued to sort through a steady stream of offers for bouts coming in from Chicago to as far as Australia.[2] Long hoped to box Taylor in a few warmups before defending the bantamweight title that summer.[3] In New York, Bushy Graham had been reinstated after a yearlong suspension, and Long was negotiating with Tex Rickard's people over the phone to match Taylor with the winner of a bout between Graham and Kid Francis. *The New York Times* suggested that matching Taylor with the winner could consolidate the NBA and New York world titles.[4] Despite the recognition of Bud as 118-pound champion by the NBA and its worldwide affiliates, New York still considered the title vacant.

On May 18, 1928, however, the NBA joined New York in vacating the world bantamweight title when its president announced the removal of Taylor as champion. NBA President Thomas Donahue noted in a statement that Taylor had repeatedly refused offers to defend his crown and that it wants a champion who will "... take an active part in keeping the division alive." The NBA had given Taylor six months to defend his title and he had not done so, Donahue said.[5]

"The Terre Haute boxer now gives every indication that he no longer is able to scale at the division poundage," read an NBA statement, and it noted that Taylor has been campaigning as a featherweight.[6] The association further announced that its 26 states and various nations would recognize the winner of the Francis-Graham bout as the new champion. The state of New York also approved the Francis-Graham fight as one for the title.[7]

"I am puzzled and surprised at the NBA action ...," Taylor told the press.[8] The title that he had gained outside the ring had been pulled from him in the same manner.

Long took the news like a hard slap. As Taylor's manager, it was his job to guide the fighter's career, and the move surely struck him as an indictment of his job performance. Whether out of outrage, or embarrassment, he complained bitterly to the press. "Why we have almost gone begging for a title match for Taylor for a year and a half and haven't found anyone who could make the weight limit and make any kind of showing. Only last week, Tex Rickard offered a match with the winner of the Bushy Graham-Kid Francis bout at New York. I accepted, but haven't heard anything from him since. Taylor has been willing to meet any challenger ever since he was crowned champion ... In order to keep Taylor active, I have been compelled to match him with featherweights. I have never received a bona fide offer from any promoter for Taylor to meet a legitimate challenger." Long fired off a scathing letter to the NBA, asking the organization to explain its action. He challenged Donahue to name one instance in which Long had received a bona fide offer to defend the title.[9]

While it is known that Long had received offers—such as the one from Ignacio Fernandez's manager 10 weeks earlier—it is not clear why he considered them less than "bona fide." Columnist Edward J. Geiger of the *Chicago American* suggested that Long had turned down the offers because he wanted more money for Bud to risk the title than any prospective opponents had offered.[10] The *Chicago Daily Journal's* Joe Foley wrote that Taylor simply had been waiting for a quality opponent. Both columnists thought the NBA acted too hastily in stripping the championship from Taylor.[11]

No formal appeal process existed, so the NBA's decision to

strip Taylor from the title would stand, and the matter had been settled. Long, desiring to give up the title on his own terms, wrote a letter to the Illinois Boxing Commission saying Taylor voluntarily surrenders the title for lack of opponents.[12]

Chapter 40

A Changing Face

Taylor left Terre Haute for two bouts in California in the summer of 1928, making the trip this time by automobile with a friend, Eddie Lynch. Taylor's mother traveled out independently to join him, bringing along curly-haired, 3-year-old Barbara Jean.[1]

Champ or ex-champ, the slugging style of The Terror of Terre Haute still filled the seats of arenas. To Californians, he remained the gutsy guy who had whipped Georgie Rivers with one arm and knocked Jimmy McLarnin from the unbeaten ranks, then beat him again. On June 29, in San Francisco, 9,000 spectators filed into the Dreamland Auditorium to watch Taylor's rematch with Santiago Zorilla, which Bud won by a slight margin.[2]

Eleven days later, Taylor entered the ring against Johnny Vacca, who owned one of the all-time greatest boxing nicknames: the "Boston Organ Grinder." Vacca entered the fight having won four of his last five, and gave Taylor and the fans an exciting 10 rounds. Vacca fought at 118 and gave away four pounds, but managed to propel his share of right hands into Taylor's face. Taylor's left, however, did the most grinding, and he won eight rounds. By the end of the fight, both sluggers' faces were badly marked.[3]

Taylor had 17 days to recover from the battering and ready himself for a third match with Zorilla, in San Francisco. Taylor told a reporter that even after 8 1/2 years of averaging 15 bouts a year, he still liked fighting frequently. "Training is harder work than fighting, so when I get in shape for one bout I might as well have a whole row of them," he said.[4]

Zorilla was a native Californian of Panamanian descent with pistonlike speed of hands and feet, although no knockout punch. His credentials were respectable: a 33-6-1 record, with two of those losses to Taylor and two to Joey Sangor. At 20, he was improving with each outing. Zorilla stood only 5 feet, 1 inch, and trying to hit the speedster was like punching at a leaf in the wind.

The fight on July 27 in Dreamland Auditorium, a rematch of their 10-rounder from a month earlier, proved disastrous for Taylor. He won the first two rounds, then took a mauling over the remaining eight. Zorilla broke Taylor's nose in the fourth round on either a punch or an accidental head butt. Taylor's seconds could not stop the bleeding, and blood splashed from the position of a gash high on the bridge of his nose into his eyes the rest of the fight, impairing his vision. The handicap gave Zorilla the freedom to thump away at his target, cutting Taylor's lips in the process. The Terror of Terre Haute left the ring resembling the victim of a terrible automobile wreck. The cut on the nose required five stitches to close and forced Taylor to cancel a bout in August.[5]

Taylor healed, but his face needed an overhaul. In its reflected image, he saw the grotesque features that his opponents had sculpted over eight years of boxing: a crooked nose, sunken left eyebrow, scarred lips, puffy ears ...[6] To strangers on the street, Ellen Taylor, Barbara Jean and Bud would have appeared as an odd threesome, the olive-skinned beauty, her pint-sized princess and the disfigured guy in their company—Delores Del Rio, Shirley Temple and their pet monster. The one most embarrassed would have been Bud, who always took meticulous care of his appearance. He wanted only to fight like The Terror of Terre Haute, not look like him as well.

On Aug. 7, Taylor visited Dr. William E. Balsinger for a series of reconstructive surgeries to renovate the damage inflicted by the blows in 136 boxing matches.[7] Balsinger had come highly recommended; he had operated on Jack Dempsey's face in August 1924 and on the features of 19 other pro fighters.[8] In five surgeries, Balsinger repaired Taylor's brow, ear, lip and nose, an overhaul that Bud described graphically in letters to Ralph White of the *Terre Haute Tribune*.[9]

"The doctor will take the cartilage that he takes from my ear to build up my nose ... [He] said [the nose] was my own flesh and bone and that there was no reason why it should not be well enough to get hit on in about two or three months ..."

Taylor added that he wanted to win the featherweight title before he quit boxing. "... If my nose shouldn't hold up I would have to call it quits, but I am sure the doctor knows what it is all about," he wrote.10

Taylor penned a letter a few weeks later, joking that his "new nose" made him look too handsome to be a fighter and that he may become a movie star. "My left eye, which was worked on, and my new ear sure look good ...," he wrote.11

Chapter 41

A Time to Retire

Taylor brought Ellen Grabski with him when he returned to Indiana in August 1928, and in the following month, they married in a small, unannounced ceremony in Indianapolis. In Terre Haute, they settled in at the Edgewood Apartments.1

The new Mrs. Bud Taylor attended Bud's fights only occasionally. Ellen Taylor neither was particularly fond of, nor offended by, the spectacles.2 Most boxers' spouses leaned to the extremes, either always attending their man's fights or staying away from them with the same dedication. Rose Julian, wife of former heavyweight champion Bob Fitzsimmons, used to stand ringside, scream at him and sway with the punches. During Fitz's title bout with Jim Corbett, she could be heard wailing "Kill him, Bob!"3 Conversely, Sammy Mandell's wife never attended one of her husband's bouts.4

Late in 1928, Bud Taylor added 600 chairs to the K of C auditorium, hoping to draw more spectators to his weekly amateur boxing shows by mixing in more pro fights.5 A strong blue-collar population always helps boxing, and Terre Haute had maintained a solid cast of regular customers for the business. The 6,285 miners living in Vigo County then—and about half that many from four surrounding counties combined—certainly helped.6 By December, Taylor had put his dad to work in the box office downstairs at the K of C, selling the $1 tickets.7

Around the nation, golfers teed off by the thousands, and Taylor occasionally played the game himself. Players donned the uniform of the era, baggy pants, V-neck sweater and pancake hat, and took to the fairways in record numbers—793 in one day in September on Terre Haute's city-owned course in Rea Park.8 Heavyweight boxing champion Gene Tunney had recommended golf to Taylor as a diversion from training, and Bud bought a new set of clubs.9 Taylor's sister had married Horace Fisbeck, who had won the city golf championship in 1926.10 With freebie tips from his expert brother-in-law, Taylor might have mastered the strokes with a modest investment of time. His devotion to fight training, however, left little time for the links.

On the boxing scene, the amateurs and young pro boxers were drawn to Taylor like minor-league baseball players would navigate to a Lou Gehrig or Rogers Hornsby. Bud took an active interest in the ones who showed promise, and guided their careers as manager/corner man. His connections got them fights in Indianapolis and occasionally, Chicago.11

One of the better up-and-comers was flyweight Johnny Nasser, the son of Terre Haute grocers Saleem and Mary Nasser.12 Johnny Nasser had quickness and a willingness to learn, and became Taylor's chief protégé of the late 1920s. Nasser had fought on the undercards in two of Taylor's bouts in Chicago early in 1928, gaining a draw in the first and losing a decision in the latter.13

Nationally, boxing had entered a post-Dempsey-era lull, not helped by the retirement of Tunney in the summer of 1928. In Chicago, business declined at promoter Jim Mullen's training gym and forced him to close in November 1928. Boxing needed people such as Mullen, a barnstormer whose "bootleg' bouts had helped keep the sport alive in the metro Chicago area for years when it still was illegal. Mullen promised to continue to promote bouts despite shutting down the gym. The death of Tex Rickard on Jan. 7, 1929, of complications from an appendectomy also contributed to boxing's slump.14

Baseball continued to flourish, and Babe Ruth reigned as king of the swatters. In October, he led the New York Yankees over the St. Louis Cardinals in the World Series, the first time a team ever won consecutive Series by four-game sweeps.

Art Nehf, a Terre Haute native who pitched in the 1920s for baseball's New York Giants, once remarked that pro baseball players loved boxing more than any other sport except their own.[15] Ruth himself was a big fight fan and had tested the ring. "There was one time I thought I would try myself out," Babe was quoted as saying. "I had a short scrap with [light-heavyweight] Gunboat Smith in a gymnasium. Smith socked me on the whiskers and then and there, Babe Ruth decided that it was very nice to be out on the field catching fly balls and hitting baseballs into bleachers."[16]

The fall of 1928 was the logical time for Taylor to retire from the ring. He had money, fame, friends, a new wife, a new face and the necessary contacts for any number of endeavors outside of boxing.

History holds a lengthy list of professional fighters who continued their boxing careers despite knowing they were past their prime. Most of them fought on for the money, either because they had earned so little in their careers and stayed bound to the steady income, or because they had squandered their fortunes.

Taylor, however, had saved more than $100,000, and owned close to $75,000 in government bonds—superb retirement figures for 1928. He also owned chunks of property in Terre Haute.[17]

A Los Angeles sportswriter had speculated in April 1928 that Taylor soon would retire, without comment from Bud on the matter.[18] When the *Terre Haute Tribune* tried to elicit comment about the possibility, Taylor dismissed the idea.

"I can still whip all the bantams and, I think, most if not all the feathers, so why should I retire?" he responded.[19] But the signs of decline were obvious. He had taken a beating in five of his previous eight fights, and lost three of them. His career bouts totaled 136, and he knew that no amount of training can compensate for the telling effects of such an accumulation. Taylor also knew about the risk of brain damage associated with extending a boxing career; he is quoted on that topic in a 1928 newspaper article.[20]

Taylor resumed serious training by mid-October, but physical problems kept him out of competition the rest of 1928.[21] First, he slipped in training and tore a ligament in his left ankle.[22] Worse were the problems with his reconstructed face. His new nose did not respond well to punches.[23]

Chapter 42

Losing With a Grin

After a career-long, six-month layoff, Taylor returned to competition on Jan. 29, 1929. He weighed 126, his heaviest ever, and looked junkyard rusty in a 10-round decision over Billy Shaw of Detroit. The *Indianapolis Star's* boxing columnist Blaine Patton covered the bout and ripped Taylor for everything but the starch in his trunks: "Taylor's judgment of distance, timing and footwork, speed and hitting power [were] far from impressive."[1]

Two days later, a Taylor left hook knocked Bobby Dempsey unconscious in a Davenport, Iowa, ring, and Dempsey's handlers had to carry him to his corner.[2] The frightening moment before Dempsey regained his senses brought to mind the tragedies of Frankie Jerome and Clever Sencio.

As much as he would have preferred otherwise, the deaths of Jerome and Sencio were part of Taylor's boxing resume'. The two tragedies were continually referenced in the publicity for his fights.[3] Sportswriters mentioned them in summaries of Taylor's career, in previews of his upcoming bouts, and even dredged them up tastelessly in their fight accounts. In reviewing the third Canzoneri fight, for example, Westbrook Pegler critiqued Taylor's performance by writing he "wasn't the same little killer who hit Frankie Jerome a smash in the flank and a clout on the base of the skull and laid him dying in the ring ..."[4] The deaths had damaged Taylor emotionally, and their continual recapitulation affected him, too.

"He was very, very sad that they happened," remembers Taylor Jr., who also said his father found it too uncomfortable to talk about the tragedies at length.5 To cope, his father apparently shoved the hurt inside. When Taylor Sr.'s friend from the late 1920s and later, drinking buddy, Howard Brokaw mentioned the fatalities, Bud immediately changed the subject.6 Ed Cummins, a friend of Taylor's, said Bud never discussed the tragedies with him.7 There is no indication Taylor ever received any kind of counseling, nor does Taylor Jr. believe his father would have sought spiritual guidance, an avenue in which his father showed little interest.8

As for Taylor's attempts to revive his career, his victories over unknowns Shaw and Bobby Dempsey were not solid indicators of progress. They were journeyman fighters, at best.9 The two bouts were warm-ups to prepare Taylor for his next marquee opponent, Al Singer.

Singer, 23, of the Bronx, began his career quietly. He had ho-hummed his way to an above-average start over a few dozen fights in New York rings before he suddenly found the formula for invincibility, beginning a run of 22-0-2 up to the bout with Taylor. His durability proved just as impressive, fighting those 24 bouts in 11 months. One of the two draws came against Tony Canzoneri in the Garden.10

The betting odds showed the onetime Terre Haute terror at a humbling three-and-a-half-to-one underdog. A fan turnout of 21,000 showed up on Feb. 8, 1929, filling Madison Square Garden, with some even standing along the walls of the balcony to watch. In the first four rounds, Singer landed two or three punches to every one of Taylor's, and the New Yorker built a sizable lead. When the punches stung the hardest, Taylor broke into smiles. The referee awarded Singer the fight in the fourth round on a foul after Taylor inadvertently struck Singer with a low punch.11 Among the sportswriters covering the bout was 27-year-old Ed Sullivan of the *New York Evening Graphic*, who later found fame in the medium of television as host of a hugely successful network variety show.12

Back home, Taylor directed a benefit boxing show for the Terre Haute Boys Club, raising $800 from paid admissions to the five bouts, for which he also served as referee.13

A rematch with Singer in New York on March 15 went the 12-round distance. Taylor kept the fight close through seven rounds, then his legs went dead. Singer landed short, savage rights at his grinning target and won by decision.[14]

There are many recorded instances of Taylor smiling during bouts. Early in his career, they often are described as spontaneous expressions of determination or confidence, or of good-naturedness, such as laughing at himself for overswinging.[15] In the latter years of his career, Taylor tended to smile after being hit.[16] There were so many instances of Taylor grinning after being punched that the displays could indicate a subconscious desire for punishment.

"Boxing is about being hit more than it is about hitting ... just as it is about feeling pain ... more than it is about winning," wrote Joyce Carol Oates, in a 1987 conjecture on the psychology of boxers.[17] History is filled with instances of people who unleashed their repressed guilt on themselves as punishment. Jesus' betrayer Judas Iscariot took the extreme measure of suicide; and Los Angeles police officer Karl Hettinger got himself caught shoplifting out of guilt over the death of a partner as recounted in the 1973 book "The Onion Field."[18]

In his book, "Raging Bull," boxer Jake LaMotta relates the details about how he thought he had killed a bookie that he had hit from behind on a dark street, and whose death he read about in the newspaper. LaMotta, a brawler who gave and took enormous amounts of punishment, boxed almost an entire career before learning, to his amazement, that the bookie was alive and well. (The newspaper had erroneously referred to the bookie as "dead" instead of "dying.") At the point LaMotta discovered that he had not killed the man after all, LaMotta lost his will to fight.[19] Frankie Jerome and Clever Sencio, however, would never return from death to "vindicate" Taylor. If Taylor's conscience demanded atonement, he may have sought it in the ring and at the receiving end of a glove.

By early April 1929, Taylor had four bouts lined up over a 26-day period, ending with an April 26 date with Canzoneri.[20]

In the first of the four bouts, Taylor decisioned Henry Falegano in Milwaukee.[21] Then, in Providence, R.I., against Young Montreal, whom Taylor had TKO'd three years earlier, Bud rated a 10-3 favorite.[22] He floored Montreal in the second round, but Montreal recovered and left-jabbed Taylor unremittingly over the distance, winning a decision.[23]

A bout with Tommy Murray spoiled Taylor's chance to fight Canzoneri again. In the Indianapolis Armory, Taylor decked Murray five times before his opponent took the full count. Taylor fractured his left thumb on Murray's head on what Bud believed was the first blow of the fight; by the time he had beaten Murray to the canvas a final time, Taylor had shattered the digit in three places.24

Cancellation of the Taylor-Canzoneri bout ended their career series and probably saved Taylor from a beating.25 Canzoneri had by that time entered the most productive part of an illustrious career that surpassed Taylor's and all other rivals. He ultimately won the lightweight and junior welterweight titles as well as the featherweight crown. History would reflect Taylor's 1-1-1 mark against Canzoneri (along with Bud's 2-1 log against Jimmy McLarnin) as The Terror of Terre Haute's most impressive head-to-head results.

Chapter 43

The Slide Continues

In the late spring of 1929, Taylor drove to Los Angeles accompanied by Terre Haute boxers Johnny Nasser and Ray Van Hook. Taylor wore a cast on his hand for his injured thumb, which he hoped would heal in the California sunshine while his younger companions boxed.1 Ellen Taylor joined Bud on the coast later, bringing Barbara Jean. The 4-year-old enjoyed her romps on the beach so much that she declared her intention to stay in California forever.2 Nasser and Van Hook (fighting as "Ray Van") met with mixed success over six weeks, with Nasser going 1-1-1 and Van Hook fighting a draw in his only fight.3

Taylor's thumb healed well enough to stir him back into action, and he took a bout for himself June 11 in Los Angeles' Olympic Auditorium. His opponent, Goldie Hess, hailed from nearby Ocean Park, California, thus attracting an enthusiastic crowd of supporters to the arena for the 10-rounder.4 Taylor's closest friends and supporters greeted the bout with a shrug. They would have rather Bud quit fighting.5 Jack Dempsey, introduced before the fight, received a rousing ovation.6

Taylor won five of the first six rounds and appeared so firmly in control of the fight that at the end of the sixth, Referee Jack Kennedy asked him, "Whaddya doin', waitin' for the eleventh round?" But Taylor was lugging his heaviest weight ever at 129, and it began to show. Hess began to dodge Taylor's left hooks and throw more punches, winning the later rounds to gain a draw.7 Bud's game had begun to resemble a flare: it still burned bright, it just didn't last.

At some point in the fight, Taylor broke his left hand on Hess' head.[8] Taylor canceled a fight scheduled in San Francisco, and his party returned to Indiana in mid-July.[9]

The highlight of boxing in Terre Haute in the summer of 1929 was the appearance of Max Schmeling to box a four-round exhibition at the city's Memorial Stadium. At the time, Schmeling stood as the No. 1 contender to heavyweight champion Jack Sharkey, whom he would defeat a year later.[10]

Taylor passed the summer running his weekly pro-am boxing shows, and for kicks, motoring his speedboat across the currents of the Wabash River.[11] He missed the Schmeling exhibition because he was in Boston, mismatched with a Massachusetts bruiser, Andy Martin.

Taylor won the first round, then took a thrashing. Martin's "stream of jabs started pouring against Bud's smiling blond head in the second round and his left hooks to the jaw almost unhinged Taylor's head," and so it went for 10 rounds. Taylor's punches "missed like a novice," probably intentionally, since Bud either re-broke his left hand or aggravated the fracture that hadn't properly healed since the Hess fight. Taylor left Boston with his hand in sorry shape and with the press speculating he would retire.[12]

With still another injury-enforced layoff, Taylor took a vacation with Ellen and Barbara Jean to Lake Wawasee in northern Indiana.[13]

Long kept the opponents coming and the money rolling in. He signed Taylor to fight Chicago native Earl Mastro on Oct. 8 in the city's new Chicago Stadium for a guarantee of $10,000.[14] At least one published report, years later, claimed that Taylor overextended his career by a few years to help Long financially.[15] Jim Long, the manager's son, recalls hearing conversations within the Long household to the contrary. Taylor, he believes, continued fighting at his own insistence.[16]

Chapter 44

Battles in Ring, Court

Earl Mastro, an Italian-American who grew up on Chicago's west side, had been a bundle-weigher in a Chicago laundry when he quit to take up boxing. Within a year, he rose from a $50 preliminaries fighter to a featherweight title contender. His victories over contenders such as Kid Francis, Fidel LaBarba, Eddie Shea and Santiago Zorilla titillated Chicagoans with the prospect of a native-born champion, a rarity for the city. The 21-year-old owned a devastating right cross.1

Promoters opportunistically had scheduled Mastro's bout with Taylor for Chicago Stadium on the evening of Tuesday, Oct. 8, sandwiched between games 1 and 2 of the 1929 World Series, Tuesday and Wednesday afternoon games in Wrigley Field.2

Trouble arose between the Taylor and Mastro camps on the Thursday before the fight. The fighters trained at separate times in a gym owned by Dave Barry, until Long accused two of Mastro's associates of spying on Taylor's practice session. The dispute seemed settled after Long told Barry he would move Taylor to a different gym to work out, but the feisty manager didn't let matters end there. When Mastro began his Friday training session, his handlers spotted Long's chubby face peering out from among the ringside spectators, prompting Mastro's people to threaten to close the workouts to everyone.3

Fifty thousand fans filled Wrigley Field to watch the Philadelphia Athletics defeat the Chicago Cubs 3-1 in Game 1 en route to winning the Series in five games. The fight attracted 20,000 fans, about 2,000 short of capacity.[4] It was a brutal fight, with no clinches. Taylor won the early rounds with left-right combinations, but Mastro's middle-round attack put a gash near Bud's eye and reopened a cut nose that Taylor had suffered in training. Both fighters weakened in the later rounds and the bout was ruled a draw.[5]

Back in Terre Haute, Taylor entered a fight of an entirely different nature: for custody of Barbara Jean. Taylor had filed court documents seeking full-time custody and the case had reached its hearing date of Oct. 10. Testimony, which took most of the day, raised questions about Iris Taylor's fitness as a mother. Witnesses said she had been living in a messy room in a seedy hotel in Chicago, where she drank a lot and partied late into the night. One witness, Margaret Terhorst, had been recruited by Bud to travel to Chicago to spy on Iris. Iris testified that she liked to drink and have fun, and admitted she had made some mistakes, but she loved Barbara Jean and had quit her job in Chicago and returned to Terre Haute. Iris' mother, Laura Shumard, told the judge that if Iris maintained custody, Shumard would help care for the child.

The witnesses on behalf of Bud spoke glowingly of Ellen Taylor in her role as stepmother to Barbara Jean.

When the case concluded the next day, Judge Linus Evans awarded full custody to Bud and Ellen Taylor. Evans ruled that Iris could visit her daughter "at reasonable times," without defining the terms, and stressed that he wanted no problems with visitation. Iris Taylor, devastated by losing custody of her 4-year-old, cried upon hearing the ruling and was comforted by friends. She continued to sob as she walked from the courtroom.[6]

Chapter 45

A Freakish Ending

After Jack Dempsey retired from the ring in 1927, he dabbled a while as a fight promoter. In October 1929, he came to Chicago to try his luck. Although his first card flopped, the second drew well, and for the third he arranged a feature match he thought would attract a great crowd: Bud Taylor vs. Santiago Zorilla, the quick-handed Panamanian who had torn up Taylor's face a year earlier in San Francisco. "Folks like Bud. Zorilla may beat him—he already has—but it'll be a fight …," Dempsey told a reporter.[1]

Dempsey liked Taylor, too, and they had more in common than their whirlwind fighting styles. Both were modest, honest men who had slugged their way out of poverty to the top. Dempsey had created the monster wave in the sport upon which Taylor and other fighters surfed to fame and prosperity, all to a lesser degree than hero Jack. Dempsey's fame towered over all the other stars in boxing because his ascent coincided with the sport's postwar boom, and, most importantly, because he was a heavyweight.

Dempsey gave Taylor an Elgin pocket watch on a gold chain, with the inscribed date of Nov. 15, 1929, and the engraved words "To my pal, Charles Bud Taylor, as a token of esteem and friendship from Jack Dempsey," with Dempsey's name written in cursive.[2]

The weight limit for the Zorilla bout of 129 pounds was the same amount Taylor weighed in his slow-footed effort against Goldie Hess. For this match, however–his fourth against Zorilla—Taylor trimmed to 125 and change, his lightest in months.[3] The gamblers remembered that Taylor had defeated Zorilla twice before the bloodbath in San Francisco, and the odds went off at about even for the fight.4

This time, Zorilla worked over Taylor in the first two rounds and opened a gash over his left eye in the second. Taylor's wild punches failed to find their mark. By the fourth, Taylor had brought his blows under control, and began to land with his left. His punches continually snapped Zorilla's head back, and Taylor won every round thence, taking the decision.5 Attendance totaled 7,678, and the gate receipts $30,646, which satisfied Dempsey.6

Taylor's performance proved that the light wasn't out on his career—only flickering. A 10-round rematch with Mastro six weeks later would give Bud a chance for back-to-back wins over respectable opponents for the first time in a year and a half.

Strange things can happen within the confines of a boxing ring, and through the years, fight fans have seen their share of the weird and wacky. In 1916, a youngster making his boxing debut inside a ring in Tacoma, Washington, forgot to put his boxing tights on and flung off his robe, naked to the crowd.7 In 1923, two flyweights in San Antonio, Texas, connected simultaneously on each other's jaws and were both counted out.8 The second Mastro-Taylor bout, Dec. 27, 1929, rates with these bouts in the realm of the bizarre.

It was plainly a one-sided bout until its memorable ending. In the second round, Mastro's punches found a cut over Taylor's eye that had thinly healed over from the Zorilla fight six weeks earlier, and the blood ran. For the next seven rounds, Taylor unyieldingly pursued his quarry, looking for an opening, landing an occasional punch while blinking off the blood in his eye and the gloves thudding off his face. Taylor was "hopelessly outclassed for eight sickening rounds," according to one writer, and had no chance to win except by knockout. He nearly pulled it off.

In the ninth, Taylor let go of a left hook that found Mastro's jaw and sent him stumbling to the canvas. He broke the fall with his hands. Mastro popped up before a count of five, and retreated to the ropes while Taylor moved in for the finish. Mastro tried to clinch, but Taylor wanted no part of it, and tried to wrestle free from his grasp as the two men lost their balance and teetered. Astonished spectators watched the two fighters fall, attached like drunken dancers. They landed between the ropes, then flat onto the ledge of the ring, Mastro pinned beneath Taylor. Referee Phil Collins strained to call out his count over the screaming crowd, and neither man moved until "five." Mastro managed to pry free, stood up and climbed inside the ropes by "nine." Taylor, who had torn a muscle in his shoulder and wrenched his back in the fall, looked up at Collins, helplessly. "I can't get up, Phil," he said. Collins had no choice but to award Mastro the victory by TKO. Eddie Long and Barney Furey carried Taylor to his corner, from where he managed eventually to leave the ring under his own power.[9]

The 17,211 fans who witnessed the freak ending would have fodder for debate for weeks, with the chief question, Would Taylor have KO'd Mastro had they not fallen?[10] Taylor insisted that he would have finished him off.[11]

Taylor ended 1929 with a win/loss mark of 6-5-2, a significant downturn from the 18-5-1 mark over the previous two years. As his boxing career limped into the new decade, his fellow Americans would encounter their own adversity as the joyful '20s gave way to the trying '30s and the Great Depression.

Chapter 46

Battling Bat, Fidel

In just two years of fighting professionally, Battling Battalino had maneuvered to the top of professional boxing with a 19-1-2 record and a victory over Andre Routis for the world featherweight championship.

Battalino grew up in Connecticut as Christopher Battaglia and had fought impressively as an amateur, winning the AAU featherweight title before turning pro. His reputation was that of a tireless, methodical fighter with little finesse, who liked to get inside and wear his opponent down.[1]

Since winning the title in the fall of 1929, Battalino had been in no hurry to defend it. His manager had taken the customary (and safe) route of accepting lucrative nontitle affairs until someone laid out the huge money for a championship fight. Detroit's Olympic Arena would be the site of his fourth such nonchampionship bout, a 10-rounder March 20, 1930, against Bud Taylor.

Long had asked for a title fight, but Battalino's camp had refused, and the weight was set at 128 pounds. "It is only too bad that the fight isn't for the title," Long said. "Bud will make Bat like it."[2]

Battalino carried a reputation of being what the press called a "cheese champion," or one undeserving of a title. He had been almost unheard of outside his native state when he won the championship, and his roster of victories showed few big names.[3] Bettors wanting to win money on the Battalino-Taylor matchup were forced to choose from between an unproven fighter and an aged one in decline. The fight went off at even money, and even is how they fought.[4] The *Detroit News* scored it 4-4-2. Bud won the official decision, however, on the strength of a decisive second round, during which he floored Battalino with a left hook. Jack Dempsey, in Detroit for an appearance at a theater, sat ringside for the fight and was one of the first to congratulate Taylor.[5]

The bout marks Taylor's last victory over a major opponent.

In Chicago, promoter Dempsey had matched Earl Mastro with one of the best featherweights in the business, Fidel LaBarba, for a fight April 21 in the Chicago Coliseum. But when Mastro's mother died, Bud took the fight as a replacement. LaBarba had his sights set on bigger game than Mastro or Taylor, and he figured to use the bout as a warmup for a more important fight in mid-May in Madison Square Garden.[6]

LaBarba, 24, the son of Italian immigrants, had been reared in Los Angeles as an all-around childhood success. He excelled at football and boxing, and served as president of his senior class. He concentrated on boxing, and won the 1924 Olympic gold medal as a flyweight before turning pro.[7] Within a year, he had won the flyweight championship of the world. At the top of his game, he quit boxing to enroll at Stanford University to fulfill his dream of attaining a college education. He did not stay in college for long.

"One day I learned that a certain professor, a very learned gentleman, for whom I had great admiration, was making only $4,500 [a year], or quite a bit less than I used to get for an ordinary fight," LaBarba told a sportswriter. "I was shocked to discover that a fine academic mind carried such a meager cash evaluation, so I decided that maybe the smart thing to do after all was to take up the gloves again and go after the money."[8] LaBarba returned to hitting human beings instead of the books, and re-established himself among the featherweights.

LaBarba's greatest asset in the ring was his quickness, which he used to his advantage particularly on defense. As one sportswriter quipped, Fidel was as easy to hit as the lottery.[9]

Taylor had little chance but to get to LaBarba early, before Fidel adapted himself to Bud's style and found the rhythm he needed to craft his defense. Taylor succeeded, crashing a right to the jaw in the first round that knocked LaBarba down. He rose at 9, dazed, and

Bud Taylor fends off Fidel LaBarba.

repeatedly clinched to survive the round. Bud also won the second and third, but landed no telling blows and LaBarba's confidence grew. LaBarba won the decision by taking rounds four through 10, and giving Taylor a pounding in the later rounds.10

Taylor returned to the Coliseum four days later as manager for Johnny Nasser, who was TKO'd in the sixth round by Tony Polacio of Chicago.11 A string of losses had stalled the progress of Taylor's No. 1 protégé, and Nasser's fortunes never would advance beyond the successes he enjoyed in Terre Haute and Indianapolis.

Around this time, Taylor stopped staging his weekly fight show at the K of C, and moved his training quarters into a building about a block to the west, at Seventh Street and Rose Court in downtown Terre Haute.[12] By May, Long had signed Taylor for a third fight against Mastro, this time in Detroit.[13]

Chapter 47

Getting Pounded

In June 1930, the Boy Scouts troop at St. Timothy's Catholic Church in Chicago needed uniforms, but the group had no money. Taylor, in the Windy City to fight a warm-up bout for Mastro, pitched in with Eddie Shea and other boxers and put on an exhibition to raise the funds.[1] Taylor held no affiliation with the church and apparently donated his time and celebrity for the satisfaction of helping the cause. In July, Taylor fought in a benefit exhibition in Chicago to raise money for Wolcott Langford, an ex-fighter left nearly blind.[2] Such acts of humanitarianism prompted sportswriters such as Dick Cullum of the *Minneapolis Journal* to write:

"Bud Taylor comes pretty close to being the strongest walking and talking exhibit the sport of boxing can advance to justify its existence." In a sport Cullum described as a "rough and scheming profession," Cullum found Taylor "has held ... to his notions of what is proper to do and what is not."[3]

Boxing, however, is a young man's game, and aged fighters put themselves at great risk for permanent damage. Earlier in the summer in Terre Haute, a huge fire burned popular St. Benedict's Catholic Church to ruins. The church sat southeast diagonally from the K of C at the intersection of Ninth and Ohio streets. Only a stiff northwest wind kept the fire from spreading to the K of C, sparing the gym so closely linked to Taylor's career.[4] Would fate likewise spare the boxer from the doom he tempted by continuing to fight?

Taylor lost the rematch with Mastro, and then, too, a rematch with Battalino over 10 rounds in Connecticut. The referee scored the latter bout 8-1-1.[5] Battalino ultimately hushed the critics who had declared him a "cheese champion." He defended his featherweight title five times, including title-bout wins over LaBarba and Mastro, and is enshrined in the International Boxing Hall of Fame.

In November, Taylor traveled to Los Angeles to fight Frenchman Maurice Holtzer. Although not known at the time, the fight marked Taylor's final show in the Olympic Auditorium, where he had performed before sold-out audiences six times over the years.[6]

Taylor fans who grimaced at his pathetic performance against Holtzer would have preferred to remember the younger version of The Terror of Terre Haute. Taylor looked slow and helpless, "absorbing terrific punishment with his usual quota of gameness." Holtzer cut Taylor near the right eye in the fifth, then jabbed away at the mark. Taylor continued into the later rounds trying to cover up from punches he no longer had the quickness to avoid. Los Angeles sportswriter Sid Ziff wrote that Taylor "leaned against the ropes ... grinning in the face of a withering barrage that bounced against his chin, a morbid grin by a man who had had enough and didn't know it."[7]

Eighteen days later, Taylor climbed back in the ring against LaBarba in Madison Square Garden. The 7,500 spectators saw "a mauling, tiresome, disappointing fight," with little punching and frequent holding. LaBarba won in a 10-round decision.[8]

At home, Taylor found the Terre Haute boxing community raving about a youngster with lightning reflexes, a wicked punch and a last name that looked great on marquees. Sammy Slaughter had begun boxing in Taylor's weekly amateur shows at the K of C as early as 1928, and seemed ready to test the big-time middleweight market. An imposing looking fellow with thick muscles above the waist and below, Slaughter combined speed and power in the ring into one awesome boxing package, often with dramatic results. His fight log included a memorable evening in Indianapolis when he knocked a fighter out in 20 seconds. When the victim awoke 30 seconds later, he remembered nothing and insisted Slaughter must have slugged him in his corner before the fight.[9] By January 1931, Slaughter had taken on Taylor as his manager.[10]

Chapter 48

Booed in Philly

A bored crowd looked on as Taylor lumbered to a lopsided 10-round decision over Joe Lucas on Jan. 13, 1931, in the Indianapolis Armory. Taylor looked "slow and wind-blown compared with the former 'Terror'," according to the *Indianapolis Times*.[1]

The name "Bud Taylor" still carried enough clout for Long to sign Bud for a bout with the world junior lightweight (130-pound] champion, Benny Bass, in Bass' home city of Philadelphia. Bass accepted the bout with the stipulation that Taylor weigh above 130 pounds, so that the title would not be on the line.[2] The requirement provided Taylor the rare opportunity to gluttonize on steaks, potatoes and long forbidden goodies, and his weight expanded to 131.[3] On Feb. 16, the two squared off before 8,000 fans.[4]

In the second round, Taylor sunk to the canvas from what appeared to some observers as a low blow. Referee Leo Houck made no count over Taylor, instead calling in a ringside physician to examine him. The physician declared that Taylor had not been struck low and Bass was awarded the fight by TKO. Angry fans jumped to their feet and protested the call. As Taylor hunched over his chair, still in pain, Bass skipped across the ring to congratulate him to a shower of peanuts, paper balls and other debris from the disapproving crowd. During a 20-minute delay, ring officials decided to let the decision stand and induced Bass to box five more rounds with Taylor as an "exhibition" to appease the fans. The consensus of newsmen at ringside was that Bass won three of the five rounds, Taylor one, and one was even. Fan support had shifted to Taylor after the questionable blow, and the crowd accorded him a wonderful ovation when he left the ring.5

Talk centered around a rematch, but it didn't happen. When Taylor returned to fight in Philadelphia on March 16, his opponent was Lew Massey. It was Taylor's 166th professional fight. Boxing experts considered Massey a lesser talent than Bass, but Massey found Taylor an easy target. Taylor "... was in retreat throughout the seven rounds and assimilated enough punishment to stop three ordinary individuals." In the eighth round, Taylor stopped punching, altogether. Referee Tommy Reilly twice warned Bud to fight, to no avail. Massey punched away at Taylor's head and body while Taylor made little or no effort to protect himself. The crowd of 7,000 booed Taylor's indifference. As Massey's blows sunk into his face and body, Taylor grinned. Reilly stepped in and stopped the fight.6 Taylor, once known as a guaranteed show-stopper who *never* quit, had been disqualified for lack of effort.

Eddie Long told reporters that Bud had injured his right hand throwing an uppercut in the first round, then hurt his left in the second round, which left him unable to punch with either mitt.7 The Pennsylvania Boxing Commission accused Taylor of stalling, held up his share of the purse and ordered him to appear before the commission on March 18. In the hearing, Taylor showed X-ray photos of his hands as proof of his injuries. The commission exonerated Taylor, and he received his money for the bout.8

Chapter 49

Adjustment

If Bud Taylor's life story had been written as fiction, he would have died in the ring in Philadelphia against Massey, a destiny dictated by his subconscious need to answer for the deaths of Frankie Jerome and Clever Sencio. Instead, Taylor returned home from Philly with sore hands and uncertain plans.1 His fight career, indeed, had ended. He never announced or acknowledged his retirement from the ring, probably because he never was certain that he had quit for good.

A *Terre Haute Star* sportswriter reported that Taylor was trying to decide between boxing and a career in the insurance business. The columnist, Bob Nesbit, recommended Bud go with the suit and tie.2 Taylor continued to work out to keep fit, and continued as manager or second for many young boxers, including Sammy Slaughter.3

In Slaughter, Taylor realized he had found a decent fighter that could go far in the business. In Taylor, Sammy had hooked up with the man who possessed the necessary connections for big-time bouts. The two seemed to enjoy each other's company in and out of the ring, although they were odds at times over training. Taylor did not think Slaughter worked hard enough.4

Taylor kept open the possibility of his own return to the ring by sparring periodically throughout 1931, and hinting to the press about the prospect of a comeback. The temptation tugged at him mightily and as late as February 1932, his friends were trying to dissuade him from a return.5

Longtime boxers often find the adjustment to retirement an excruciating process. Taylor had fought an average of once every three weeks for 11 years. Boxing had become far more to him than a job or an adrenaline rush—it had become an *existence*. What he ate and drank, how and when he exercised, when he slept and even the nature of his thoughts all had been dictated by his next fight. It had been a life lived in segments, 166 chunks of time, each ending with fight day, each beginning with the day after fight day.

Ironically, in the year Taylor retired from the ring, the Indiana Legislature provided for the formation of a state athletic commission to regulate professional bouts. Boxing became legal in Indiana in 1931, and the no-decision bout a thing of the past.[6]

That Bud stayed close to boxing in these early days of retirement surely added to the urge to lace 'em up. Along with helping young fighters, he refereed bouts and ran the affairs of his downtown gym.[7] In his spare time, he led a Boy Scouts troop and hunted rabbits and birds.[8] By the fall of 1931, Taylor had scuttled plans for a career in the insurance business for another choice: boxing promoter.

On Sept. 4, 1931, Taylor debuted as a promoter with a five-bout card in the Zorah Shrine Temple in Terre Haute. The card featured Slaughter against Norman Brown of Chicago in a middleweight matchup and a popular Terre Haute-area fighter, Frankie Hughes, against Babe Amos of Syracuse, New York in a welterweight clash. The Elks Lodge of Sullivan sent its 25-piece band to play, in appreciation for the many times Taylor had appeared in Sullivan for charitable functions. Taylor himself hopped into the ring during introductions and the ovation lasted minutes. The bouts drew 1,800 customers, and the rookie promoter pronounced the affair a success.[9]

Chapter 50

Sammy's Big Chance

Bud Taylor promoted at least 15 professional boxing shows over the winter of 1931-32, featuring such Indiana favorites as Slaughter; West Terre Haute light-heavyweight Andy Kellett; Indianapolis' Tiger Jack Fox, later a world light-heavy contender; and lightweight Harold "Bones" Farris of Marshall, Ill.[1]

History has forgotten thousands of Kelletts and Farrises of the times, talented, crowd-pleasing warriors who scratched out a living traveling the Midwest, fighting two or three times a month for years and winning far more than they lost, never to widespread acclaim. Farris fought more than a hundred career bouts and never earned more than $140 in one fight.[2]

The following spring, Taylor financed the building of a boxing stadium near 27th Street and Wabash Avenue on Terre Haute's east side. The outdoor arena cost $5,500, seated 3,500 and among its amenities featured reclining ringside seats with comfortable slanting backs, and footrests. It had floodlights, two ticket offices, concession areas and a spacious lot for parking. Taylor's weekly shows on Mondays matched the best of the local fighters with others from the Midwest, and sometimes beyond. The Taylor Bowl, often referred to as the "Taylor Punch Bowl," hosted its first card on June 28, 1932.[3]

In the meantime, Slaughter blazed the trail on the boxing circuit of middleweights. When he banged his way to a 10-round decision over notable Dave Shade of Chicago, boxing folks nationwide began to take particular notice, and Taylor began to book his protégé for main events in cities such as Milwaukee, Chicago and St. Louis.4

On Oct. 12, Ellen Taylor gave birth to Charles Bernard Taylor Jr. As newborn "Buddy" wriggled in the nursery in St. Anthony's Hospital, sportswriter Ralph White wrote that the kid already flashed a neat jab.5 In a tradition common to the times, Bud passed out cigars to his friends to celebrate the birth.6 The growing family required more space, and Bud and Ellen moved to a fabulous home at 247 Barton Ave. Their residence stood less than 50 feet off Ohio Boulevard, an exclusive area of elegant homes on Terre Haute's east side. Their Barton Avenue neighbors included Birch and Leah Bayh, the parents of a toddler, Birch Jr., who later became a U.S. senator and the father of Sen. Evan Bayh.7 Taylor drove an L-29 Cord four-door convertible, an impressive sight on the city streets.8

Slaughter had won six straight bouts by late October and 11 of 12 by January 1933, when Taylor negotiated Sammy's golden opportunity. Slaughter would fight Gorilla Jones in Cleveland on Jan. 30.

William "Gorilla" Jones was the best middleweight boxer in the United States at the time.9 He had held the National Boxing Association's title for that division for five months in early 1932 before losing it in a title-consolidating bout in France to Marcel Thil, International Boxing Union champ. Since the Thil contest, Jones had not lost in seven fights. The NBA endorsed Jones-Slaughter as the "American Middleweight Championship."10

For six rounds before 7,914 fans, Slaughter fought Jones on even terms. In the seventh, Jones found a gap in Slaughter's defense. As Slaughter fired a right, Jones whipped a short right uppercut that met Sammy's jaw with its full force. Slaughter pitched forward on his face, out.11

Slaughter's boxing career had peaked with the one big chance, and he won only about half his fights for the remainder of 1933. In January 1934, he and Taylor severed boxing ties.12 Slaughter pushed his boxing career on until 1939, with more losses than wins in his final six years in the ring.13

In December 1933, Congress repealed Prohibition, legalizing the sale of alcoholic beverages. The Terre Haute Brewing Co.

resumed business making beer, and Taylor took a job as a salesman. The company's Champagne Velvet, $1.90 a case to consumers in 1934, sold well nationwide and the job left Taylor with little time to promote boxing shows.[14]

The Taylor Bowl soon closed its gates, a business casualty of the hard times. In the 1930s, boxing did not draw customers in Terre Haute as the sport did in the 1920s. Boxing's big names still excited the fans, but Taylor's arena could not seat enough people to attract superstar fighters to Terre Haute. In addition, the shortage of money during the Great Depression limited what families could spend on live entertainment. Furthermore, other forms of entertainment emerged to compete, such as pro wrestling. Former heavyweight champs Jack Dempsey and Jess Willard added to the attraction of wrestling shows by touring the nation separately as referees in 1934, with Dempsey making a thousand dollars or more for an evening's work, depending on the draw.[15] Dempsey refereed a pro wrestling card in the Shrine auditorium in Terre Haute in September, and Willard in November.[16] The Taylor Bowl also could host wrestling matches, of course, but it couldn't compete with the year-round indoor venues.

Taylor continued to promote fights at other sites. In April 1934, he wanted to bring Max Baer, the No. 1 heavyweight contender for Primo Carnera's title, to Terre Haute for a boxing exhibition. Taylor ditched the idea after deciding that the demands by Baer's people for $200 in guaranteed appearance money and 50 percent of the gate amounted to too much. Baer won the heavyweight title two months later.[17]

In the first few years after he quit boxing, Taylor's weight rose dramatically. Significant weight gain among ex-boxers is common, as they adjust to freedom from the restraints of constantly making weight for a fight. Taylor's job with the beer company required that he meet with clients, which usually meant drinking with them.[18] In addition, once he gave up any pretense of returning to the ring, his rate of exercise fell. By November 1934, he had ballooned to 180 pounds. "I used to weigh every ounce of food I ate, but now I'm a banquet hound," he told a reporter.[19]

Over the summer of 1934, Taylor lost $15,000 promoting boxing in Terre Haute.[20] His job with the brewing company ended and he decided to relocate and enter some other line of business.[21] He considered opening a tavern in the Loop in Chicago, but Ellen Taylor felt the ache of missing her mother and the rest of her family, who were in California.[22] In December, the Taylor family of four moved to Los Angeles.[23]

Chapter 51

L.A. Descent

Bud Taylor returned to Los Angeles in 1935 as manager and part owner of a downtown restaurant/nightclub. His business partner, Suey Welch, had managed world middleweight champion Gorilla Jones. Taylor and Welch rounded up well-known ex-fighters Fidel LaBarba, Mushy Callahan and Jackie Fields to serve the establishment's quarter beers and 65-cent steak dinners. Over the next four years, Taylor tended to the workings of the business at Washington Boulevard and Vermont Avenue. He never strayed far from the fight game, refereeing and managing, and at one point actually set up a ring for bouts inside his "Ringside Cafe," with customers' tables set on its perimeter.[1]

For a while, things worked out well. Taylor had remained a popular sports celebrity in a city whose fight fans had witnessed some of his greatest triumphs. The restaurant/bar business succeeded, at least at first, and Barbara Jean made new friends and blossomed. Bud and Ellen Taylor lived the high life. They mingled with other celebrities, attended Hollywood parties and lived in a hacienda-style home in the hills near Hollywood.[2] But the party did not last.

Taylor earned the kind of income from his years as a boxing headliner that should have provided for a comfortable retirement. But by the end of the 1930s, all the money was gone. He had invested tens of thousands in government bonds, and during the collapse of the economy, Uncle Sam defaulted, leaving investors across the nation with nothing.[3] LaBarba and Sammy Mandell were among a spate of other ex-boxers who got KO'd by the economy. LaBarba lost $250,000 in the stock-market crash. By 1934, Mandell had lost all his cash in a bank foreclosure and the stock market.[4] Taylor lost money in other investments, too, such as $10,000 he had sunk into the lavish boxing stadium in Terre Haute and possibly worse losses from his restaurant business.[5]

Taylor also took a hit from "friends" to whom he lent money and from unscrupulous business partners. "He was abused at times because of his generosity," said Taylor's granddaughter, Judy Christine, a point with which there exists unanimous agreement among family members. "He was not a businessman," Charles Rutz said, "and he was very trusting."[6]

Some of the money disappeared with the lifestyle change. Taylor had been a teetotaler throughout most of his fight career, to keep himself in top shape.[7] But as his career fizzled in the late 1920s, he no longer practiced abstinence.[8] Eddie Long, who had developed a serious drinking problem, and Taylor, with his own inclination for self-destruction, "used up all the money in the form of entertainment for one and for all," wrote newspaper columnist Gene Coughlin.[9]

Taylor's weight problem worsened, and he reached at or near 200 pounds for much of the mid- to late-1930s. The sportswriters seemed fascinated by Taylor's weight, or at least they believed their readers were. They dutifully reported the latest readings in the tidbit news parts of their columns: 195 pounds, 200, 205.[10] "Bud Taylor, former featherweight boxer, is a heavyweight now," one wrote.[11] "He's so fat in the face, he can hardly open his eyes," wrote another.[12] At one point, Taylor bought a punching bag to try to lose 50 pounds, because, as a newsman wrote, "Bud, once one of the trimmest athletes in the ring, is tired of being called 'blimp'."[13] Taylor drank and caroused excessively, and his relationship with Ellen deteriorated.[14]

Despite his mounting personal problems, Taylor's cache in the fight business was never greater, and the young and ambitious of the game sought him out. One of the more talented ones that he managed was Ritchie Fontaine, a Montana featherweight fighting out on the West Coast and considered a contender for Henry Armstrong's world title.[15] Taylor and Fontaine, master and understudy, fared well together until Bud crashed his car in Bakersfield, Calif., while the two were en route to a fight in January 1938. In a heavy rainstorm, the car rear-ended a truck and the car in turn was hit from behind by a vehicle, seriously injuring both Taylor and Fontaine. Fontaine suffered broken ribs and initially it appeared he might not fight again.[16] He managed to return to the ring eight months later, without Taylor in his corner, and without the success he had enjoyed before the crash. He won just three of the last 18 bouts of his career.

Taylor's marriage also crashed. On July 12, 1939, he and Ellen split, and the following month, she sued him for divorce, complaining to a judge about his drinking and womanizing. She also claimed that he had struck her, although Ellen's daughter by a later marriage has said that Bud only threatened to strike his wife, and that no blow was delivered.[17] Ellen won her divorce in August, was granted custody of the children and a judge ordered Taylor to pay $20 a month in child support apiece for daughter Barbara Jean and son Buddy.[18]

In November, Fontaine sued Taylor over the accident and won a $4,500 judgment after a trial.[19]

The decade ended with Taylor single and broke. If matters were not bad enough, his mother back in Terre Haute was suffering from failing health.[20] Taylor decided to go home.[20]

Chapter 52

The Final Rounds

When Bud Taylor moved back to Terre Haute in January 1940, no professional boxing cards had shown in his home city for more than two years.1 Amateur boxing had surfaced to take its place, with the major event being the annual Golden Gloves tournament. The city served as a regional site for the Golden Gloves beginning in 1936, and within a few years drew thousands of spectators to the city for the matches. The winners in their respective divisions advanced to the national tournament in Chicago.2

That January, Taylor's mother died at age 70. Bud had been devoted to the woman who seems to have been his greatest influence in the character traits of kindness and compassion. A *Terre Haute Star* columnist described Tillie Taylor as "a genial lady with a wide circle of local friends, who we had come to admire immensely through our long association with Bud."3 Sam Taylor, Bud's father and from whom Bud adopted the tenets of hard work and self-discipline, died a few months later.

Bud decided to help coach a Golden Gloves team in February 1940. The older Golden Gloves competitors, in their early twenties, remembered Taylor's days of glory in the sport well and were thrilled at the opportunity to learn from him. When Taylor traveled with the team for a show in Anderson, Indiana, in March 1940, fans cheered the announcement of his name as a coach, and admirers gathered around him after the show.4

Taylor scrounged out a living in the early 1940s in laborer-type jobs in the Terre Haute area, while occasionally promoting and coaching boxing.5 He promoted an outdoor card in Indianapolis in the summer of 1941 that happened to land on a Friday the 13th. "I'm not superstitious and I believe we'll have good weather for the show even though it's Friday the 13th," he told a reporter. "I fought twice on that date during my own days in the ring and the only bad luck either time happened to my opponent."6

In February 1942, Eddie Long suffered a heart attack and died in his home in Chicago. Taylor did not attend the funeral or visitation. Instead, he wrote to Long's family, expressing his grief over the loss of his friend and the man who had guided his career so competently. "He was broke," son Jim Long said about Taylor. "He wrote a letter and said that he wanted to come but 'all I had was a dollar in my pocket'."7

To his credit, Eddie Long had quit drinking around 1932 and stayed sober the rest of his life, saving himself and his family from almost certain personal and financial ruin.8

A testament to Taylor's trust in Eddie Long was the nature of their business relationship. During their seven-year association, Long negotiated bouts and picked up checks from promoters for Taylor's ring earnings that totaled more than a half million dollars, yet the two men trusted each other so deeply that they worked the entire time without a contract.9

Taylor revisited Chicago in March 1943, when he accompanied a Golden Gloves team to the national finals in Chicago Stadium. He ran into old friends and well-wishers all evening in the city where he had thrilled fight fans a generation earlier. He told Bob Nesbit of the *Star* it was one of the happiest evenings of his life.10

Taylor helped coach the Indiana State University team in the Golden Gloves in 1943, along with Paul Selge, a former amateur boxer who had just begun his college teaching career. Taylor coached boxing with the same crash-bang philosophy and fearlessness that he practiced it.

"I didn't agree [with him] 100 percent," Selge said in 2005. "He advised sticking your head out and taking blows in order to land some. That may be all right if you're a lighter weight and you can handle that, but if you're a heavyweight and some of the bigger weights that hit so goddamn hard, I didn't think it was a great idea. Other than that, we got along real well."11

In California, Barbara Jean had graduated high school and won an academic scholarship to UCLA to study music. In December 1943, Taylor moved back to the West Coast.[12]

"She was the brightest girl in her class at Hollywood High School," he boasted about the girl to a reporter, "and the prettiest. She takes after her mother, not me."[13] After the 1927 divorce, Iris Taylor remained in Terre Haute for the rest of her life and never remarried. Barbara Jean maintained a relationship with her biological mother, visiting occasionally over the years.

After her divorce from Bud, Ellen Taylor remarried a military man named Paul Potter and in the mid-1940s moved to Atlanta, where Bud Jr. was raised. The bitterness from the divorce eventually faded, and Bud and Ellen thereafter associated amicably. Over the years, Taylor Jr. periodically visited his father on the coast.[14]

In the years after World War II, Bud Taylor worked on the sets of RKO Studios in Hollywood. He also worked at the Sports Club bar in downtown Los Angeles, owned by Suey Welch, one of his best friends. "Bud manages the place," a journalist wrote about the bar. "He could handle obstreperous customers as adroitly as a professional boxer. One word from Bud and they docilely take off as if mesmerized."[15]

In September 1947, Barbara Jean married her high-school sweetheart, Charles Rutz. Both finished UCLA, with Charles Rutz earning his degree in 1949 and beginning a successful career as an accountant. Bud Taylor's first grandchild, Carol, was born to the Rutzes in 1951.[16]

In the early 1950s, Charles Rutz used to attend the fights with his father-in-law in Los Angeles and remembers the streams of people who approached to speak to Taylor or shake his hand. "We'd get to the Hollywood Legion [Auditorium] and everybody knew him. We wouldn't walk 10 feet ..."[17]

In 1953, Nat Fleischer, the founder and editor of Ring magazine, named Taylor the fifth-greatest bantamweight of all time, an honor of distinction considering Fleischer's status as an authority in the sport and coming nearly 30 years past Taylor's boxing prime.[18]

On June 1, 1954, Taylor thought he was suffering from indigestion when it was actually the early part of a massive heart attack. While recovering in a Los Angeles hospital, members of his family counted the cards and telegrams from well-wishers and found they

Bud Taylor clowns with Jack Dempsey.

numbered more than 1,000. Taylor recovered, but it was months before he was even driving his car again. His weight, which had reached as high as 210 since his retirement, fell to 169.[19]

Taylor took a job as a public relations agent with the California Western Freight Association, a trucking company. "He would go around and drum up business, and of course, everyone loved to talk sports with him because he was a big celebrity," Charles Rutz said.[20]

Taylor joined the Roorag, a social organization in Los Angeles, described in a newspaper article as "a whimsical luncheon group devoted to the cultivation of the belly laugh." Taylor contributed to the merriment "by regaling friends with anecdotes of his lusty experiences both in and out of the ring," according to the press.[21]

In his fifties, he still loved to compete, just mostly at gin rummy.[22]

As for the deaths of Taylor's two opponents, it is not known if, or how, he forgave himself. A magazine writer's account of an interview with Taylor in 1962 depicts him as still obsessed with—even haunted by—Jerome's death.[23]

"How do you live with something like that on your conscience?" is one of the questions in the interview. But it is not the writer, but Taylor himself posing the question, rhetorically, back to the reporter. The article also suggests that Taylor may have found solace in reports that Jerome's fight with Johnny Curtin—two weeks before the Taylor fight—could have contributed to the injury that caused Frankie's death, and that a car wreck in which Jerome was involved also could have been a factor.[24]

Rutz, the son-in-law, believes Taylor came to terms with the tragedies in his own way that he kept private.[25] The passage of time heals, and as a man changes, so does his perspective about his burdens.

In 1956, Taylor was enshrined in the national Helms Foundation Boxing Hall of Fame, a widely respected, privately owned sports museum established in 1948 to honor the greats of sports.[26] Ring magazine also named Taylor to its Hall of Fame, which began inducting in 1954 and stopped in 1987. Taylor also remarried late in life, to his third wife, Lillian.

On March 4, 1962, Taylor played gin rummy most of the afternoon with retired fighter Art Aragon. "He seemed in such good health," Aragon said. "He would be hopping mad when I ginned. He's the only guy I ever beat." Taylor lost $2.47 and it would have been like him to stew over the loss and wear out a handful of decks practicing for a rematch.[27]

It would not happen. Two days later, a second heart attack sounded the final bell.

More than 500 people attended a rosary for Taylor in Church of the Precious Blood in Los Angeles.[28] Barbara Jean considered the diversity of the visitors a great tribute to her father. "There were people who were very well-to-do and also people who couldn't afford the price of a tie. At some time Dad had touched their lives," she wrote in a letter to a family friend.[29]

The family moved his body to Terre Haute for burial. Taylor fought in 43 other cities across 20 states over his 11-year career, yet always returned to the banks of the Wabash to make his home. In 1962, he returned forever. "Indiana is a great state," Taylor said during the prime of his boxing career. "It is a wonderful state. I hope to die there and be buried beneath one of those beautiful sycamore trees."[30]

The hundreds who visited Callahan Funeral Home to pay their respects covered the spectrum of Terre Haute society, and provided a walking timeline of Taylor's life: Bud Perrill and Billy Long, early '20s boxers from whom Bud learned the game; fans such as Ed Withrow, who cheered Taylor's victories in the K of C and Grand Opera House; friends, admirers and former neighbors; and prominent citizens such as Anton "Tony" Hulman and the police chief, county treasurer and county controller. The ex-boxers were easy to spot, once tough, agile sparring partners of Taylor's from the '20s and '30s, such as Jackie Barnhart and Harold Farris, slow-moving fellows with crooked noses and faces mapped with scars and loose cartilage.[31] Jack Dempsey was among the friends who telephoned the funeral home to extend long-distance condolescences.[32]

Chapter 53

Legacy

The sport of boxing experienced rises and declines throughout the 20th century, but never regained its lofty status from the 1920s in terms of participation, publicity and fan hysteria. In Terre Haute, the sport enjoyed a resurgence in the mid- to late-1990s, when its fans rallied behind their own Terry Ray. Ray started off 25-1, rose to national prominence under the management of Hall-of-Famer Angelo Dundee and briefly held the World Boxing Federation's cruiserweight title.[1] A blond like Taylor, Ray knew about Taylor ever since he began boxing at age 12. Ray's grandfather Ralph Tucker, mayor of Terre Haute 1948 to 1968, had been a big fan of boxing and a friend of Taylor's. Ray retired from the ring in 2001, ending a brief but memorable flashback to the '20s for city boxing fans.[2]

The Terre Haute of the 21st century offers few visible reminders of Taylor, except his gravestone in Highland Lawn Cemetery and an occasional mention in a newspaper story about notable sports celebrities in the city's past. The houses where Taylor lived as a child and the school whose playground served as a battleground for his earliest fistic encounters have long since been replaced by other structures. Taylor's closest blood relatives living in Terre Haute are distant cousins.

On a mid-August day in 1972, a steel clam swinging from a cable slammed into the former K of C building in downtown Terre Haute, and stone and timbers fell like uneven rows of KO'd fighters.[3] Along with the millions of bits of dust from the rubble rose a cloud of irony: Dick Brokaw owned the B&C Wrecking company that was tearing down the premises where his boyhood idol, Taylor, launched his championship career.

Never sentimental over stone, mortar and wood, Brokaw had not given the matter a second thought when his company was offered the $8,000 demolition. If his heavy machinery had not razed the building, some other company would have profited by leveling the decrepit structure that no longer served any useful function.[4]

A segment of Taylor's jogging route along the Vandalia Railroad tracks was paved over in 2002 as part of, appropriately, a 13-mile exercise route across the city known as the National Road Heritage Trail. Bikers, runners, walkers and skateboarders of the 21st century who never heard of Taylor beat the same path as he plodded in the 1920s, with their own dreams of superstardom in their chosen sports.

A showroom for Taylor's earliest ring triumphs, the Grand Opera House, tumbled to the wrecking ball decades ago and the 3-I baseball park is long gone. The Hippodrome, Memorial Stadium and Zorah Shrine venues remain standing, but not for use as boxing arenas, and their role in the momentum of Taylor's career in the sport's golden years is known by few.

Instead, Taylor's place in the history of the sport he loved is celebrated in Canastota, New York, inside a building maintained by an organization dedicated to preserving boxing history and honoring its greats. On June 12, 2005, the International Boxing Hall of Fame in Canastota enshrined Taylor in its annual ceremonies. Taylor joined the class of 2005: Bill Cayton, Bobby Chacon, Eugene Criqui, Don Fraser, Jersey Jones, Duilio Loi, Joe Lynch, Barry McGuigan, Harry Mullan, Terry Norris, Jack Randall, Lope Sarreal, Bert Sugar and Marcel Thil.

Taylor's family and friends who traveled to the ceremony from California, Georgia and Ohio included his son, a stepdaughter, a son-in-law, grandchildren and great-grandchildren. In acknowledging the honor of induction, Bud Taylor Jr. spoke from a stage to a crowd of about 1,500 from a podium backed by seated boxing celebrities such as Angelo Dundee, Carmen Basilio, Marvin Hagler and Jake LaMotta.

"He loved boxing and he loved the people involved in the sport, and I'm just delighted to be here to accept this," Bud Jr. said of his father. He kept the speech brief, just as his microphone-shy dad would have done if accepting it himself.

Taylor Sr.'s daughter, Barbara Jean Rutz, died in 1986 and Bud Taylor Jr. passed in 2006. Eight grandchildren of Bud Taylor were living in 2008.

One of them, Judy Rutz Christine, watched the ceremony in Canastota with particular interest. She was only 6 years old when her grandfather died, but feels connected with him beyond the bloodline and into the essence of the man. When she had played with toys as a child, she chose balls over dolls, and feels like she had been born to compete.

"Sports and competition is what drove me," she says of her youth in Ohio in the 1960s and 70s. As a teenager, she arrived first to softball and volleyball practices, and left last. Her mother recognized the inbred source of Judy's passion for competition.

Although not particularly gifted athletically, Judy worked hard to master the skills necessary to excel. She earned a sports scholarship to Youngstown State University.[5]

Now in her fifties, Christine works as a teacher, coach and mother, ever mindful of a Taylor legacy she regards as one of reward through discipline, hard work and sacrifice.

Notes

Introduction

Intro-1. Thousands turned out is from *Terre Haute Tribune*, 27 March 1927.
Intro-2. Ibid., 23, 24 March 1927.
Intro-3. *Terre Haute Tribune-Star*, 23 Jan. 2000.
Intro-4. Six times is from *Los Angeles Times*, 9 Nov. 1930.
Intro-5. *Terre Haute Tribune*, 9 March 1962.
Intro-6. *Indianapolis Star*, 10 March 1962.

Chapter 1

1. *Terre Haute Tribune*, 16 Dec. 1916.
collection.
3. U.S. Census, 1900 and 1910.
4. *Chicago Daily News*, 12 Nov. 1929.
5. U.S. Census; *Cleveland Plain Dealer*, 27 Aug. 1924.
6. U.S. Census, 1900, 1920; Bud Taylor Jr., telephone interview with author 17 Dec. 2004.
7. International Brotherhood of Teamsters Web site, http://development04.teamster.org/
8. Ibid.
9. Photo in *Terre Haute Tribune*, 16 July 1922.
10. Blond hair from *Cleveland Plain Dealer*, 27 Aug. 1924. Sam's birth date is given variously; likely it was Dec. 16, 1857, as listed in Gillis Funeral Home records in the Special Collections Department of the Vigo County Public Library.
11. *Terre Haute Tribune*, 16 July 1922.
12. Taylor Jr., 4 April 2005.

13. *Terre Haute Tribune*, 16 July 1922.
14. Noel Jacob Kent, *America in 1900*, (New York: M.E. Sharpe, 2000), 80.
15. Ibid, 51,79.
16. Terre Haute city directories from 1900 to 1915.
17. U.S. Census 1870, 1880.
18. Ibid., 1900, 1910.
19. Number of autos in Terre Haute is from *Saturday Spectator*, 24 Jan. 1914.
20. *Chicago Daily Tribune*, 10 March 1962.
21. *Indianapolis Star,* 10 March 1962.
22. *Chicago Daily News*, 12 Nov. 1929.
23. Halpern and Joyce Carol Oates, *Reading the Fights* (New York: Henry Holt & Co., 1988), 118.
24. Joe Frazier with Phil Berger, *Smokin' Joe The Autobiography* (New York: Macmillan, 1996), 8.
25. *Los Angeles Record*, 4 Dec. 1925; *Chicago Daily News*, 12 Nov. 1929.
26. *Los Angeles Record*, 4 Dec. 1925.
27. Roller skating popularity from www.hickoksports.com/history/rollerstatix.shtml. Taylor's childhood skating from *Chicago Daily News*, 12 Nov. 1929.
28. *Terre Haute Tribune*, 18 Nov. 1914.
29. Taylor's early jobs from *Terre Haute Star*, 26 Nov. 1922; *Wisconsin News*, 19 April 1926; *Chicago Daily News*, 12 Nov. 1929.
30. All Orville Taylor death information from *Terre Haute Tribune*, 24, 27 Nov. 1913.
31. Bud did not indicate any doubts about the cause in reports of how Orville died in *Los Angeles Times*, 31 May, 1925; *Terre Haute Tribune*, 17 Sept. 1922.
32. *Los Angeles Times*, 31 May 1925; *Terre Haute Tribune*, 17 Sept. 1922.
33. *Terre Haute Tribune*, 16 July 1922.

Chapter 2
1. Joyce Carol Oates, *Joyce Carol Oates on Boxing* (New York: Dolphin Doubleday, 1987), 31-39.

2. Guy Reel, "The Rise of Modern American Prizefighting," *Journalism History* 27(2), (2001): 73.
3. *Chicago American*, 24 Feb. 1927.
4. *Los Angeles Times*, 20 March 1939.
5. The three fights are reported in *Terre Haute Evening Gazette*, 16, 19 Dec. 1902; 1, 13, 14 Jan., 1903.
6. Ibid., 14 Jan. 1903.
7. *Chicago Daily Tribune*, 20 Nov. 1906.
8. Sullivan's visit is from *Terre Haute Star*, 7 March 1905. Johnson's visit is from *Terre Haute Tribune*, 3 Jan. 1910.
9. *Terre Haute Star*, 18 Feb. 1905.
10. Ibid., 18 Feb. 1905; *Terre Haute Tribune-Star*, 24 June 2001.
11. *Chicago Daily Tribune*, 14 Aug. 1909.
12. Ibid., 14 Aug. 1909; 27 April 1912.
13. *Boston Globe*, 12 Nov. 1909.
14. *Theodore Roosevelt, the Rough Riders, an Autobiography* (New York: Library of America, 2004), 295, 297.
15. *Los Angeles Times*, 29 April 1911.
16. *New York Times*, 28 Aug. 1911.
17. *Terre Haute Star*, 5 June 1934.
18. *Terre Haute Tribune*, 16 Dec. 1915.
19. Information on the mayors and promoters is from *Chicago Daily Tribune*, 27 April 1912; *Terre Haute Tribune*, 4 April 1912, 24 Dec. 1913, 2 Jan., 7 Feb., and 25 Nov. 1914; and *Terre Haute Star*, 25 Nov. 1922.
20. *Terre Haute Tribune*, 24 Dec. 1913.
21. Scandal information is from *Terre Haute Tribune-Star*, 18 Sept. 1995, 4 May 2003.
22. *Terre Haute Tribune*, 16 Dec. 1915; also, the absence of mention of boxing in Terre Haute newspapers over subsequent months.
23. Johnson information from *Terre Haute Star*, 25 Nov. 1922.
24. *Chicago Tribune*, 19 Dec. 1971.
25. Declaration and subsequent military information is from *Terre Haute Tribune*, 27 Dec. 1917, 14 Sept. 1918.
26. *Terre Haute Tribune*, 12 Oct. 1918.
27. Ibid., 24 May 1919.
28. Bert Randolph Sugar, telephone interview with author, 18 Feb. 2005.

29. *Terre Haute Tribune*, 5 Jan. 1919.
30. Ibid.
31. Ibid., 31 Jan. 1940. B.J. Griswold and Edward M. Lucas, *Some Terre Haute Phizes* (Fort Wayne, Ind.: Archer Printing Co., 1905), 132. Terre Haute city directory, 1905.
32. An example is reported in *Terre Haute Tribune*, 22 Nov. 1914.
33. *Terre Haute Tribune* 28 Feb., 29 March, 28 Oct., and 4 Dec., 1919.
34. Ibid., 26, 29 March 1919.
35. Ibid., 19 Jan. 1919.
36. Ibid., 14 Feb. 1919.
37. Ibid., 16, 20 April 1919.
38. Ibid., 17 April 1919.
39. Ibid.
40. Ibid., 16 April 1919.
41. Ibid.
42. Ibid., in separate article of same date.
43. Ibid.
44. Accounts of Dempsey's appearance in *Terre Haute Tribune* and *Terre Haute Star* on 20 April 1919 make no mention of takers on the $1,000 offer.
45. *Terre Haute Star*, 7 Jan. 1920.
46. Return date is given in *Terre Haute Tribune*, 9 March 1919.
47. *Terre Haute Star*, 19 Nov. 1922; *Chicago Daily Tribune*, 12 Jan. 1921.
48. *Terre Haute Star*, 19 Nov. 1922.
49. Jane Mauk, interview with author, Terre Haute, 15 July 2005.
50. Ibid; *Terre Haute Star*, 19 Nov. 1922.
51. Incomes figures are from *Terre Haute Star*, 3 Jan. 1920; *Terre Haute Tribune*, 5 Aug. 1919.
52. *Chicago Herald-Examiner*, 20 March 1927.
53. *Los Angeles Times*, 4 Dec. 1925; *Illinois State Register* (Springfield), 9 June 1930.
54. *Terre Haute Tribune*, 1 Sept. 1921; *Chicago Daily News*, 12 Nov. 1929; *Terre Haute Tribune-Star*, 13 May 1962.
55. *Terre Haute Star*, 26 Nov. 1922; *Chicago Daily News*, 12 Nov. 1929.
56. Rink incident from *Chicago Herald-Examiner*, 20 March 1927. Roberts' age from *Terre Haute Star*, 20 Nov. 1922.

57. Training information is from *Terre Haute Tribune*, 10 June 1919; *Chicago Daily News*, 12 Nov. 1929; *Indianapolis Star*, 7 June 1954; Bud Taylor Jr., telephone interview with author, 17 Dec. 2004.
58. Taylor Jr., 17 Dec. 2004.
59. *Terre Haute Tribune*, 16 July 1922.

Chapter 3
1. *Terre Haute Star*, 25 Nov. 1922; Taylor descendants' family photos.
2. Ibid., 25 Nov. 1922; *Terre Haute Tribune*, 29 May 1909.
3. *Terre Haute Star*, 25 Nov. 1922.
4. Ibid.
5. *Terre Haute Tribune*, 28 Oct. 1919; *Terre Haute Star*, 3 Dec. 1919.
6. *Terre Haute Tribune*, 28 Sept., 3 Dec. 1919.
7. Ibid., 4 Dec. 1919. *Terre Haute Star*, 3 Dec. 1919.
8. *Chicago Daily News*, 12 Nov. 1929.
9. *Terre Haute Tribune*, 25 Jan. 1920; *Terre Haute Star*, 26 Jan. 1920.
10. Weight is from *Los Angeles Record*, 4 Dec. 1925.
11. *Terre Haute Star*, 27 Jan. 1920; *Terre Haute Tribune*, 27 Jan. 1920.
12. Taylor's first boxing pay total is recounted similarly from many sources, among them *Los Angeles Record*, 4 Dec. 1925; *Terre Haute Tribune*, 9 Jan. 1927; *Indianapolis Star*, 7 June 1954.
13. *Chicago Daily News*, 12 Nov. 1929.
14. *Terre Haute Tribune*, 27 Jan. 1920.
15. Much of Langford information is from Bert Randolph Sugar, *The 100 Greatest Boxers of All Time* (New York: Bonanza Books, 1984), 35; and www.boxrec.com.
16. *Terre Haute Tribune*, 17 Feb. 1920.
17. Bert Randolph Sugar, telephone interview with author, 18 Feb. 2005.
18. *Terre Haute Tribune*, 11 Sept. 1924.
19. Ibid., 16 July 1924.
20. Ibid., 28 June 1925.

21. Battle royal number comes from author's count beginning with *Vincennes Morning Commercial*, 6 June 1920, to *Terre Haute Tribune*, 19 March 1929.
22. *Terre Haute Star*, 16 Feb. 1920.
23. Accounts of Everett fight are from *Los Angeles Evening Herald*, 7 Dec. 1925; *Terre Haute Tribune*, 17 Feb. 1920.
24. *Terre Haute Star*, 17 Feb. 1920; *Terre Haute Tribune*, 5 March 1920.
25. *Terre Haute Tribune*, 9 Jan. 1927.
26. *Terre Haute Star*, 26 Nov. 1922; *Terre Haute Tribune*, 17 April 1920.
27. *Terre Haute Tribune*, 12, 14 March, 1920.
28. *Terre Haute Star*, 7 March 1920.
29. Ibid., 17, 20, 21, 22, Nov., 1922. *Terre Haute Tribune*, 17 May 1920.
30. *Terre Haute Star*, 16 March 1920.
31. *Terre Haute Tribune*, 16 March 1921.
32. Ibid., 17 April 1920. U.S. Census for Sullivan County, 1920.
33. *Terre Haute Tribune*, 14 May 1920.
34. *Muncie Morning Star*, 25 May 1920. Unidentified newspaper clipping dated 25 May 1920 from private collection of Vigo County historian B. Michael McCormick.
35. *Muncie Morning Star*, 25 May 1920.
36. Edwards' biography is from *Marion Chronicle-Tribune*, 14 Jan. 1998; *Marion Chronicle Tribune Magazine*, 2 Nov. 1975.
37. *Terre Haute Tribune*, 25 May, 1920; *Terre Haute Star*, 25 May 1920.
38. *Terre Haute Tribune*, 7 March 1921; *Terre Haute Star*, 6 June 1920.
39. *Terre Haute Tribune*, 22 Aug. 1920, 7 March 1921.
40. Ibid., 27 March, 1921; 9 July 1922.

Chapter 4
1. *Milwaukee Sentinel*, 10 March 1962.
2. Twenty-five dollars is from *Terre Haute Tribune*, 9 Jan. 1927.
3. Attendance, admission, from *Muncie Morning Star*, 2 Aug. 1920.
4. *Vincennes Morning Commercial*, 6 June 1920.
5. *Chicago Daily Times*, 12 Jan. 1921.

6. *Terre Haute Tribune*, 10-17 Oct. 1920.
7. Amount paid is from Ibid., 9 Jan. 1927.
9. *Terre Haute Tribune*, 5 Oct. 1920; *Terre Haute Star*, 11 Oct. 1920.
10. *Terre Haute Star*, 5 Oct. 1920.
11. *Terre Haute Tribune*, 17 Sept. 1922.
12. Scandinavian reference is from *Cleveland Plain Dealer*, 27 Aug. 1924.
13. *Terre Haute Star*, 28 June 1925.
14. *Terre Haute Tribune*, 2 Nov. 1920.
15. Quote is from Ibid., 1 Nov. 1920.
16. *Terre Haute Star*, 2 Nov. 1920.
17. *Terre Haute Tribune*, 9 Jan. 1927; *Terre Haute Star*, 2 Nov. 1920.
18. *Cincinnati Enquirer*, 5 Nov. 1920.
19. Fight accounts from Ibid., 9 Nov. 1920; *Terre Haute Tribune*, 9 Nov. 1920.
20. *Terre Haute Tribune*, 14 Dec. 1920.
21. Ibid.

Chapter 5

1. The French being there as early as the 1600s is from Blackford Condit, *The History of Early Terre Haute from 1816 to 1840* (New York: A.S. Barnes, 1900), 12.
2. The date of 1811 is from Ibid., p. 37.
3. H.C. Bradsby, *History of Vigo County, Indiana, With Biographical Selections* (Chicago: S.B. Nelson & Co., 1891), 238-241. Terre Haute Tribune, 4 June 1931. U.S. Censuses, early 1800s.
4. Condit, pp. 12, 64. Dorothy J. Clark, *Terre Haute Wabash River City* (Woodland Hills, Calif.: Windsor Publications, 1983), 16.
5. Population is from F.J. Gardon, *Twentieth Century Souvenir of Terre Haute* (Terre Haute: Moore & Langen, 1903), Introductory.
6. Ibid., Introductory. Clark, p. 48.
7. http://en.wikipedia.org. Also, http://specials.tribstar.com/hulman/building/philanthropy
8. Examples: *Terre Haute Tribune*, 29 Aug., 29 Oct. 1920; 20 June 1921. *Terre Haute Star*, 6 Sept. 1920.

9. *Terre Haute Star*, 6 Sept. 1920.
10. *Terre Haute Tribune*, 20 June 1921.
11. Ibid., 31 March 1928.
12. Ibid., 8-10 Dec., 1919.
13. Ibid., 10 Dec., 1919.
14. Wagner information from *Los Angeles Times*, 12 Aug. 1924; *Terre Haute Tribune-Star*, 20 Sept. 2002.
15. Mason's record and cities are from www.boxrec.com
16. Weight is from *Fort Wayne Journal-Gazette*, 17 July 1929. www.boxrec.com
17. *Terre Haute Tribune*, 18 Jan. 1921; *Fort Wayne Journal-Gazette*, 17 July 1929.
18. *Terre Haute Tribune*, 18 Feb. 1920.
19. Ibid.
20. *South Bend News-Times*, 19 Nov. 1919.
21. Ibid.
22. *Fort Wayne Journal-Gazette,* 4 Sept. 1920; *Terre Haute Tribune*, 3 Sept. 1920.
23. *Terre Haute Tribune*, 10 Jan. 1921; 12 March 1922.
24. Tierney and Baker's pre-fight opinions are from Ibid., 18 Jan. 1921.
25. *Terre Haute Star*, 2 Jan. 1921.
26. Ibid.
27. *Terre Haute Tribune*, 9, 16 Jan. 1921.
28. Quotes are from Ibid., 17 Jan. 1921.
29. Ibid., 18 Jan. 1921.
30. Ibid., in two separate articles.
31. *Terre Haute Tribune*, 18 Jan. 1921; *Terre Haute Star*, 18, Jan. 1921.
32. *Fort Wayne Journal-Gazette*, 17 July 1929.

Chapter 6

1. Various references to nickname as early as *Terre Haute Tribune*, 28 Dec. 1922.
2. Ibid., 1 Feb. 1921. *St. Louis Post-Dispatch*, 1 Feb. 1921.
3. *Terre Haute Tribune*, 1 Feb. 1921. *Terre Haute Star*, 1 Feb. 1921.
4. *Terre Haute Star*, 1 Feb., 1921. *St. Louis Post-Dispatch*, 1 Feb. 1921.

5. *Los Angeles Herald Express*, 28 Aug. 1937.
6. *Terre Haute Tribune*, 1 Feb. 1921.
7. Training and Bud's involvement in the boxing subculture are from *Terre Haute Tribune*, 24, 28 Dec. 1920; 8, 24 Feb., 15 March, 22 Nov. 1921; 8 April, 11 Nov. 1922.
8. Ibid., 27 Sept. 1921; 9 January, 26 March 1923.
9. Ibid., 23 Feb. 1921.
10. *Terre Haute Star*, 17 Feb. 1920.
11. Ibid, 1 March 1921; *Terre Haute Tribune*, 1 March 1921.
12. *Terre Haute Tribune*, 13 March 1921.
13. Ibid., 23 March 1921. *Terre Haute Star*, 22 March 1921.
14. *Terre Haute Tribune*, 22 March 1921.
15. Ibid., 24 March, 30 Oct. 1921.
16. Ibid., 4 April 1921.
17. Fight account is from Ibid., 5 April 1921; *Terre Haute Star*, 5 April 1921.
18. *Terre Haute Tribune*, 25 Feb., 1 April 1921.
19. Ibid., 5 April 1921.
20. Long and Kane's first encounter with Taylor as recounted in Ibid., 31 Dec. 1922, 1 April 1923; *Los Angeles Record*, 18 June 1925.
21. O'Keefe anecdote is from *Chicago Daily Calumet*, 21 June 1962.
22. Unknown newspaper clipping dated 19 July 1921 from collection of Vigo County historian B. Michael McCormick.
23. Ibid.
24. Wide disagreement on who won, thus a "draw." See Ibid., 19, 26 July 1921; *Louisville Courier-Journal*, 26 July 1921. Chink's real name is from *Terre Haute Tribune*, 18 Jan. 1923.
25. *Terre Haute Tribune*, 21 Aug. 1921.

Chapter 7

1. *Los Angeles Times*, 27 Oct. 1925; *Terre Haute Tribune*, 29 June 1924. Dick Brokaw, interview with author, Terre Haute, 19 Nov. 2004.
2. *Evansville Courier*, 15 Sept. 1929.
3. *Terre Haute Tribune*, 7, 9 Oct. 1921.
4. Ibid., 9 Oct. 1921.

5. Quotes are from Ibid., 7, 9 Oct. 1921.
6. Ibid., 11 Oct. 1921. *Terre Haute Star*, 11 Oct. 1921.
7. *Terre Haute Star*, 13 Oct. 1921.
8. Ibid., 11, 13 Oct. 1921; *Terre Haute Tribune*, 11 Oct. 1921.
9. *Terre Haute Tribune*, 30 Oct., 1921.
10. Jim Long, telephone interview with author, 11 April, 2006.
11. *Chicago Daily Calumet*, 29 June 1962.
12. Ibid., 30 June 1962.
13. Sites and results are from *Chicago Herald-Examiner*, 5 Dec. 1921; *Terre Haute Star*, 30 Dec. 1921; *Terre Haute Tribune*, 26 Feb., 1922.
14. *Chicago Daily Calumet*, 29 June 1962.
15. Dick Brokaw, interview with author, Terre Haute, 11 March 2005.
16. Examples: *Terre Haute Star*, 22 March 1921; *Terre Haute Tribune*, 26 July 1921; *Logansport Morning Press*, 16 May 1922; *Los Angeles Evening-Herald*, 20 Nov. 1925.
17. Nigel Collins, *Boxing Babylon* (New York: Citadel Press, 1990), 50.
18. Taylor quotes on Greb are from *Los Angeles Times*, 10 Jan. 1926; *Los Angeles Record*, 23 Oct. 1925.
19. Peter Heller, *In This Corner* (New York; Simon & Schuster, 1973), 247.
20. *Terre Haute Star*, 29 Dec. 1921.

Chapter 8

1. *Terre Haute Star*, 13 Oct. 1921.
2. Ibid.
3. Ibid., 3 Jan. 1922.
4. Valentino note is from *Ring* magazine, 23 Nov. 1923.
5. *Terre Haute Tribune*, 4 Jan. 1922; *Terre Haute Star*, 4 Jan. 1922.
6. *Terre Haute Tribune*, 5 Jan. 1922.
7. *Terre Haute Star*, 5 Jan. 1922.
8. Ibid., separate article.
9. Weigh-in and fight accounts from *Terre Haute Star*, 6 Jan. 1922; *Terre Haute Tribune*, 6 Jan. 1922; *Indianapolis News*, 6 Jan. 1922.

Chapter 9

1. *Terre Haute Star*, 22 July 1923 says Blackburn had been tutoring Taylor for a year, although Taylor was working out as early as January 1922 with Mandell under Blackburn's supervision per *Terre Haute Tribune*, 17 Jan. 1922.
2. *Chicago Defender*, 2 May 1942.
3. Ronald K. Fried, *Corner Men, Great Boxing Trainers* (New York: Four Walls Eight Windows, 1991), 117. Richard Bak, *Joe Louis, the Great Black Hope* (Dallas: Taylor Publishing, 1996), 48. Also, www.harrygreb.com at the Blackburn biography page.
4. Bak, p. 45; Fried, pp. 117, 120, 126; *Chicago Defender*, 2 May 1942.
5. Blackburn's intimidating presence and astute teaching methods are from Fried, pp. 112, 117, 120; Bak, p. 24.
6. *Terre Haute Tribune*, 5 Sept. 1923; Dick Brokaw, interview with author, Terre Haute, 5 Nov. 2004.
7. *Terre Haute Tribune*, 3 Jan. 1922.
8. Ibid., 15 Jan. 1922. *Chicago American*, 14 Jan. 1922.
9. *Chicago American*, 14 Jan. 1922.
10. End of bout is from Ibid.; *Los Angeles Herald-Express* 21 Nov. 1938.
11. *Chicago Daily Tribune*, 7 Feb. 1922.
12. Ibid., 9 Feb. 1922.
13. Ibid., 21 Sept. 1922.
14. Walker was Taylor's favorite is from *Chicago American*, 9 Feb. 1928; *Chicago Evening Post*, 29 Feb. 1928.
15. *Terre Haute Tribune*, 2 March 1922.
16. Ibid., 17 Jan. 1922.
17. Ibid., 3 Aug. 1924.
18. Ibid., 17, 18, 24 Jan. 1922.
19. Ibid., 30 Jan. 1922.
20. *Chicago Daily Tribune*, 17 March 1922; *Milwaukee Journal*, 21 March 1922.
21. *Chicago Daily Tribune*, 10 Feb. 1922.
22. Unknown newspaper clipping dated 10 Feb. 1922 from Joyce Boxing Collection, Hesburgh Library, University of Notre Dame, Bud Taylor file.

23. Fight account is from *Chicago American*, 11 Feb., 1922; Terre Haute Tribune, 11 Feb. 1922; *Chicago Daily Tribune*, 11 Feb. 1922.
24. *Chicago American*, 11 Feb. 1922.
25. *Terre Haute Tribune*, 18 March 1922.
26. *Chicago Daily Tribune*, 23 March 1922; *Terre Haute Tribune*, 23 March 1922.
27. *Terre Haute Tribune*, 23 March 1922.
28. Ibid., 26 Feb., 1922.
29. Year of discovery is from Judith S. Baughman, *American Decades 1920-1929* (Detroit: Gale Research, 1995), 344-45.
30. *Los Angeles Times*, 23 Oct. 1927.
31. *Terre Haute Tribune*, 17 Oct. 1923.
32. Brokaw, interview with author, Terre Haute, 19 Nov. 2004.
33. Description of human hand from www.bartleby.com.
34. Brokaw, interview with author, Terre Haute, 8 Dec. 2004.
35. Seating capacity is from *Chicago Daily Tribune*, 3 May 1922.
36. Records courtesy www.boxrec.com
37. Moore's record, Ibid.
38. *Chicago Daily Tribune*, 23, 24 June 1922.
39. *Indianapolis Daily Times*, 16 June 1922; *Terre Haute Tribune*, 13 June 1922.
40. *Terre Haute Tribune*, 24 June 1922.
41. *Los Angeles Herald-Express*, 21 Nov. 1938.
42. Fight account is from *Chicago Daily Tribune*, 24 June 1922; *Terre Haute Tribune*, 24 June 1922.

Chapter 10
1. *Terre Haute Tribune*, 25 June 1922. Asher's results from www.boxrec.com
2. *Terre Haute Tribune*, 30 June 1922.
3. Dick Brokaw, interview with author, Terre Haute, 9 Dec. 2004.
4. Ibid.
5. *Terre Haute Tribune*, 30 June, 30 Aug. 1922; 28 Aug. 1923.
6. Ibid., 30 June 1922.
7. Ibid., 25 May 1924.
8. *Chicago American*, 23 Feb. 1927.
9. Jim Long, telephone interview with author, 20 Dec. 2006.

10. *Terre Haute Tribune*, 5 July 1922.
11. Ibid.
12. Ibid., 21 July 1921.
13. Number of Terre Haute taverns is from Ibid., 30 Jan. 1921. Selling liquor on the sly is deduced from the numerous newspaper accounts of arrests and their location.
14. Bill Lowe, interview with author, 20 Feb. 2005. Brokaw, 23 Dec. 2004.
15. Jeffries court information from *Terre Haute Star*, 16 July 1922; *Terre Haute Tribune-Star*, 19 Aug. 1956. Light sentences is from *Terre Haute Tribune*, 2 March 1922.
16. *Terre Haute Tribune*, 2 March 1922.
17. Ibid., 17 Feb. 1925.
18. Ibid., 2 Aug. 1924.
19. *Terre Haute Star*, 12 Feb. 1922.
20. *Terre Haute Tribune*, 29 Nov. 1920. Used conversion chart at U.S. Department of Labor Bureau of Statistics Web site: www.bls.gov/cpi.
21. *Terre Haute Tribune*, 4 Feb. 1921.
22. Hip containers referred to in Ibid., 5 July 1922; Brokaw, 23 Dec. 2004.
23. *Terre Haute Tribune*, 5 July 1922.
24. Judith Baughman, *American Decades 1920-1929* (Detroit: Gale Research, 1995), pp. 152, 154, 156, 269.
25. *Terre Haute Tribune-Star*, 26 Aug. 1995.
26. *Terre Haute Tribune*, 10 April, 4 May 1921.
27. Ibid., 5 July 1922.
28. Ibid., 5, 16 July 1922.
29. Edith Taylor interview Ibid., 16 July 1922.
30. Earnings deduced from Ibid., 1 April 1923. Third Avenue home from *Terre Haute Star*, 26 Nov. 1922.
31. *Terre Haute Star*, 26 Nov. 1922.
32. Ibid.
33. *Terre Haute Tribune*, 31 July 1922.
34. *Terre Haute Star*, 26 Nov. 1922.
35. *Terre Haute Tribune*, 5 July 1922.

36. Ibid., 1 Jan. 1924. *Terre Haute Star*, 28 June 1925. *Terre Haute Tribune-Star*, 8 Oct. 1994. Various newspaper photos. Bud Taylor Jr., telephone interview with author, 17 Dec. 2004. Patty Ewald, "Re Bud Taylor info" e-mail interview with author, 7 Dec. 2006.
37. Nasal drawl is from *Terre Haute Star*, 28 June 1925.
38. Taylor Jr., 17 Dec. 2004; Brokaw, 23 Dec. 2004.
39. Edginess before a fight is from *Los Angeles Herald-Express*, 21 Nov. 1938.

Chapter 11
1. *Terre Haute Tribune*, 16 July 1922.
2. Ibid., 5 Sept. 1922. *Terre Haute Star*, 5 Sept. 1922.
3. www.boxrec.com
4. *Chicago American*, 19 Sept. 1922.
5. *Terre Haute Tribune*, 19 Sept. 1922. *Chicago Daily Tribune*, 19 Sept. 1922.
6. www.boxrec.com
7. *Terre Haute Tribune*, 19 Sept. 1922.
8. Open air and fan who was a packer details are from *Chicago American*, 19 Sept. 1922.
9. Ibid., 17 Sept. 1922.
10. *Chicago Daily Calumet*, 21 June 1962.
11. Fight account and Taylor's resolve are from *Gary Post-Tribune*, 22 Sept. 1922; *Terre Haute Tribune*, 23, 25 Sept. 1922. Smith career facts from www.boxrec.com
12. *Terre Haute Star*, 27 Sept. 1922; *Terre Haute Tribune*, 12 Nov. 1922.
13. *Terre Haute Tribune*, 27 Sept. 1922.
14. *Chicago American*, 5 Sept. 1923.
15. Jim Long, telephone interview with author, 29 Dec. 2005.
16. *Chicago Daily Tribune*, 12 Aug. 1900.
17. *Los Angeles Times*, 1 April 1928.
18. Long, 16 May 2006.
19. *Los Angeles Times*, 16 March 1962.
20. Long, 29 Dec. 2005.
21. *Terre Haute Star*, 23 Dec. 1922.
22. *Terre Haute Tribune*, 26 Dec. 1922.

23. *Chicago Herald-Examiner*, 26 Dec. 1922; *Chicago Daily Tribune*, 23 Dec. 1922; *Indianapolis Times*, 27 Dec. 1922; *Chicago Daily Journal*, 23 Dec. 1922.
24. *Chicago Herald-Examiner*, 26 Dec. 1922.
25. Summary of 1922 year in boxing are from *Indianapolis Star*, 31 Dec. 1922.
26. Quote and information about deal are from *Terre Haute Tribune*, 28 Dec., 1922.

Chapter 12
1. Fight details are from *Indianapolis Star*, 2 Jan. 1923; *Terre Haute Star*, 2 Jan. 1923; *Terre Haute Tribune*, 2 Jan. 1923.
2. *Terre Haute Tribune*, 5 Jan. 1923.
3. *Chicago Daily Tribune*, 25 March 1927.
4. *Los Angeles Times*, 20 March 1939.
5. Fight details from *Chicago Daily Tribune*, 16 Jan. 1923; *Terre Haute Tribune*, 16 Jan. 1923; *East Chicago Times*, 16 Jan. 1923. Inaugural event from Times, 25 Jan. 1924. Arena location from *Chicago Daily Journal*, 8 Jan. 1923.
6. Bud's pay revealed in *Terre Haute Tribune*, 14 Feb. 1923.
7. Ibid., 20 Feb. 1923.
8. *Chicago Daily Tribune*, 14 Feb. 1923. Site of Hall is from Labor History Map of Indianapolis, www.labormap.org/sites.asp?12
9. Number of paved miles is from *Terre Haute Tribune*, 31 Oct. 1922. Number of Hauteans is from Tribune, 14 Feb. 1923.
10. *Chicago Daily Tribune*, 14 Feb. 1923.
11. *Terre Haute Tribune*, 14 Feb. 1923; *Terre Haute Star*, 14 Feb. 1923.
12. *Terre Haute Tribune*, 14 Feb. 1923.
13. *Chicago Daily Tribune*, 14 Feb. 1923.
14. *Terre Haute Tribune*, 4 March 1928; 13 June 1938.
15. Ibid., 13 April 1921; 13 June 1938.
16. Davis' accomplishments from Ibid., 13 June 1938.
17. Ibid., 13, 17 March, 28 April 1923; *Chicago Daily Tribune*, 14 Feb. 1923.
18. *Terre Haute Tribune*, 3 June 1923.
19. Ibid., 15 Oct. 1924.
20. Ibid., 27 April 1928.

21. Ibid., 1 Aug. 1924.
22. Ibid., 10 May 1925.
23. *Terre Haute Star*, 28 June 1925.

Chapter 13
1. *Terre Haute Tribune* , 23 Feb. 1923.
2. *Terre Haute Star*, 13 May 1923.
3. *Terre Haute Tribune*, 24 Feb. 1923.
4. Ibid., 24 Feb., 3 March 1923.
5. Restless days is from Ibid., 28 Feb. 1923. Dyer's call from Ibid., 27 Feb. 1923.
6. Ibid., 3 March 1923.
7. Ibid.
8. Genaro as described in *Milwaukee Journal*, 5 May 1926.
9. *Terre Haute Tribune*, 3 April 1923.
10. *Chicago American*, 4 April 1923.
11. *Terre Haute Tribune*, 3 April 1923. Gym location is from Chicago Daily News, 20 July 1926.
12. *Terre Haute Tribune*, 3 April 1923.
13. Ibid., 20 March, 11 April 1923.
14. Low: *Chicago Evening Post*, 5 April 1923. High: *Chicago Daily News*, 5 April 1923.
15. *Terre Haute Tribune*, 3 April 1923.
16. Ibid., 5 April 1923. *Chicago Daily Journal*, 5 April 1923; *Chicago Evening Post*, 5 April 1923; *Chicago Daily Tribune*, 5 April 1923; *Chicago American*, 5 April 1923; *Chicago Daily News*, 5 April 1923.
17. *Chicago Daily Tribune*, 5 April 1923.
18. *Los Angeles Times*, 24 June 1925.
19. *Terre Haute Tribune*, 28 Jan., 3 April 1921; 10 May 1924.
20. Ibid., 9 Jan. 1927.
21. *Terre Haute Star*, 3 Aug. 1923; *Los Angeles Times*, 15, 24 June 1925.
22. *Terre Haute Star*, 3 Aug. 1923; *Los Angeles Times*, 15, 24 June 1925.
23. *Terre Haute Tribune*, 20 Feb., 8 March 1924.
24. *Chicago Evening Post*, 21 May 1928.
25. *Terre Haute Tribune*, 23 April 1923.

26. *Terre Haute Tribune-Star*, 3 Dec. 2004.
27. Ticket prices and sales are from *Terre Haute Tribune*, 19, 26 June, 1923.
28. Ibid., 30 May 1923.
29. Ibid., 26 June, 22 July 1923.
30. Ibid., 8 Jan. 1923. *South Bend Times*, 6 Sept. 1921.
31. *Terre Haute Tribune*, 25 Nov. 1923.
32. *Terre Haute Star*, 3 Aug. 1923.
33. *Terre Haute Tribune*, 5 July 1923.
34. *Terre Haute Star*, 5 July 1923.
35. Sources on Dempsey-Gibbons: Roger Kahn, *A Flame of Pure Fire, Jack Dempsey and the Roaring Twenties* (New York: Harcourt Brace & Co., 1999), 307-319; Tim Gibbons of Tommy and Mike Gibbons Preservation Society, "Re boxing, Bud Taylor," 13 Dec. 2005, personal e-mail, 13 Dec. 2005; *Terre Haute Tribune*, 25 Nov. 1923.

Chapter 14

1. *Chicago Daily Tribune*, 13 July 1923. Gordon's record from www.boxrec.com
2. *Terre Haute Star*, 22 July 1923. Richard Bak, *Joe Louis, the Great Black Hope* (Dallas: Taylor Publishing, 1996), 45, 48.
3. Taylor-Gordon fight account is from *Chicago Daily Tribune*, 8 June 1944; *Los Angeles Herald-Express*, 21 Nov. 1938; *Sports Weekly*, 17 Nov. 1939; *Chicago Daily Tribune*, 21 July 1923; *Terre Haute Tribune*, 21 July 1923.
4. White's words from *Terre Haute Tribune*, 11 Aug. 1923. Mrs. Pfeiffer's first name from Terre Haute city directory listings.
5. "Poor" is deduced from neighborhood location, number of members of household and household head occupation in U.S. Census and city directories.
6. Various newspaper photographs.
7. Patty Ewald, interview with author, Canastota, N.Y., 11 June 2005. Definition of "flapper" from William and Mary Morris, *Morris Dictionary of Word and Phrase Origins* (New York: Harper & Row, 1977), 223.
8. *Terre Haute Tribune*, 11 Aug. 1923.

9. Vigo County Clerk's office records lists the divorce filings as for 25 April 1924 and 13 Aug. 1927. *Chicago American*, 5 Sept. 1923. Bud Taylor Jr., telephone interview with author, 28 April 2005; 8 Dec. 2004. Custody hearings, *Terre Haute Tribune*, 10, 11 Oct. 1929; *Terre Haute Star*, 10, 11, 1929. *Star*, 3 Aug. 1923 calls Bud an "exceptionally clean liver."
10. *Terre Haute Tribune*, 28 Aug. 1923.
11. Ibid., 31 Aug. 1923.
12. www.boxrec.com
13. *Chicago American*, 25 Feb. 1927.
14. Villa's record from www.boxrec.com
15. Fight account from *Terre Haute Star*, 4 Sept. 1923; *Sports Weekly*, 17 Nov. 1939.
16. *Terre Haute Star*, 4 Sept. 1923.
17. *Terre Haute Tribune*, 5, 6 Sept. 1923.

Chapter 15

1. Nigel Collins, *Boxing Babylon* (New York: Citadel Press, 1990), 44-49.
2. Bert Randolph Sugar, *The 100 Greatest Boxers of All Time* (New York: Bonanza Books, 1984), 112.
3. Ibid.
4. Collins, p. 44-49.
5. *Chicago Daily Tribune*, 10 March 1934.
6. *Terre Haute Tribune*, 8 Sept. 1923.
7. Ibid., 7 Sept. 1923.
8. Ibid., 5 Sept. 1923
9. Ibid., 9 Sept. 1923. *Indianapolis Star*, 9 Sept. 1923.
10. *Terre Haute Tribune*, 9 Sept. 1923.
11. Ibid., 8 Sept. 1923.
12. Ibid., 10 Sept. 1923.
13. *Terre Haute Star*, 9 Sept. 1923.
14. *Terre Haute Tribune*, 9 Sept. 1923.
15. Ibid.
16. *Chicago Daily Tribune*, 9 Sept. 1923.
17. *Terre Haute Tribune*, 9 Sept. 1923; *Chicago Herald-Examiner*, 9 Sept. 1923; Chicago Daily News, 9 Sept. 1923.

18. *Chicago Daily Tribune*, 9 Sept. 1923.
19. Ibid.
20. *Terre Haute Tribune*, 9 Sept. 1923.
21. Ibid., 10 Sept. 1923.
22. *Terre Haute Star*, 16 Nov. 1922; 5 June 1934.
23. Examples: *Terre Haute Tribune*, 27 Nov. 1922; 24 June 1923; 18, 22 July 1923,
24. *Terre Haute Tribune*, 13 March, 30 May 1923; 14 Sept. 1924.
25. *Ring* magazine, October 1923.
26. *Time* magazine, 23 June, 1924, www.time.com/time/archive
27. Bud Taylor Jr., telephone interview with author, 17 Dec. 2004.
28. *Terre Haute Tribune*, 17 Oct. 1923.
29. Roger Kahn, *A Flame of Pure Fire*, Jack Dempsey and the Roaring Twenties (New York: Harcourt Brace & Co., 1999), 38-39, 43. International Boxing Hall of Fame Web site at www.ibhof.com.
30. Kahn, pp. 38-39, 43. Also, www.ibhof.com.
31. *New York Times*, 19 March 1929.
32. *Terre Haute Tribune*, 2, 8 Oct. 1923.
33. Ibid., 17 Oct. 1923.
34. Ibid., 20, 22 Oct. 1923. *Terre Haute Star*, 22 Oct. 1923.
35. *Terre Haute Tribune*, 22 Oct. 1923.
36. Ibid., 29 Nov. 1923.
37. Ibid., 25 Nov. 1923.
38. Ibid., 29 Nov. 1923. Capacity of theater from *Terre Haute Tribune-Star*, 10 Dec. 2004.
39. *Terre Haute Star*, 2 Dec. 1923.
40. Ibid, 3 Dec. 1923.
41. Moore fight results from www.boxrec.com
42. Moore's age, fight details and quote from *Terre Haute Tribune*, 6 Dec. 1923.
43. Ibid., 7 Dec. 1923; *Terre Haute Star*, 8 Dec. 1923.
44. *Indianapolis Star*, 4 Jan. 1924.
45. Among sources that document his goal was a championship: *Terre Haute Tribune*, 3 March, 17 Oct., 4 Dec. 1923.

Chapter 16

1. http://en.wikipedia.org/wiki/20th_Century_Limited.
2. Fragile hands felt strong is from *Terre Haute Tribune*, 6 Jan. 1924. Fight details are from *Tribune*, 2 Jan. 1924; *Indianapolis Star*, 8 Jan. 1924.
3. *Terre Haute Tribune*, 6, 15 Jan. 1924.
4. *New York Times*, 24 Jan. 1923.
5. Early life and electric fan anecdote from *Ring* magazine, Dec. 1923.
6. *New York Tribune*, 14 Jan. 1923.
7. *Ring*, Dec. 1923.
8. "Likable" from *Ring*, Jan. 1925. Facial description from photo in *Ring*, Feb. 1924.
9. *Ring*, Jan. 1925.
10. *New York Times*, 24 Nov., 29 Dec. 1923.
11. Ibid., 12 March 1943.
12. Ibid., 24, 25 Nov. 1923.
13. Ibid., 29 Dec., 1923.
14. Ibid., 14 Jan. 1924.
15. Ibid., 12 Jan. 1924.
16. *New York Tribune*, 12 Jan. 1924.
17. *New York World*, 12 Jan. 1924.
18. *New York Tribune*, 12 Jan. 1924.
19. Details about the felling blow are from Ibid., 12 Jan. 1924; *Terre Haute Tribune*, 15 Jan. 1924; *New York Times*, 15 Jan. 1924.
20. *New York Tribune*, 12 Jan. 1924.
21. *New York Times*, 15 Jan. 1924.
22. Last round action is from Ibid., 12 Jan. 1924; *New York Tribune*, 12 Jan. 1924.
23. *New York Tribune*, 12 Jan. 1924.
24. *New York Times*, 15 Jan. 1924.
25. *Beloit (Wisc.) Daily News* clipping with unknown publication date, datelined 15 Jan. 1924, New York, in archives of Antiquities of the Prize Ring, Hilliard, Ohio.
26. Visitors, diagnosis, surgery and Jerome's quote from Terre Haute Tribune, 14 Jan. 1924. Taylor visited Jerome is from *Boxing Illustrated Wrestling News*, June 1962.

27. *Terre Haute Tribune*, 14 Jan. 1924.
28. Ronald K. Fried, *Corner Men, Great Boxing Trainers* (New York: Four Walls, Eight Windows, 1991), 197.
29. Quoted material is from *Terre Haute Tribune*, 15 Jan. 1924.
30. Ibid., 14 Jan. 1924, two separate articles.
31. *New York Times*, 15 Jan. 1924.
32. Ibid.
33. Ibid.
34. *Terre Haute Tribune*, 15 Jan. 1924.
35. *Terre Haute Star*, 16 Jan. 1924.
36. *New York Times*, 15 Jan. 1924.
37. Ibid., 16 Jan. 1924.
38. *Chicago Daily Tribune*, 15 Jan. 1924.
39. *New York Times*, 16 Jan. 1924.
40. Ibid., 12, 14 Jan. 1924. *Terre Haute Tribune*, 14 Jan. 1924.
41. Attendance at funeral and Pegler's passage from *Atlanta Constitution*, 18 Jan. 1924; www.poynter.org
42. *Sports History*, vol. 3, No. 5, 1990, p. 12.
43. *Terre Haute Tribune*, 16 Jan. 1924.
44. *Terre Haute Star*, 19 Jan. 1924.
45. *New York Times*, 16 Jan. 1924.
46. *Terre Haute Tribune*, 16 Jan. 1924; *Chicago Daily Tribune*, 16 Jan. 1924; Vermont Boxing History Web site under "History Worth Repeating" at http://esf.uvm.edu/vtbox/.
47. *Washington Post*, 20 Feb. 1924.
48. *Terre Haute Tribune*, 14 Jan. 1924.
49. *Beloit [Wis.] Daily News*, clipping with unknown publication date, datelined 15 Jan. 1924, New York, in archives of Antiquities of the Prize Ring, Hilliard, Ohio.
50. *New York Times*, 7 Dec. 1924.
51. *Terre Haute Tribune*, 28 Nov. 1924.
52. Ibid., 9 Dec. 1923.
53. Ibid., 18 Jan. 1924.

Chapter 17
1. Phenomenon mentioned in *Chicago Daily Tribune*, 24 Jan. 1924, 16 Dec. 1968; *Los Angeles Times*, 12 Aug. 1965; *Fort Wayne News-Sentinel*, 17 July 1929; *East Chicago Times*, 26 Jan. 1924.

2. *Terre Haute Tribune*, 22, 29 Jan. 1924; *Terre Haute Star*, 29 Jan. 1924; *East Chicago Times*, 29 Jan. 1924.
3. *Terre Haute Tribune*, 22 Jan. 1924.
4. Ibid., 24 Jan. 1924.
5. Ibid., 23 Jan. 1924.
6. Schaeffer spectator incident from *Chicago Daily Journal*, 29 Jan. 1924.
7. *Ohio State Journal* (Columbus), 6 Feb. 1924.
8. Ibid., 8 Feb. 1924. *Terre Haute Tribune*, 9 Feb. 1924.
9. *Los Angeles Times*, 22 Sept. 1924.
10. *Terre Haute Tribune*, 8 Feb. 1924.
11. Ibid., 22 Oct. 1923; 20 Feb. 1924; *Chicago Daily Tribune*, 27 May 1924; *St. Louis Post-Dispatch*, 22 March 1921.
12. Roger Kahn, *A Flame of Pure Fire, Jack Dempsey and the Roaring Twenties* (New York: Harcourt Brace & Co., 1999), 73-74, 83.
13. *Indianapolis Star*, 19 Feb. 1924.
14. *Terre Haute Tribune*, 20 Feb. 1924.
15. Ibid., 6, 26 Jan., 25, 26, 27 Feb., 1924.
16. Ibid., 27 Feb. 1924.
17. Ibid., 17, 27 Feb., 2 March 1924; *Indianapolis Star*, 16 March 1924.
18. *Milwaukee Journal*, 6 March 1924.
19. *Chicago Daily Tribune*, 7 March 1924.
20. Ibid.
21. *Milwaukee Leader*, 7 March 1924.
22. *Milwaukee Journal*, 7 March 1924.
23. *Wisconsin News*, 7 March 1924.
24. Gate total is from *Chicago Daily Tribune*, 7 March 1924.
25. *Terre Haute Tribune*, 8 March 1924; *Milwaukee Journal*, 8 March 1924.
26. *Terre Haute Tribune*, 2, 8 March 1924.
27. *New York Times*, 18 March 1924.
28. *Terre Haute Tribune*, 11 March 1924.
29. Ibid., 14, 18 March, 1924.
30. Ibid., 16 March 1924.
31. Ibid., 22 March 1924.
32. Ibid., 23 March, 6 May 1924.

33. Ibid., 23 March, 6 May 1924. Record from www.boxrec.com
34. *Indianapolis News*, 1 April 1924; *Terre Haute Tribune*, 20 April 1924.
35. *Terre Haute Tribune*, 27 May 1924 shows Taylor had signed to fight Villa.
36. www.boxrec.com.
37. *Terre Haute Tribune*, 8 April 1924.
38. *Aurora Beacon-News*, 21 May 1924.
39. Lester Bromberg, *Boxing's Unforgettable Fights* (New York: The Ronald Press Co., 1962), 133.
40. *New York Times*, 11 June 1924.
41. Ibid; *Terre Haute Tribune*, 11 June 1924.
42. *New York Times*, 11 June 1924; *Terre Haute Tribune*, 11 June 1924.
43. *New York Times*, 11 June 1924.
44. *Terre Haute Tribune*, 11 June 1924.
45. Quote is from *New York Times*, 11 June 1924.

Chapter 18

1. Deduced from *Terre Haute Star*, 27 June 1924.
2. Fight account is from Ibid., 28 June 1924; *Cleveland Plain Dealer*, 28 June 1924; *Terre Haute Tribune*, 28 Dec. 1924; 2 July 1925.
3. *Terre Haute Star*, 27 June 1924; *Terre Haute Tribune*, 11, 18 July 1924.
4. *Terre Haute Star*, 22 July 1924; *Terre Haute Tribune*, 23 July 1924.
5. Fishing examples: *Terre Haute Tribune*, 20 June, 6 July, 1924.
6. Pre-fight Ryan dispute recounted in Ibid., 2 Aug. 1924; *Los Angeles Record*, 15 June 1925.
7. *Los Angeles Herald-Express*, 21 Nov. 1938.
8. *Indianapolis Star*, 17 Aug. 1924.
9. Fight account from fourth round is from *Terre Haute Star*, 2, 3 Aug. 1924; *Terre Haute Tribune*, 2 Aug. 1924; *Indianapolis Star*, 17 Aug. 1924.
10. *Terre Haute Tribune*, 2 Aug. 1924.
11. *Terre Haute Star*, 8 Aug. 1924.
12. Odds are from *Terre Haute Tribune*, 10 Aug. 1924. Right hand sparingly from *Chicago Daily Tribune*, 5 Aug. 1924.

13. *Chicago Daily Tribune*, 26 Jan. 1940.
14. Ibid., 12 Aug., 1940.
15. *Terre Haute Tribune*, 12 Aug. 1924; *Chicago Daily Tribune*, 12 Aug. 1924.
16. Unknown publication dated 26 Nov. 1956, written by Gene Couglin, clipping from Bud Taylor file in Joyce Collection, Hesburgh Library, University of Notre Dame.
17. *Chicago Daily Tribune*, 26 Jan. 1940.
18. See n. 16 above.
19. *Terre Haute Tribune*, 22 Aug. 1924.
20. Ibid., 23 Aug. 1924.
21. Ibid., 24 Aug. 1924. Tremaine's record from www.boxrec.com.
22. *Terre Haute Tribune*, 21 Aug. 1924.
23. *Cleveland Plain Dealer*, 23 Aug. 1924.
24. Attendance figure from Ibid., 29 Aug. 1924.
25. *Terre Haute Star*, 26 Aug. 1924.
26. *Cleveland Plain Dealer*, 29 Aug. 1924.
27. *Cleveland News*, 29 Aug. 1924.
28. *Terre Haute Star*, 30 Aug. 1924.
29. *Terre Haute Tribune*, 2, 5, 7 Sept. 1924.
30. *Ring* magazine, Sept. 1924.
31. *Terre Haute Tribune*, 12 Sept. 1924.
32. Ibid., 5, 7 Sept. 1924. *Terre Haute Star*, 7 Sept. 1924.
33. *Terre Haute Tribune*, 13 Sept. 1924. Speed limit from *Tribune*, 26 July 1925.
34. *Los Angeles Times*, 19, 21, 23, 24, Sept. 1924.
35. William Deverell and Tom Sitton, *Metropolis in the Making: L.A. in the 1920's* (University of California Press, 2001), 7, 19, 32, 107, 128, 129.
36. *Terre Haute Tribune*, 30 Nov. 1924.
37. *Indianapolis Star*, 16 Nov. 1924.
38. Taylor's pay is from *Los Angeles Times*, 16 Feb. 1926. Rivers' best bantamweight from *Los Angeles Examiner*, 25 Sept. 1927.
39. Fight account is from *Los Angeles Times*, 23 Sept. 1924; *Los Angeles Record*, 24 Sept. 1924; *Terre Haute Tribune*, 24, 29 Sept. 1924; 26 March 1927.
40. *Terre Haute Tribune*, 26 March 1927; *Los Angeles Herald-Express*, 28 Aug. 1937, 21 Nov. 1938; *Los Angeles Times*, 8 Dec. 1940.

41. *Terre Haute Tribune*, 16 Oct. 1924.
42. Ibid.
43. Ibid.
44. Ibid., 16 Oct., 2 Nov. 1924.
45. Ibid., 2 Nov. 1924.
46. Ibid., 29 Oct. 1924.
47. *Milwaukee Journal*, 15 April 1926.
48. *Los Angeles Times*, 20 March 1939.
49. *Terre Haute Tribune*, 13 Jan. 1925.
50. Ibid., 23 Dec. 1924.
51. *Washington Post*, 24 Dec. 1924.
52. *Terre Haute Tribune*, 29 Dec. 1924.

Chapter 19

1. Entire Harter anecdote is from *Los Angeles Record*, 30 Oct. 1925. The show referred to is probably 30 May 1924, based on other information provided in the Record article.
2. Fight account is from *Terre Haute Tribune*, 2 Jan. 1925; *Indianapolis Star*, 2 Jan. 1925; *Sports Weekly*, 17 Nov. 1939; *Los Angeles Herald-Express*, 28 Aug. 1937.
3. *Terre Haute Tribune*, 24 May 1927.
4. *Los Angeles Times*, 14 June 1925.
5. *Terre Haute Tribune*, 25 Jan. 1925.
6. Ibid., 12 Feb. 1925.
7. *Los Angeles Times*, 14 June 1925; *Terre Haute Star*, 21 March 1931.
8. *Los Angeles Times*, 14 June 1925; *Terre Haute Tribune*, 27 Jan. 1925.
9. *Los Angeles Times*, 14 June 1925.
10. Ibid.
11. Ibid.

Chapter 20

1. *Terre Haute Star*, 2 July 1925.
2. Ibid.
3. *Terre Haute Tribune*, 31 July 1921.
4. *Chicago Daily Tribune*, 21 April 1925.
5. *Terre Haute Tribune*, 22 April 1925.

6. *Los Angeles Evening Herald*, 26 Oct. 1925.
7. *Terre Haute Tribune*, 27 Jan., 18 July 1924; 23 May 1926.
8. Terre Haute city directories. Divorce filings also indicate the address.
9. *Terre Haute Tribune*, 23 April 1925.
10. Ibid.
11. *Los Angeles Evening Herald*, 26 Oct. 1925.
12. *Terre Haute Tribune*, 27 Jan. 1924; 23 May 1926.
13. *Los Angeles Evening Herald*, 26 Oct. 1925.
14. *Terre Haute Star*, 25 April 1926.
15. *Terre Haute Tribune*, 28 May 1925.
16. Ibid., 14, 16 May, 1925.
17. Fight result and attendance are from *Indianapolis Star*, 9 April 1926; *Terre Haute Tribune*, 19 May 1925.
18. *Los Angeles Evening Herald*, 30 May 1925 indicates he had the sock while in New York.
19. *New York Times*, 18 March 1924 on club's capacity. Bud carried sock in waist of trunks is from NEA News Service, by Dan Thomas, unknown date or publication, clipping from Vigo County historian B. Michael McCormick.
20. Fight account is from *Terre Haute Tribune*, 27 May 1925; *Los Angeles Times*, 27 May 1925.
21. *Los Angeles Evening Herald*, 30 May 1925.
22. *Terre Haute Tribune*, 24 Nov. 1922; 21, 27 May, 1925; 5 July 1925. U.S. Census for Vigo County, Indiana, 1930.
23. *Terre Haute Tribune*, 27 May 1925.
24. htpp://aerofiles.com
25. *Los Angeles Times*, 28 May 1925.
26. Ibid., 24 May 1925.
27. *Terre Haute Tribune*, 27 May 1925.
28. *Ring Record Book & Boxing Encyclopedia* (New York: Athenium, 1981), 610, lists McLarnin at 29-0-2 going into the fight with Taylor, probably as reliable a source as any. McLarnin's pay is from *Ring* magazine, April 1928. Taylor's pay from *Los Angeles Times*, 16 June 1926.
29. *Los Angeles Times*, 2 June 1925.
30. McLarnin background from *Ring*, April 1928; *Los Angeles Times*, 1 June 1925; www.irishboxing.com.

31. Author's observation from fight films.
32. *Los Angeles Times*, 1 June 1925.
33. Ibid.
34. Unknown publication, 1957 article datelined Los Angeles, by George T. Davis, clipping from files of Vigo County, Indiana historian B. Michael McCormick.
35. *Los Angeles Times*, 8 May 1936.
36. See n. 34 above.
37. Ibid; *Sports Weekly*, 17 Nov. 1939; *Los Angeles Herald-Express*, 21 Nov. 1938/
38. *Los Angeles Times*, 16 June 1926; unknown publication, 1957 article datelined Los Angeles, by George T. Davis, clipping from files of Vigo County, Indiana historian Mike McCormick.
39. *Los Angeles Times*, 8 May 1936; Sports Weekly, 17 Nov. 1939.
40. *Los Angeles Times*, 15 Nov. 1925.
41. *Terre Haute Tribune*, 24 June 1925.
42. Ibid.
43. *Los Angeles Times*, 18 June 1925.
44. Ibid.
45. *Terre Haute Tribune*, 24 June 1925.
46. Ibid., 19 June 1925.
47. *Los Angeles Times*, 17 June 1925.
48. Ibid., 18 June 1925.
49. *Terre Haute Star*, 28 June 1925.
50. *Terre Haute Tribune*, 25 Sept. 1927
51. *Terre Haute Star*, 28 June 1925.

Chapter 21
1. *Terre Haute Tribune*, 21 June 1925.
2. Ibid., 18 June 1925.
3. Ibid., 28 June 1925; *Terre Haute Star*, 28 June 1925.
4. *Terre Haute Star*, 30 June 1925; *Terre Haute Tribune*, 1 July 1925.
5. *Terre Haute Tribune*, 1 July 1925; photo of Taylor in parade from collection of Bud Taylor Jr.
6. *Terre Haute Star*, 2 July 1925.
7. Ibid., 1 July 1925.
8. Ibid., 5 July 1925; *Terre Haute Tribune*, 5 July 1925.

9. *Terre Haute Star,* 5 July 1925; *Terre Haute Tribune*, 5 July 1925.
10. *Terre Haute Tribune*, 13 July 1925.

Chapter 22
1. *Terre Haute Tribune*, 15 July 1925.
2. Lester Bromberg, *Boxing's Unforgettable Fights* (New York: The Ronald Press, 1962), 133.
3. www.ibhof.com. Record is from www.boxrec.com.
4. www.boxrec.com
5. *Washington Post*, 3 Feb. 1927.
6. Ibid.
7. Fight account is from *Terre Haute Tribune*, 1 Aug. 1925; Chicago Daily Tribune, 1 Aug. 1925.
8. *Terre Haute Tribune*, 3 Aug. 1925.
9. Ibid., 6 Aug. 1925.
10. Ibid.
11. Fight account is from *New York Times*, 25 Aug. 1925; Terre Haute Tribune 25 Aug. 1925.
12. *Los Angeles Record*, 23 Oct. 1925.
13. *Terre Haute Tribune*, 27 Aug. 1925.
14. Ibid.
15. Ibid., 28 Sept. 1925.
16. *Los Angeles Evening Herald*, 26 Oct. 1925.
17. *Los Angeles Times*, 9 Nov. 1925.
18. Ibid., 28 Oct. 1925; *Terre Haute Star*, 19, 27 March 1926; *Cleveland Plain Dealer*, 25 March 1926.
19. *Los Angeles Examiner*, 25 Oct. 1925.
20. *Los Angeles Times*, 25 Oct. 1925.
21. *Los Angeles Examiner*, 28 Oct. 1925.
22. Bud's pay is from *Los Angeles Times*, 26 Feb. 1926.
23. Examples: *Terre Haute Tribune*, 11 Jan. 1926; *Milwaukee Journal*, 31 Jan., 30 April 1926; *Wisconsin News*, 17 April 1926.
24. *Terre Haute Tribune*, 9 Nov. 1925.
25. *Los Angeles Times*, 16 Nov. 1925.
26. Ibid., 28 May 1925.
27. *Terre Haute Star*, 28 March 1926.

28. *Los Angeles Record*, 5 Nov. 1925.
29. *Los Angeles Times*, 9 Nov. 1925.
30. Ibid., 15 Nov. 1925.
31. Ibid., 15, 17 Nov. 1925.
32. *Los Angeles Examiner*, 17 Nov. 1925.
33. *Terre Haute Tribune*, 19 Nov. 1925; *Los Angeles Times*, 15 Sept. 1929.
34. *Los Angeles Evening Herald*, 5 Dec. 1925.
35. *Los Angeles Times*, 19 Nov. 1925.
36. *Terre Haute Tribune*, 19 Nov. 1925.
37. *Los Angeles Record*, 19 Nov. 1925.
38. *Los Angeles Evening Herald*, 20 Nov. 1925.

Chapter 23
1. *Los Angeles Times*, 25 Nov., 7 Dec. 1925.
2. *Terre Haute Tribune*, 11 Oct. 1925.
3. Weight negotiations and quote are from *Los Angeles Times*, 17, 18 Nov. 1925.
4. Ibid., 18 Nov. 1925.
5. Ibid., 4 Dec. 1925.
6. Ibid., 7 Dec. 1925.
7. *Terre Haute Tribune*, 19 Dec. 1925.
8. *Los Angeles Record*, 9 Dec. 1925; *Los Angeles Times*, 9 Dec. 1925.
9. *Los Angeles Record*, 9 Dec. 1925; *Los Angeles Times*, 10 Dec. 1925; *Terre Haute Tribune*, 9 Dec. 1925.
10. *Los Angeles Times*, 9 Dec. 1925; *Los Angeles Record*, 9 Dec. 1925; *Terre Haute Tribune*, 9 Dec. 1925.
11. *Terre Haute Tribune*, 10 Dec. 1925.
12. Ibid; *Los Angeles Examiner*, 9 Dec. 1925; *Los Angeles Evening Herald*, 9 Dec. 1925.
13. *Los Angeles Record*, 10 Dec. 1925; *Los Angeles Times*, 10 Dec. 1925; *Terre Haute Tribune*, 20 Dec. 1925.
14. *Los Angeles Times*, 10 Dec. 1925.
15. Ibid.
16. Ibid.
17. www.spookyfx.com/book/archery.html
18. *Terre Haute Tribune*, 20 Dec. 1925.

19. Ibid., 24 Dec. 1925.
20. Ibid., 20 Dec. 1925.
21. *Terre Haute Star*, 27 Dec. 1925.
22. Ibid; *Terre Haute Tribune*, 27 Dec. 1925.
23. *New York Times*, 18 Dec. 1925; *Los Angeles Times*, 7 Dec. 1925.\
24. *Terre Haute Tribune*, 25 Sept. 1927.
25. NEA News Service, by Dan Thomas, unknown date or publication, clipping from Vigo County, Indiana historian B. Michael McCormick.
26. *Los Angeles Times*, 10 Jan. 1926.
27. Ibid., 12 Jan. 1926.
28. Ibid., 14 Jan. 1926; 8 May 1936.
29. Ibid.
30. Ibid.
31. Size 7 is from *Los Angeles Evening Herald*, 24 Oct. 1925.
32. Fight account is from *Los Angeles Times*, 13, 14, 31 Jan. 1926; *Los Angeles Examiner*, 13 Jan. 1926.
33. NEA News Service, by Dan Thomas, unknown date or publication, clipping from Vigo County Indiana historian B. Michael McCormick.
34. McLarnin comments made in *Seattle Weekly*, 4 Nov. 1998 (www.seattleweekly.com); *Los Angeles Times*, 2 Dec. 1966; *Chicago Daily Tribune*, 21 Oct. 1935; *Los Angeles Times*, 19 Jan. 1930.

Chapter 24
1. Rankings and possibility of elimination tourney are from *Washington Post*, 20 Jan. 1926.
2. *New York Times*, 23 Jan. 1926.
3. nationmaster.com encyclopedia: WBA. Also, www.britannica.com under "Boxing professional organizations."
4. *New York Times*, 19 Oct. 1926; 31 Aug. 1927.
5. Ibid., 20 Oct. 1926.
6. Ibid., 27 Jan. 1925.
7. Ibid.
8. www.nationmaster.com Encyclopedia: WBA. Also, www.britannica.com under "Boxing professional organizations."

9. *Los Angeles Times*, 1 Feb. 1926.
10. Ibid., 3 Feb. 1926.
11. Fight account is from *Los Angeles Record*, 4 Feb. 1926; *Los Angeles Times*, 4 Feb. 1926; unknown clipping dated 3 Feb. 1926, by Bill Yeager, found in Joyce Collection of Hesburgh Library at University of Notre Dame.
12. *Los Angeles Times*, 16 Feb. 1926; *Terre Haute Star*, 18 March 1926.
13. *Los Angeles Record*, 1 March 1926.
14. *Los Angeles Times*, 8 March 1926.
15. *Los Angeles Evening Herald*, 10 March 1926.
16. *Terre Haute Tribune*, 7 March 1926.
17. *Los Angeles Times*, 10 March 1926.

Chapter 25
1. *Milwaukee Journal*, 8 April 1926.
2. *Los Angeles Times*, 4 March 1926.
3. Fight account is from *Terre Haute Star*, 27 March 1926. Snell record from www.boxrec.com
4. Theater capacity is from *Indianapolis Star*, 9 April 1926.
5. *Terre Haute Tribune*, 31 March 1926.
6. Quote is from Ibid., 6 April 1926. Goldstein's record is from www.boxrec.com
7. *Terre Haute Tribune*, 9 April 1926; *Terre Haute Star*, 9 April 1926; *Indianapolis Star*, 9 April 1926.
8. *Terre Haute Tribune*, 13 April 1926; *Terre Haute Star*, 10 April 1926.
9. *Terre Haute Star*, 10 April 1926.
10. Ibid.
11. *Terre Haute Tribune*, 10 April 1926.
12. *Chicago Daily Tribune*, 11 April 1926.
13. *Terre Haute Tribune*, 13 April 1926.
14. Ibid., 15 April 1926.

Chapter 26
1. Moldez's childhood and early boxing career are from *Milwaukee Journal*, 19 April 1926; *Terre Haute Tribune*, 21 April 1926.
2. *Ring* magazine, Sept. 1925.

3. Earnings and plan are from *Milwaukee Journal*, 17 April 1926; *Milwaukee Leader*, 20 April 1926.
4. *Milwaukee Journal*, 15 April 1926.
5. *New York Times*, 8 Sept. 1925.
6. Ibid., 24 Nov. 1925.
7. *Milwaukee Leader*, 21, 23 April, 1926.
8. *Milwaukee Journal*, 19 April 1926.
9. *Los Angeles Times*, 19 Sept. 1926.
10. Ibid., 21 Jan., 28 March 1926.
11. Examples: *Wisconsin News*, 19 April 1926; *Milwaukee Journal*, 20 April 1926.
12. Lisa Elorde, interview with author, Canastota, N.Y., 12 June 2005. Also, *Milwaukee Journal*, 19 April 1926 refers to Moldez as having been hired out to the fields as a child.
13. *Wisconsin News*, 20 April 1926.
14. *Terre Haute Tribune*, 9 Jan. 1927; *Milwaukee Leader*, 23 April 1926.
15. *Terre Haute Tribune*, 19 April 1926.
16. *Milwaukee Journal*, 20 April 1926.
17. *Chicago Daily Tribune*, 19 April 1926. *Wisconsin News*, 14 April 1926.
18. *Milwaukee Leader*, 20 April 1926.
19. *Milwaukee Journal*, 20 April 1926.
20. Early rounds are from Ibid., 20 April 1926; *Indianapolis Star*, 20 April, 1926; *Milwaukee Leader*, 20 April 1926.
21. *Milwaukee Journal*, 20 April 1926.
22. Rounds five through nine account is from *Terre Haute Tribune*, 20 April 1926.
23. *Milwaukee Journal*, 20 April 1926.
24. *Indianapolis Star*, 20 April 1926.
25. *Terre Haute Tribune*, 20, 21 April 1926.
26. *Milwaukee Leader*, 20 April 1926; *Chicago American*, 22 April 1926.
27. Account is from *Milwaukee Leader*, 20 April 1926; *Indianapolis Star*, 20 April 1926; *Milwaukee Journal*, 20 April 1926; *Terre Haute Tribune*, 21 April 1926.
28. *Terre Haute Star*, 20 April 1926.
29. *Wisconsin News*, 20 April 1926.

30. Ibid.
31. Ibid.
32. *Milwaukee Leader*, 20 April 1926.
33. Wallace's involvement and Eckwart response are from Ibid; *Milwaukee Journal*, 20 April 1926; *Wisconsin News*, 20 April 1926.
34. *Milwaukee Leader*, 20 April 1926.
35. Quotes in Wengert's office are from *Wisconsin News*, 20 April 1926.
36. *New York Times*, 21 April 1926.
37. *Milwaukee Journal*, 23 April 1926.
38. *Chicago American*, 22 April 1926.
39. *Terre Haute Tribune*, 21 April 1926.
40. *Chicago Daily Tribune*, 23 April 1926.
41. *New York Times*, 22 April 1926.
42. *Chicago Daily Tribune*, 23 April 1926.
43. *Milwaukee Journal*, 23 April 1926.

Chapter 27
1. *Terre Haute Tribune*, 23 April 1926
2. Ibid., 12 May 1926.
3. Information on negotiations and quote are from Ibid., 24 April 1926; *Terre Haute Star*, 27 April 1926; *Washington Post*, 30 April 1926.
4. *Terre Haute Tribune*, 5 May 1926.
5. Fight account and Ryan's style are from *Terre Haute Tribune*, 15, 17 May 1926; *Chicago Daily Tribune*, 16 May, 16 July 1926; *Terre Haute Star*, 15 May 1926.
6. *Terre Haute Tribune*, 2 June 1926.
7. Ibid., 8 June 1926.
8. Ibid., 19 June 1926.
9. Ibid., 26 June 1926; *Terre Haute Star*, 20 June 1926.
10. *Terre Haute Star*, 30 June 1926.
11. *Terre Haute Tribune*, 29 June 1926.
12. Ibid., 3 July 1926.
13. *Rockford (Ill.) Register*, 26 Feb. 1968.
14. Ibid.; *Los Angeles Times*, 4 July 1926.

15. *Rockford Register*, 26 Feb. 1968.
16. *Terre Haute Tribune*, 13 July 1926.
17. *Terre Haute Star*, 24 July 1926.
18. *Washington Post*, 26 July 1926.
19. *Terre Haute Tribune*, 6 July 1926.
20. *Terre Haute Star*, 26 July 1926.
21. *Chicago Daily Tribune*, 16 July 1926.
22. *Washington Post*, 26 July 1926.
23. *Chicago Daily Tribune*, 25 July 1926; *Terre Haute Star*, 25 July 1926.
24. *Los Angeles Times*, 17 Aug. 1926.
25. Ibid., 15, 19 Aug. 1926; *Terre Haute Star*, 19 Aug. 1926. That LaHood had some big-name wins is from www.boxrec.com.
26. *Terre Haute Tribune*, 27 Aug. 1926.

Chapter 28
1. *Terre Haute Star*, 12 Sept. 1926; *Terre Haute Tribune*, 12, 14 Sept. 1926; *Chicago Daily Tribune*, 8 Sept. 1926.
2. *Terre Haute Tribune*, 8 Sept. 1926.
3. Ibid., 19 April, 8 Sept. 1926.
4. www.boxrec.com
5. *Milwaukee Journal*, 30 April 1926.
6. *Terre Haute Tribune*, 14 Sept. 1926.
7. Quote is from Ibid., 12 Sept. 1926.
8. Quote is from *Terre Haute Star*, 12 Sept. 1926.
9. Ibid., 14 Sept. 1926. Also, www.boxrec.com.
10. *Terre Haute Tribune*, 15 Sept. 1926.
11. Ibid.
12. Ibid.
13. Ibid.
14. Ibid., 13, 15 Sept. 1926. *Chicago Herald-Examiner*, 15 Sept. 1926.
15. *Chicago Daily Journal*, 15 Sept. 1926.
16. *Terre Haute Tribune*, 15 Sept. 1926.
17. *Chicago Herald-Examiner*, 15 Sept. 1926.
18. *Chicago Daily Journal*, 15 Sept. 1926.
19. *Chicago Daily Tribune*, 25 Jan. 1940.
20. *New McClures*, Vol. 62, No. 3, March 1929.

21. *Terre Haute Tribune*, 16 Sept. 1926.
22. Ibid., 15 Sept. 1926.
23. *Los Angeles Times*, 15 Sept. 1926.
24. Peter Heller, *In This Corner* (New York: Simon & Schuster, 1973), 93.
25. *Terre Haute Tribune*, 15 Sept. 1926.
26. Ibid.
27. *Los Angeles Times*, 16 Sept. 1926.
28. *Terre Haute Tribune*, 16 Sept. 1926.
29. *Chicago Daily Journal*, 22 May 1928.
30. *New York Times*, 15 Sept. 1926.
31. *Terre Haute Star*, 16 Sept. 1926.
32. Ibid., 24 Sept. 1926.
33. *New York Times*, 19 Oct. 1926.
34. *Terre Haute Star*, 19 Oct. 1926.
35. Ibid., 22, 23 Oct. 1926.
36. *Los Angeles Times*, 28, 29 Oct. 1926.
37. *Los Angeles Record*, 6 Nov. 1926.
38. Arms described in *Los Angeles Times*, 6 Nov. 1926.
39. *Los Angeles Record*, 4 Nov. 1926.
40. *Terre Haute Tribune*, 1 Oct. 1926.
41. *Los Angeles Times*, 5 Nov. 1926.
42. *Los Angeles Record*, 6 Nov. 1926.
43. Ibid., *Terre Haute Tribune*, 3 Nov. 1926.
44. *Los Angeles Times*, 15 Aug. 1926.
45. *Los Angeles Evening Herald*, 3 Nov. 1926.
46. *Terre Haute Tribune*, 7 Nov. 1926.
47. Ibid., separate article on same date.
48. Ibid., 14 Jan. 1927.
49. *Terre Haute Star*, 14 Nov. 1926.
50. Nat Fleischer, *A Pictorial History of Boxing* (New Jersey: Citadel Press, 1975), 354-355.
51. *Terre Haute Tribune*, 18 Nov. 1926.
52. Ibid., 16 Nov. 1926.
53. Ibid.
54. Ibid., 18 Nov. 1926.
55. Ibid., 2 March 1927. Also, www.ibhof.com. Taylor's income is estimated from his known income from five bouts in 1927.
56. Sangor's record is from www.boxrec.com

57. Sangor's typical boxing weight: *Los Angeles Record*, 29 Jan. 1926.
58. Fight account is from *Chicago Daily Tribune*, 30 Nov. 1926; *Los Angeles Times*, 30 Nov. 1926.
59. *Chicago Daily Tribune*, 1 Dec. 1926.
60. Ibid., 6 Dec. 1926; *New York Times*, 11 Dec. 1926; *Terre Haute Tribune*, 13 Dec. 1926.
61. *Washington Post*, 23 Dec. 1926.
62. *Terre Haute Tribune*, 4 Feb. 1927.

Chapter 29
1. The $50,000 figure comes from *Chicago Herald-Examiner*, 26 Feb. 1927, after the business had been open three months. The initial investment probably was closer to $10,000, a figure cited in *Terre Haute Tribune*, 6 Dec. 1926.
2. *Terre Haute Tribune*, 5, 6 Dec. 1926.
3. Ibid.
4. *Time* magazine, 2 Nov., 1981, reported on the fitness trend.
5. Opening night is recapped in *Terre Haute Tribune*, 7 Dec. 1926; *Terre Haute Star*, 7 Dec. 1926.
6. *Terre Haute Star*, 7 Dec. 1926.
7. *Terre Haute Tribune*, 3 Jan. 1927.
8. Training regimen mostly from Ibid., 9 Jan. 1927. Also, *Los Angeles Herald Express*, 21 Nov. 1938.

Chapter 30
1. *Terre Haute Tribune*, 5 Feb. 1927.
2. *Washington Post*, 9 Feb. 1927.
3. *New York Times*, 12 Feb. 1927.
4. *Terre Haute Tribune*, 15, 16, 1927.
5. Ibid, Feb. 13, 1927; *Chicago Daily Tribune*, 23 Feb. 1927.
6. *Chicago Daily Tribune*, 25 Feb. 1927; *New York Times*, 25 Feb. 1927.
7. *Washington Post*, 26 Feb. 1927.
8. *Chicago American*, 25 Feb. 1927.
9. *Terre Haute Tribune*, 1 March 1927.
10. Sarmiento record is from www.boxrec.com.
11. *Terre Haute Tribune*, 4, 9 March 1927.

12. Ibid., 13 March 1927.
13. Ibid., 16 March 1927.
14. Ibid., 18 March 1927/
15. *Atlanta Constitution*, 3 July 1910.
16. *Wisconsin News*, 27 Nov. 1926; *Terre Haute Tribune*, 14 Sept. 1926.
17. White's words are from *Terre Haute Tribune*, 21 March 1927.

Chapter 31

1. *New York Times*, 11 Dec. 1959; *Chicago Evening Post*, 21 March 1926; Ring magazine, July 1927.
2. *Chicago Daily Tribune*, 31 Dec. 1927.
3. *Chicago American*, 22 March 1927.
4. Bert Randolph Sugar, *The 100 Greatest Boxers of All Time* (New York: Bonanza Books, 1984), 36; *Chicago Herald-Examiner*, 20 June 1927.
5. *Terre Haute Star*, 12 Feb. 1928.
6. *Chicago Evening Post*, 19 March 1927.
7. *Terre Haute Tribune*, 20 March 1927.
8. Ibid., 20, 21 March 1927.
9. Ibid., 26 March 1927.
10. Ibid.
11. Ibid., 23, 24 March 1927.
12. *Los Angeles Herald-Express*, 21 Nov. 1938.
13. Ibid.; *Terre Haute Tribune*, 14 Sept. 1926; *Chicago American*, 24 March 1927.
14. Treatment of sparring partners is from *Terre Haute Tribune*, 24 March 1927; *Chicago Herald-Examiner*, 24 March 1927; *Chicago American*, 24 March 1927.
15. *Terre Haute Tribune*, 26 March 1927.
16. Various newspaper accounts include Ibid., 25 March 1927.
17. Fralick there is reported in *Chicago Herald-Examiner*, 20 March 1927.
18. *Terre Haute Tribune*, 27 March 1927.
19. Clayton W. Henderson, *On the Banks of the Wabash*, The Life and Music of Paul Dresser (Indianapolis: Indiana Historical Society Press, 2003), 210.
20. *Terre Haute Tribune*, 27 March 1927; *Chicago American* undated article, from materials supplied by Bud Taylor Jr.

21. *Terre Haute Tribune*, 27 March 1927.
22. Fite account is from Ibid., 28 March 1927; *Chicago Daily Tribune*, 27 March 1927; *New York Times*, 27 March 1927; *Chicago Herald-Examiner*, 23 June 1927.
23. *Chicago Daily Tribune*, 27 March 1927; *New York Times*, 27 March 1927; *Terre Haute Tribune*, 28 March 1927.
24. *Chicago Daily Tribune*, 27, 29 March 1927.
25. *Ring* magazine, July 1927.
26. *Chicago Herald-Examiner*, 29 March 1927.
27. *Terre Haute Tribune*, 28 March 1927.
28. *Ring*, July 1927.
29. *Terre Haute Tribune*, 25, 28 March 1927.
30. *New York Times*, 28 March 1927; Chicago Herald-Examiner, 29 March 1927.
31. *Chicago Daily Tribune*, 1 April 1927.
32. Account of the ceremony is from *Terre Haute Tribune*, 31 March, 1 April, 1927; *Terre Haute Star*, 1 April 1927.
33. *Terre Haute Tribune*, 2 April 1927; *Terre Haute Star*, 2 April 1927.
34. Fundraiser and cost of gym are from *Terre Haute Star*, 30 March, 2 April 1927; *Terre Haute Tribune*, 1, 2, 18 April 1927.
35. *Terre Haute Tribune*, 13 June 1927.
36. *Los Angeles Times*, 19 April 1927.
37. Ibid, 18 April 1927.
38. *Chicago Daily Tribune*, 3 May 1927.
39. *Chicago Daily Journal*, 30 April, 3 May 1927.
40. *Chicago Daily Tribune*, 4 May 1927; *Chicago Evening Post*, 4 May 1925.
41. *Indianapolis Star*, 4 May 1927.

Chapter 32
1. *Terre Haute Tribune*, 10 May 1927.
2. Ibid., 15 May, 1927; *Chicago Daily News*, 22 June 1927.
3. *Terre Haute Tribune*, 16 May 1927.
4. Ibid., 20 May 1927; *Los Angeles Times*, 20 May 1927.
5. *Los Angeles Times*, 1 June 1927.
6. *Chicago Daily Tribune*, 10 June 1927.
7. Moore and Mandell's help are from *Terre Haute Tribune*, 17, 21 June 1927.

8. *Chicago Herald-Examiner*, 18 June 1927.
9. Ibid., 20 June 1927.
10. *Chicago American*, 23 June 1927.
11. Ibid., 24 June 1927; *Terre Haute Tribune*, 23 June 1927.
12. *Chicago Daily News*, 21 June 1927.
13. *Terre Haute Tribune*, 10 July 1927.
14. Ibid., 22 June 1927
15. *Chicago American*, 22 June 1927.
16. Under weight is from *Chicago Herald-Examiner*, 22 June 1927. Lincoln Park is from *Chicago Daily News*, 22 June 1927.

Chapter 33
1. *Terre Haute Tribune*, 23 June 1927.
2. Ibid., 24 June 1927.
3. Ibid.
4. *Chicago American*, 23 June 1927.
5. *New York Times*, 25 June 1927 estimated the crowd at 15,000 to 20,000.
6. Those present and their occupations are from *Terre Haute Tribune*, 24 June 1927, 18 Nov. 1946; Terre Haute city directories of the 1920s.
7. *Terre Haute Tribune*, 24 June 1927.
8. *Chicago Herald-Examiner*, 26 June 1927.
9. First round account is from *Chicago Daily Tribune*, 25 June 1927.
10. *Terre Haute Tribune*, 25 June 1927.
11. *Chicago Daily Tribune*, 25 June 1927.
12. *New York Times*, 25 June 1927; *Terre Haute Tribune*, 25 June 1927.
13. *Chicago American*, 25 June 1927.
14. Of 10 sportswriters' accounts, seven had Canzoneri ahead after five rounds, two had Taylor ahead, and one scored it even. The five-round scoring is based on fight accounts from the 24, 25 June 1927 editions of the following: *Chicago Daily Tribune, New York Times, Sullivan Daily Times* (United Press report); *Terre Haute Tribune, Chicago American* (two accounts), *Chicago Daily News, Chicago Evening Post, Chicago Herald-Examiner* and *Milwaukee Journal*. How the judges ultimately scored the fight by rounds is not revealed in these accounts. It is clear from all the accounts that Taylor won the fight in the later rounds.

15. *Milwaukee Journal*, 25 June 1927.
16. Round Six is from *New York Times*, 25 June 1927; *Chicago American*, 25 June 1927; *Terre Haute Tribune*, 25 June 1927.
17. *Chicago Evening Post*, 25 June 1927 reported Canzoneri slowed after the fifth round.
18. *Chicago Daily Tribune*, 25 June 1927.
19. Ibid.
20. *Chicago American*, 25 June 1927.
21. Ibid.
22. *Chicago Daily News*, 25 June 1927.
23. See n. 14 above.
24. *Terre Haute Tribune*, 25 June 1927.
25. Ibid.
26. *Sullivan Daily Times*, 25 June 1927.

Chapter 34
1. *Terre Haute Star*, 27 June 1927.
2. *Terre Haute Tribune*, 25 June 1927.
3. Ibid., 28 June 1927.
4. Ibid.
5. Ibid.
6. Ibid., 4, 6 July 1927.
7. Ibid., 16 March, 3 Aug. 1927; 15 Jan., 27 March 1928.
8. Tom Jennings, interview with author, Terre Haute, 14 Jan. 2005.
9. *Chicago Daily Tribune*, 16 Aug. 1927; *Washington Post*, 16 Aug. 1927.

Chapter 35
1. *Indianapolis Star*, 8 Sept. 1927.
2. *Chicago Daily Tribune*, 9 Feb. 1928.
3. *Terre Haute Tribune*, 16 Oct. 1927.
4. Baldock passage is from *Los Angeles Examiner*, 10 Sept. 1927; *Ring* magazine, Aug. 1927.
5. *Los Angeles Record*, 19 Sept. 1927.
6. Spy, poster anecdotes are from *Los Angeles Times*, 18, 20 Sept. 1927.
7. *Los Angeles Record*, 17 Sept. 1927.
8. Ibid.

9. Ibid.
10. Ibid. 21 Sept. 1927.
11. Entire Lindbergh anecdote and Taylor's quote are from *Terre Haute Tribune*, 27 Sept. 1927; *Los Angeles Times*, 21 Sept. 1927.
12. Fight account is from *Los Angeles Record*, 21 Sept. 1927; *Los Angeles Times*, 21 Sept., 23 Oct. 1927.
13. Jim Long, telephone interview with author, 14 Jan. 2006.

Chapter 36

1. *Los Angeles Times*, 22 Oct. 1927. Also, www.boxrec.com.
2. *Los Angeles Times*, 21 Oct., 5 Nov. 1927.
3. Ibid., 9, 13 Nov. 1927.
4. *Los Angeles Examiner*, 8 Nov. 1927.
5. *Los Angeles Times*, 10 Nov. 1927.
6. *Terre Haute Tribune*, 10 Nov. 1927.
7. *New York Times*, 10 Nov. 1927.
8. *Terre Haute Tribune*, 12 Nov. 1927.
9. News about these boxers is from *Terre Haute Tribune*, 23 Dec. 1927; 7 March 1929; Terre Haute city directories. An absence of fight news about Barnhart and Perrill in the daily sports sections supports conclusion they were no longer boxing.
10. *Terre Haute Tribune*, 10 Feb., 11, 22 May 1927; 12 Feb. 1928 for Cooper. *Tribune*, 13 Dec. 1928 for Sparks. *Tribune*, 28 Jan., 6, 10 Feb., 14 April 1927; 1 April 1929 for McDermott.
11. Results of these cards were published weekly in the *Terre Haute Tribune*. Sullivan's name appears occasionally, such as 13 July 1927. Tom Jennings, interview with author, Terre Haute, 14 Jan. 2005. Dick Brokaw, interview with author, Terre Haute, 19 Nov. 2004.
12. *Terre Haute Tribune*, 6 Nov. 1927.
13. Brokaw, 23 Dec. 2004.
14. Ibid, interview dates 5 Nov., 8, 9, 23 Dec. 2004; 11 Jan., 11 March 2005. Miners' show was on 24 Dec. 1924.
15. *Terre Haute House* and big buildings: *Terre Haute Tribune*, 13 March, 10 May, 8 June, 23 Oct. 1927; 6 July 1928.
16. Ibid., 27 Nov. 1927.
17. Ibid., 13 June 1928.

18. Traffic items are from Ibid., 11 Aug. 1923; 19, 28 April 1925.
19. *Chicago Daily Tribune*, 1 May 1927; *Chicago Herald-Examiner*, 19 June 1927.
20. *Terre Haute Tribune*, 28 April 1927.
21. Ibid., 29 Nov. 1927; *New York Times*, 3 Dec. 1927.
22. *Terre Haute Tribune*, 25 Dec. 1927.
23. Ibid.
24. Ibid., 4 Nov. 1927.
25. *Terre Haute Tribune*, 30 Dec. 1927.
26. Ibid, same date, separate article.
27. Fight account is from *Los Angeles Times*, 31 Dec. 1927; *New York Times*, 31 Dec. 1927; *Chicago Daily Tribune*, 31 Dec. 1927; *Terre Haute Tribune*, 31 Dec. 1927; *Terre Haute Star*, 31 Dec. 1927.

Chapter 37

1. Fight account is from *Terre Haute Tribune*, 25 Jan. 1928.
2. Smith: *Terre Haute Tribune*, 13 Dec. 1927. Francis: *Tribune*, 3 Jan. 1928.
3. Ibid., 6 Feb. 1928.
4. Ibid., 7 Feb. 1928.
5. Ibid., 8 Feb. 1928; *New York Times*, 10 Feb. 1928.
6. *Terre Haute Tribune*, 5 Feb. 1928. Gas price from *Tribune*, 11 Feb. 1928.
7. *New York Times*, 10 Feb. 1928.
8. Fight account is from Ibid., *Chicago Daily Tribune*, 10 Feb. 1928; *Terre Haute Tribune*, 10 Feb. 1928; *Los Angeles Times*, 10 Feb. 1928.
9. *Chicago Daily Tribune*, 11 Feb. 1928; *Los Angeles Times*, 11 Feb. 1928.
10. *Chicago Daily Tribune*, 10 Feb. 1928.
11. *Los Angeles Times*, 23 Oct. 1927, reports Taylor had "haunting desire to redeem himself after the loss." Same paper, separate article reports Taylor and Sangor "personally don't like each other."
12. *Chicago American*, 10 Feb. 1928.
13. *Chicago Daily Tribune*, 10 Feb. 1928.

Chapter 38

1. Patty Ewald, "Re Bud Taylor the Terre Haute Terror" personal e-mail, 4 Dec. 2006. Ewald, Ellen's daughter by a later marriage, vaguely recalls hearing that they met through a showbiz friend of her mother's who had a Terre Haute connection.
2. *Los Angeles Times*, 18 Feb., 30 Sept. 1928; *Terre Haute Tribune*, 12 June 1928; Bud Taylor Jr., telephone interview with author, 17 Dec. 2004.
3. *Terre Haute Tribune*, 29 Sept. 1928. Ewald, 4 Dec. 2006; Taylor Jr., 4 April 2005.
4. *Terre Haute Tribune*, 12 June 1928. Also, www.imdb.com.
5. Ankles analogy from Ewald, 11 June 2005.
6. Taylor Jr., 4 April 2005.
7. Ibid.
8. *Los Angeles Times*, 4 March 1928; *New York Times*, 18 March 1928.
9. *Los Angeles Times*, 7 March 1928; Unknown publication, 1957 article datelined Los Angeles, by George T. Davis, clipping from Vigo County, Indiana historian Mike McCormick.
10. *Terre Haute Tribune*, 31 March 1928; *Los Angeles Times*, 7 March 1928.
11. *Terre Haute Tribune*, 31 March 1928.
12. *Los Angeles Times*, 3, 4 April 1928.

Chapter 39

1. *Terre Haute Tribune*, 1, 3, 4 May 1928.
2. Ibid., 3, 4 May 1928.
3. Ibid, 4 May 1928.
4. *New York Times*, 12 May 1928.
5. *Terre Haute Tribune*, 19 May 1928.
6. Ibid.
7. *Chicago American*, 22 May 1928; *New York Times*, 28 Aug. 1928.
8. *Terre Haute Tribune*, 19 May 1928.
9. Ibid., 19, 21 May 1928.
10. *Chicago American*, 22 May 1928.
11. *Chicago Daily Journal*, 22 May 1928.
12. *Terre Haute Tribune*, 21 Aug. 1928.

Chapter 40
1. *Terre Haute Tribune*, 9, 12 June, 6 Aug. 1928.
2. *Los Angeles Times*, 30 June 1928.
3. Accounts from *Los Angeles Times*, 6, 8, 11 July 1928.
4. Ibid., 10 July 1928.
5. Fight accounts from Ibid., 26 Aug. 1928; *Terre Haute Tribune*, 31 July, 10 Aug. 1928; *Chicago Daily Tribune*, 10 Nov. 1928.
6. *Terre Haute Tribune*, 10 Aug. 1928.
7. *Los Angeles Times*, 26 Aug. 1928.
8. Ibid.
9. Ibid., on number of surgeries.
10. *Terre Haute Tribune*, 10 Aug. 1928.
11. Ibid., 22 Aug. 1928.

Chapter 41
1. *Terre Haute Tribune*, 29 Sept. 1928.
2. Bud Taylor Jr., telephone interview with author, 4 April 2005.
3. *Washington Post*, 15 Jan. 1933.
4. *Rockford Register*, 14 June 1968.
5. *Terre Haute Tribune*, 20 Nov. 1928.
6. Ibid., 18 Nov. 1928.
7. Ibid., 11 Dec. 1928.
8. Ibid., 7 Oct. 1928.
9. Ibid., 24 May 1928.
10. Ibid., 19 May, 1928; *Terre Haute Star*, 10 Oct. 1926.
11. Dick Brokaw, interview with author, Terre Haute, 23 Dec. 2004; Tom Jennings, interview with author, Terre Haute, 14 Jan. 2005; Bill Lowe, interview with author, Terre Haute, 20 Feb. 2005.
12. Nasser's parents' names from John Nasser, interview with author, Terre Haute, 10 April 2005.
13. *Terre Haute Tribune*, 15 Jan., 22 May 1928. *Chicago Daily Tribune*, 10 Feb. 1928.
14. Rickard and Mullen information is from *Chicago Daily Tribune*, 9 Nov. 1928, 6 June 1945.
15. *Ring* magazine, June 1926.
16. *Ring*, June 1928.
17. *Los Angeles Times*, 1 April 1928, 9 June 1929, 9 Nov. 1930.
18. *Los Angeles Examiner*, 10 April 1928.

19. *Terre Haute Tribune*, 26 Sept. 1928.
20. Ibid., 10 Feb. 1924, 17 Oct. 1928.
21. *Terre Haute Star*, 16 Oct. 1928.
22. *Terre Haute Tribune*, 20 Oct. 1928.
23. Ibid., 17 Dec. 1928.

Chapter 42
1. *Terre Haute Tribune*, 30 Jan. 1929; *Indianapolis Star*, 30 Jan. 1929.
2. *Terre Haute Tribune*, 1 Feb. 1929.
3. Examples: *Evansville Courier*, 20 Sept. 1929; *Washington Post*, 21 July 1928; *Chicago Daily Tribune*, 31 Dec. 1927; *Los Angeles Times*, 4 March 1928; *Chicago Evening Post*, 21 April 1930.
4. *Chicago Daily Tribune*, 31 Dec. 1927.
5. Bud Taylor Jr., interview with author, Canastota, N.Y., 11 June 2005.
6. Dick Brokaw, interview with author, Terre Haute, 19 Nov. 2004.
7. *Terre Haute Tribune-Star*, 8 Oct. 1994.
8. Taylor Jr., telephone, 3 Feb. 2006.
9. Dempsey: *Terre Haute Tribune*, 1 Feb. 1929.
10. Singer's record is from www.boxrec.com
11. Fight account is from *Chicago Daily Tribune*, 8, 9 Feb. 1929; *New York Times*, 9 Feb. 1929; *New York Herald-Tribune*, 9 Feb. 1929. The *Herald-Tribune* reported the smiles.
12. *Terre Haute Tribune*, 11 Feb. 1929.
13. Ibid., 19 March 1929.
14. Fight account is from *Chicago Daily Tribune*, 16 March 1929; *Terre Haute Tribune*, 17 March 1929.
15. Examples: *Terre Haute Tribune*, 20 April, 2 Aug. 1924; 25 Aug. 1925; *Los Angeles Times*, 11 June, 23 Sept. 1924; *St. Louis Post-Dispatch*, 22 March 1921; *Aurora Beacon-News*, 12 Aug. 1924.
16. Examples: *Terre Haute Tribune*, 25 Jan. 1928; 17 March 1929; 8 April 1930; 14 Jan., 17 March 1931; *Terre Haute Star*, 23 July 1929; 17 March 1931; *Chicago Daily Tribune*, 31 Dec. 1927; *New York Herald-Tribune*, 9 Feb. 1929.
17. Joyce Carol Oates, *Joyce Carol Oates on Boxing* (New York: Dolphin Doubleday, 1987), 25.
18. Joseph Wambaugh, *The Onion Field* (New York: Delacorte Press, 1973).

19. Jake LaMotta, Joseph Carter and Peter Savage, *Raging Bull* (Englewood Cliffs, N.J.: Prentice-Hall, 1970) 1, 7, 168, 170-171, 178.
20. *Milwaukee Journal*, 26 March 1929.
21. *Terre Haute Tribune*, 3 April 1929.
22. Odds are from Ibid., 10 April 1929.
23. *Providence Evening Bulletin*, 11 April 1929.
24. Fight schedule and details are from *Terre Haute Tribune*, 17 April 1929; *Chicago Daily Tribune*, 18 April 1929; *Indianapolis Star*, 18 April 1929.
25. That the bout was canceled is from *Washington Post*, 18 April 1929.

Chapter 43
1. *Terre Haute Tribune*, 24 May 1929.
2. Ibid., 4 June 1929.
3. Ibid., 24 June 1929.
4. *Los Angeles Times*, 10 June 1929; *Los Angeles Record*, 12 June 1929; Los Angeles Evening Herald, 12 June 1929.
5. *Los Angeles Times*, 9 June 1929.
6. *Los Angeles Record*, 12 June 1929.
7. Fight account is from *Los Angeles Evening Herald*, 12 June 1929.
8. *Terre Haute Tribune*, 18 June 1929.
9. *Los Angeles Times*, 13 June 1929.
10. *Terre Haute Tribune*, 17-20 July 1929.
11. Ibid., 16 July 1929.
12. Fight account and press speculation are from Ibid., 23 July 1929; *Terre Haute Star*, 23 July 1929; *Chicago Daily Tribune*, 23 July 1929.
13. *Terre Haute Star*, 25 July 1929.
14. *Terre Haute Tribune*, 8 Sept. 1929.
15. Associated Press, by Bob Myers, obituary for Taylor, unknown publication or date, clipping found in personal collection of Vigo County, Indiana historian Mike McCormick.
16. Jim Long, telephone interview with author, 29 Dec. 2005.

Chapter 44
1. *Terre Haute Tribune*, 1, 8 Oct. 1929; *Chicago Daily Tribune*, 5 Aug. 1949.
2. *Terre Haute Tribune*, 7, 8 Oct. 1929.
3. Ibid., 6 Oct. 1929.
4. Ibid., 9 Oct. 1929; *Chicago Daily Tribune*, 26 Dec. 1929.
5. *Terre Haute Tribune*, 9 Oct. 1929.
6. Custody hearing accounts from Ibid., 10, 11 Oct. 1929; *Terre Haute Star*, 11 Oct. 1929.

Chapter 45
1. Dempsey's success promoting boxing in Chicago and the quote are from *Chicago Daily Tribune*, 1 Nov. 1929.
2. Bud Taylor Jr., telephone interview with author, 28 Feb. 2005.
3. *Chicago Daily Tribune*, 12 Nov. 1929; *Terre Haute Tribune*, 16 Nov. 1929.
4. *Chicago Daily Tribune*, 12 Nov. 1929.
5. Fight account is from Ibid., 16 Nov. 1929; *Terre Haute Tribune*, 16 Nov. 1929.
6. *Chicago Daily Tribune*, 16 Nov. 1929.
7. *Terre Haute Tribune*, 9 Dec. 1916.
8. *Atlanta Constitution*, 30 Sept. 1923.
9. Fight account is from *Chicago Herald-Examiner*, 28 Dec. 1929; *Chicago American*, 28 Dec. 1929; *Los Angeles Times*, 28 Dec. 1929; *Chicago Daily News*, 28 Dec. 1929; *Terre Haute Tribune*, 29, 30 1929.
10. Attendance is from *Terre Haute Tribune*, 28 Dec. 1929.
11. Ibid., 30 Dec. 1929.

Chapter 46
1. *Terre Haute Tribune*, 21 March 1930.
2. Ibid., 20 March 1930.
3. Ibid., same date, separate article.
4. See n.2 above.
5. Fight account and Dempsey item are from *Terre Haute Tribune*, 21 March 1930.
6. *Chicago Daily Tribune*, 13 April, 7 May 1930.
7. LaBarba's childhood is from *Los Angeles Times*, 22 April 1971; *Terre Haute Tribune*, 30 March, 6 Sept. 1925.

8. *Terre Haute Star*, 4 Nov. 1930.
9. *Los Angeles Times*, 22 April 1971.
10. Fight account is from *Chicago Daily Tribune*, 22 April 1930.
11. Ibid., 26 April 1930.
12. *Terre Haute Tribune*, 21 May 1930.
13. *Chicago Daily Tribune*, 3 June 1930.

Chapter 47
1. *Chicago Daily Tribune*, 30 May 1930.
2. Ibid., 9 July 1930.
3. *Terre Haute Tribune*, 8 April 1930.
4. Ibid., 31 July 1930.
5. Ibid., 19 Aug. 1930.
6. *Los Angeles Times*, 9 Nov. 1930.
7. Fight account is from *Los Angeles Examiner*, 11 Nov. 1930; *Terre Haute Tribune*, 31 July 1932.
8. *Terre Haute Star*, 29 Nov. 1930; *Chicago Daily Tribune*, 29 Nov. 1930.
9. *Terre Haute Tribune*, 4 Sept. 1930.
10. *Terre Haute Star*, 11 Jan. 1931.

Chapter 48
1. *Terre Haute Star*, 14 Jan. 1931; *Indianapolis Times*, 14 Jan. 1931.
2. *Terre Haute Star*, 5 Feb. 1931.
3. Ibid.; *Chicago Daily Tribune*, 17 Feb. 1931.
4. Attendance is from *Terre Haute Star*, 17 Feb. 1931.
5. Fight account is from Ibid., 17, 20 Feb. 1931; *Chicago Daily Tribune*, 17 Feb. 1931; Associated Press account datelined Feb. 17, unknown publication, clipping in personal collection of Vigo County, Indiana historian Mike McCormick.
6. Fight account is from *Terre Haute Star*, 17 March 1931; *Terre Haute Tribune*, 17 March 1931.
7. *Terre Haute Tribune*, 17 March 1931.
8. *New York Times*, 19 March 1931; unknown publication, dated 19 March 1931, clipping in personal collection of Vigo County, Indiana historian Mike McCormick.

Chapter 49
1. Sore hands is from *Terre Haute Star*, 19 March 1931.
2. Ibid., 15 May, 25 June, 8 July 1931.
3. *Chicago Daily Times*, 16 June 1931; *Terre Haute Star*, 11 June, 28 July, 1 Aug. 1931.
4. At odds over training is from Dick Brokaw, interview with author, Terre Haute, 9 Dec. 2004.
5. *Terre Haute Star*, 15 May, 5, 11 June, 3 Sept. 1931; 4, 9 Feb. 1932.
6. *Terre Haute Tribune*, 9 Feb. 1932.
7. Refereeing example is from *Terre Haute Star*, 18 April 1931.
8. Ibid., 15 Oct., 17 Nov. 1931.
9. Account of promoting debut is from Ibid., 4, 5 Sept. 1931.

Chapter 50
1. *Terre Haute Star*, 13 Jan., 1, 15 Feb., 11 Dec. 1931.
2. *Marshall (Ill.) Choice*, 21 Nov. 1988.
3. *Terre Haute Tribune*, 30 June 1932.
4. Shade a noticeable victory is from *Chicago Daily Tribune*, 2 Aug. 1932.
5. *Terre Haute Tribune*, 12, 13 Oct. 1932.
6. Ibid., 13 Oct. 1932.
7. Terre Haute city directories; U.S. Census 1930.
8. Frank Kleptz, interview with author, Terre Haute, 9 Jan. 2005; Tom Jennings, interview with author, Terre Haute, 18 Jan. 2005; Patty Ewald, "Re Bud Taylor the Terre Haute Terror" personal e-mail, 4 Dec. 2006.
9. Slaughter was the eighth fight in 13 by Jones without a loss since Jones' loss to Frenchman Marcel Thil for the world middleweight title, according to www.boxrec.com.
10. *Chicago Daily Tribune*, 24 Jan. 1933.
11. *Cleveland News*, 31 Jan. 1933.
12. *Terre Haute Tribune*, 4 March 1934. Also, www.boxrec.com
13. www.boxrec.com.
14. *Terre Haute Star*, 10 May, 21 July 1934; *Los Angeles Herald-Express*, 21 Jan. 1938.
15. *Terre Haute Star*, 15 May 1934 reports Dempsey made $1,100 refereeing in Memphis, Tenn.

16. *Terre Haute Tribune*, 24 Sept. 1934; Terre Haute Star, 30 Nov. 1934.
17. *Terre Haute Tribune*, 3, 9 April 1934.
18. *Los Angeles Herald-Express*, 21 Jan. 1938.
19. *Los Angeles Times*, 16 Nov. 1934.
20. *Chicago Daily Tribune*, 12 Jan. 1935.
21. *Terre Haute Tribune*, 23 Nov. 1934.
22. Tavern in Loop is from *Chicago Daily Times*, 11 Sept. 1934. Ellen missed is from Ewald, 4 Dec. 2006.
23. *Terre Haute Tribune*, 23 Nov., 16 Dec. 1934.

Chapter 51
1. *Chicago Daily Tribune*, 15 April 1935; *Los Angeles Times*, 25 April, 21 Dec. 1936; 1 Jan., 22 July, 17 Dec. 1937; 21 Jan. 1938; 20 Feb. 1939; Bud Taylor Jr., telephone interview with author, 28 Feb. 2005; copy of menu from restaurant and photo of same provided by surviving family of Bud Taylor.
2. Taylor Jr., 4 April 2005; Patty Ewald, "Re Bud Taylor, the Terre Haute Terror," personal e-mail, 4 Dec. 2006.
3. Bonds from *Los Angeles Times*, 1 April 1928; 9 Nov. 1930.
4. Peter Heller, *In This Corner* (New York; Simon & Schuster, 1973), 104; *Terre Haute Tribune*, 3 July 1934.
5. Ten thousand is from Dick Brokaw, interview with author, Terre Haute, 23 Dec. 2004.
6. Taylor Jr., 28 April 2005; Charles Rutz, telephone interview with author, 10 Feb. 2007; Judy Ruth Christine, interview with author, Canastota, N.Y., 12 June 2005.
7. *Terre Haute Star*, 2 July 1925; Brokaw, 23 Dec. 2004.
8. Brokaw, 23 Dec. 2004.
9. Unknown publication dated 26 Nov. 1956, written by Gene Coughlin, clipping from Bud Taylor file in Joyce Collection, Hesburgh Library, University of Notre Dame; Long material is from Jim Long, telephone interview with author, 29 Dec. 2005.
10. *Terre Haute Tribune*, 22 July 2004; *Los Angeles Times*, 16 Nov. 1934; 25 April 1936; *Chicago Daily Tribune*, 25 Dec. 1936; 22 July 1937; 20 Feb., 13 March 1939; unknown publication, clipping dated 14 Aug. 1954, from Bud Taylor file in Joyce Collection.

11. *Chicago Daily Tribune*, 25 Dec. 1936.
12. *Los Angeles Times*, 16 Nov. 1934.
13. *Chicago Daily Tribune*, 13 March 1939.
14. Divorce papers from Los Angeles County Clerk's office.
15. *Chicago Daily Tribune*, 22 July 1937.
16. *Los Angeles Times*, 20 Jan. 1938.
17. Ibid., 23 Aug. 1939; Patty Ewald, interview with author, Canastota, N.Y., 11 June 2005.
18. See n. 14 above.
19. *Chicago Daily Tribune*, 26 Nov. 1939.
20. *Terre Haute Tribune*, 3 Feb. 1940. Tillie had suffered a stroke three years earlier, according to *Saturday Spectator*, 3 Feb. 1940. Sam had suffered a fractured hip five weeks earlier, according to Tribune, 8 March 1940.

Chapter 52
1. *Terre Haute Tribune*, 29 Jan. 1940.
2. *Chicago Daily Tribune*, 25 Jan. 1936.
3. *Terre Haute Tribune*, 31 Jan., 4 Feb. 1940.
4. Dick Brokaw, interview with author, Terre Haute, 23 Dec. 2004. *Terre Haute Tribune*, 23, 24 March 1940.
5. *Terre Haute Tribune*, 15 Feb., 9 June 1941; 3 Feb., 18 Dec. 1942; 25 Feb. 1943; Bill Taylor, telephone interview with author, 9 July 2005.
6. *Indianapolis Star*, 13 June 1941.
7. Jim Long, telephone interview with author, 11 April 2006.
8. Long, 29 Dec. 2005.
9. *Los Angeles Herald-Examiner*, 21 Aug. 1938.
10. *Terre Haute Tribune*, 7 March 1943.
11. Paul Selge, interview with author, Terre Haute, 3 Nov. 2005.
12. *Chicago Daily Tribune*, 18 Dec. 1943.
13. Ibid., 8 June 1944.
14. Bud Taylor Jr., telephone interview with author, 9 Dec. 2004.
15. RKO Studios is from Charles Rutz, interview with author, Canastota, N.Y., 12 June 2005. Quote is from an unknown published article, clipping in the Bud Taylor file in the Joyce Collection at Hesburgh Library, University of Notre Dame.
16. Rutz, telephone, 21 July 2006.

17. Ibid.
18. *New York Times*, 10 March 1962.
19. Heart attack information is from three sources: *Los Angeles Examiner*, 9 March 1962; and two published articles of unknown source in the Bud Taylor file in the Joyce Collection, one undated, the other dated 14 Aug. 1954.
20. Rutz, 21 July 2006.
21. *Los Angeles Times*, 17 March 1954; 10 March 1962.
22. Taylor Jr., telephone, 17 Dec. 2004; Rutz, 12 June 2005.
23. *Boxing Illustrated, Wrestling News*, June 1962.
24. Ibid.
25. Rutz, telephone, 10 Feb. 2007.
26. *Terre Haute Tribune*, 21 April 1956; *Los Angeles Times*, 6 Jan. 1957.
27. *Los Angeles Times*, 16 March 1962.
28. Ibid., 14 March 1962.
29. Barbara Jean Taylor Rutz to Paul Frisz, May 1962, Taylor family collection.
30. *Los Angeles Evening Herald*, 15 June 1925.
31. Visitation list before funeral of Bud Taylor, courtesy Taylor family. Among those who signed were former sparring partners Jackie Barnhart and Harold Farris. Withrow items from *Terre Haute Tribune*, 18 Jan., 1 March 1921.
32. Taylor Jr., telephone, 28 Feb. 2005.

Chapter 53
1. www.boxrec.com
2. Terry Ray, interview with author, Terre Haute, 11 Jan. 2007.
3. Date is from *Terre Haute Tribune-Star*, 17 Aug. 1997.
4. Dick Brokaw, interview with author, Terre Haute, 11 March 2005.
5. Judy Rutz Christine, interview with author, Canastota, N.Y., 12 June 2005.

Bibliography

Bak, Richard, *Joe Louis, The Great Black Hope*. Dallas: Taylor Publishing. 1996.

Baughman, Judith S. *American Decades 1920-1929*. Detroit: Gale Research, 1995

Bradsby, H.C. *History of Vigo County, Indiana, With Biographical Selections*. Chicago: S.B. Nelson & Co., 1981.

Clark, Dorothy J., *Terre Haute, Wabash River City*. Woodland Hills, Calif.: Windsor Publications, 1983.

Collins, Nigel, *Boxing Babylon*. New York: Citadel Press, 1990.

Condit, Blackford. *The History of Early Terre Haute From 1816 to 1840*. New York: A.S. Barnes, 1900.

Deverell, William and Tom Sitton. *L.A. Metropolis in the Making*. University of California Press, 2001.

Fleischer, Nat, and Sam Andre. *A Pictorial History of Boxing*. New Jersey: Citadel Press, 1975.

Frazier, Joe and Phil Berger. *Smokin Joe The Autobiography*. New York: Macmillan, 1996.

Fried, Ronald K. *Corner Men, Great Boxing Trainers*. New York: Four Walls Eight Windows, 1991.

Gardon, F.J. *Twentieth Century Souvenir of Terre Haute*. Terre Haute, Ind.: Moore & Langen, 1903.

Griswold, B.J. and Edward M. Lucas. *Some Terre Haute Phizes*. Fort Wayne, Ind.: Archer Printing Co., 1905.

Halpern, Daniel, and Joyce Carol Oates. *Reading the Fights*. New York: Henry Holt & Co., 1988.

Heller, Peter. *In This Corner, Great Boxers in Their Own Words*. New York: Simon & Schuster, 1973.

Henderson, Clayton W. *On the Banks of the Wabash, The Life and Times of Paul Dresser*. Indianapolis: Indiana Historical Society Press, 2003.

Kahn, Roger. *A Flame of Pure Fire, Jack Dempsey and the Roaring Twenties*. New York: Harcourt Brace & Co., 1999.

Kent, Noel Jacob. *America in 1900*. New York: M.E. Sharpe, 2000.

La Motta, Jake. Joseph Carter and Peter Savage. *Raging Bull*. New Jersey: Prentice-Hall, 1970.

Man, John. *Attila*. New York: Thomas Dunne Books, St. Martin's Press, 2005.

McNeil, Jim. *They Could've Been Contenders*. London: Robson, 2001.

Morris, William and Mary Morris. *Morris Dictionary of Word and Phrase Origins*. New York: Harper & Row, 1977.

Oates, Joyce Carol. *Joyce Carol Oates on Boxing*. New York: Dolphin Doubleday, 1967.

Roosevelt, Theodore. *Theodore Roosevelt, The Rough Riders an Autobiography*. New York: Library of America, 2004.

Sugar, Bert Randolph. *The 100 Greatest Boxers of All Time*. New York: Bonanza Books, 1984.

Sugar, Bert Randolph, ed. *Ring Record Book and Boxing Encyclopedia*. New York: Athenium, 1981.

Wambaugh, Joseph. *The Onion Field*. New York: Delacorte Press, 1973.

Bud Taylor Professional Fight Record

"W" indicates a win and "L" a loss. "(N)" denotes the bout officially was a "no decision," and the outcome listed here was determined by newspaper accounts. "WF" or "LF" indicates referee disqualification, usually by a foul.

Date	Opponent	Site	Result
1/26/20	Davy Templeton	Terre Haute	W3 (N)
2/16/20	Everett Shepherd	Terre Haute	TKO 3
3/15/20	Walter Gering	Terre Haute	TKO 3
5/24/20	Jackie Edwards	Muncie, Ind.	TKO 2
6/7/20	Davy Templeton	Vincennes, Ind.	KO 4
7/6/20	Artie Armstrong	Vincennes, Ind.	W (N)
7/26/20	Bruce Michael	Clinton, Ind.	KO 2
8/2/20	"Dutch" Davison	Muncie, Ind.	TKO 3
10/4/20	Artie Armstrong	Terre Haute	W 10 (N)
11/1/20	Jimmie Burns	Terre Haute	TKO 9
11/8/20	Tom "Whitey" Murrette	Cincinnati, Ohio	W 6
11/25/20	"Young" Dempsey	Terre Haute	TKO 2
12/13/20	Tom "Whitey" Murrette	Terre Haute	W 10 (N)
1/1/21	Bobby Moon	Terre Haute	W 10 (N)
1/17/21	Frankie Mason	Terre Haute	W 10 (N)
1/31/21	Jimmy Murphy	St. Louis, Mo.	D 6 (N)
2/28/21	Jimmy Murphy	Terre Haute	D 10 (N)
3/21/21	Jimmy Murphy	St. Louis, Mo.	W 8 (N)
4/4/21	"Dutch" Davison	Terre Haute	KO 1

4/24/21	Phil O'Dowd Terre Haute	D 10 (N)
4/29/21	Battling Chink Terre Haute	W 10 (N)
7/18/21	Eddie O'Dowd Louisville, Ky.	L 12 (N)
7/21/21	Johnny McGrath Springfield, Ill.	KO 3
7/25/21	Battling Chink Louisville, Ky.	D 12 (N)
8/22/21	Patsy Drennan Terre Haute	KO 1
9/5/21	Herbie Schaeffer South Bend, Ind.	W 8 (N)
10/10/21	Solly Epstein Terre Haute	KO 9
11/7/21	"Chick" Allman Terre Haute	W 10 (N)
12/3/21	Harold Smith Chicago, Ill.	W 6 (N)
12/5/21	Herbie Schaeffer Omaha, Neb.	D 10 (N)
12/12/21	Stanley Everett Terre Haute	W 10 (N)
12/29/21	Harold Smith La Salle, Ill.	W 10 (N)
1/5/22	Solly Epstein Terre Haute	KO 1
1/13/22	George Corbett Chicago, Ill.	TKO 3
1/24/22	Ollie O'Neill Chicago, Ill.	W 8 (N)
2/10/22	Jimmy Kelly Chicago, Ill.	TKO by 6
2/23/22	Harold Smith LaSalle, Ill.	D 10 (N)
3/10/22	Herbie Schaeffer Chicago, Ill.	W 10 (N)
3/22/22	Jimmy Kelly Kenosha, Wis.	W 10 (N)
4/21/22	Frankie Henke Chicago, Ill.	TKO 7
5/15/22	Kid Buck Logansport, Ind.	W 10 (N)
6/14/22	Herbie Schaeffer Indianapolis, Ind.	W 10 (N)
6/23/22	"Memphis" Pal Moore Aurora, Ill.	D 10 (N)
7/4/22	Babe Asher Terre Haute	W 10 (N)
9/4/22	Jimmy Kelly Terre Haute	W 10 (N)
9/21/22	Harold Smith E. Chicago, Ind.	L 10 (N)
10/13/22	Stanley Everett Chicago, Ill.	KO 5
11/1/22	Battling Chink Terre Haute	W 10 (N)
11/27/22	Billy O'Brien Peoria, Ill.	W 8 (N)
11/30/22	Eddy Santry Terre Haute	TKO 5
12/22/22	"Memphis" Pal Moore Chicago, Ill.	L 10 (N)
1/1/23	Benny Vogel Indianapolis, Ind	KO 1
1/8/23	Jimmy Kelly Chicago, Ill.	W 10 (N)
1/15/23	"Memphis" Pal Moore East Chicago, Ind.	D 10 (N)
2/13/23	"Memphis" Pal Moore Indianapolis, Ind.	D 10 (N)

4/4/23	Frankie Genaro Chicago, Ill.	L 10 (N)
5/29/23	Johnny Sheppard Indianapolis, Ind.	W 10 (N)
6/25/23	Battling Murray Terre Haute	W 10 (N)
7/5/23	Johnny Sheppard Indianapolis, Ind.	W 10 (N)
7/20/23	Harry Gordon Aurora, Ill.	W 10 (N)
7/30/23	Tommy Murray Terre Haute	W 10
8/24/23	Hilly Levine Aurora, Ill.	W 10 (N)
9/3/23	Harry Gordon Terre Haute	W 10 (N)
9/8/23	Pancho Villa Chicago, Ill.	L 10 (N)
10/19/23	Phil Rosenberg New York City	W 10
12/5/23	Roy Moore Terre Haute	W 10 (N)
1/1/24	Sammy Nable New York City	W 12
1/7/24	Johnny Brown Indianapolis, Ind.	KO 3
1/11/24	Frankie Jerome New York City	KO 12
1/28/24	Herbie Schaeffer E. Chicago, Ind.	W 10 (N)
2/7/24	Eddie O'Dowd Columbus, Ohio	L 10 (N)
2/18/24	Sammy Nable Indianapolis, Ind.	W 10 (N)
3/6/24	Pancho Villa Milwaukee, Wis.	W 10 (N)
4/7/24	Al Pettingill Indianapolis, Ind.	KO 2
4/15/24	Charles "Rosy" Stoy Youngstown, Ohio	D 12 (N)
5/26/24	Connie Curry Aurora, Ill.	D 10 (N)
5/30/24	Tommy Ryan Indianapolis, Ind.	D 10 (N)
6/10/24	Pancho Villa Brooklyn, N.Y.	L 12
6/23/24	Eddie Coulon Indianapolis, Ind.	KO 1
6/27/24	Al Ziemer Cleveland, Ohio	W 10 (N)
8/1/24	Tommy Ryan Terre Haute	W 10 (N)
8/11/24	Pete Sarmiento Aurora, Ill.	W 10 (N)
8/28/24	Carl Tremaine Cleveland, Ohio	L 10 (N)
9/23/24	George Rivers Vernon, Calif.	W 4
1/1/25	Al Ziemer Indianapolis, Ind.	D 10 (N)
4/20/25	Midget Smith E. Chicago, Ind.	W 10 (N)
5/18/25	Mike Moran Terre Haute	W 10 (N)
5/26/25	Abe Goldstein Long Island, N.Y.	W 10
6/2/25	Jimmy McLarnin Vernon, Calif.	W 10
6/16/25	Ernie Goozeman Vernon, Calif.	TKO 7
6/24/25	"Dynamite" Murphy Oakland, Calif.	W 10

7/4/25 Bobby Wolgast Terre Haute	W 10 (N)
7/31/25 "Bushy" Graham Aurora, Ill.	W 10 (N)
8/24/25 "Bushy" Graham Long Island, N.Y.	L 12
10/27/25 "Doc" Snell Vernon, Calif.	W 10
11/18/25 Pete Sarmiento Los Angeles, Calif.	W 10
12/8/25 Jimmy McLarnin Vernon, Calif.	LF 2
1/12/26 Jimmy McLarnin Vernon, Calif.	W 10
2/3/26 Joey Sangor Los Angeles, Calif.	W 10
3/9/26 Johnny Brown Vernon, Calif.	W 10
3/26/26 "Doc" Snell Cleveland, Ohio	W 12
4/8/26 Abe Goldstein Terre Haute	D 10 (N)
4/19/26 Clever Sencio Milwaukee, Wis.	W 10
5/14/26 Tommy Ryan Louisville, Ky.	W 12 (N)
6/18/26 "California" Joe Lynch San Francisco, Calif.	W 10
6/25/26 Chuck Hellman Portland, Ore.	D 10
6/26/26 Young Nationalista Seattle, Wash.	W 6
7/24/26 Tommy Ryan Chicago, Ill.	WF 3
8/19/26 Dixie LaHood Los Angeles, Calif.	TKO 8
10/22/26 Vic Burrone St. Paul, Minn.	W 10 (N)
11/6/26 Young Montreal Vernon, Calif.	TKO 3
11/26/26 Joey Sangor Milwaukee, Wis.	L 10
2/15/27 Midget Smith Indianapolis, Ind.	W 10 (N)
2/24/27 Eddie Shea Chicago, Ill.	W 10
3/15/27 Pete Sarmiento Terre Haute	W 10 (N)
3/26/27 Tony Canzoneri Chicago, Ill.	D 10
4/18/27 Young Nationalista Los Angeles, Calif.	TKO 5
5/3/27 Abe Goldstein Chicago, Ill.	W 10
5/9/27 "Memphis" Pal Moore Memphis, Tenn.	W 8 (N)
5/31/27 Chick Suggs Los Angeles, Calif.	TKO 5
6/11/27 Johnny Hughes St. Paul, Minn.	KO 2
6/24/27 Tony Canzoneri Chicago, Ill.	W 10
9/1/27 Don "Midget" Smith Culver City, Calif.	KO 1
9/20/27 Joey Sangor Los Angeles, Calif.	L 10
11/8/27 Johnny Farr Los Angeles, Calif.	W 10
12/30/27 Tony Canzoneri New York City	L 10

1/10/28 Roy "Babe" Ruth Chicago, Ill.   W 10
1/24/28 Phil Zwick Milwaukee, Wis.   KO 2
2/9/28 Joey Sangor Chicago, Ill.   TKO by 7
3/6/28 Ignacio Fernandez Los Angeles, Calif.   W 10
3/23/28 Vic Foley Vancouver, B.C.   L 10
4/3/28 Santiago Zorilla Los Angeles, Calif.   W 10
5/21/28 Joe Lucas Chicago, Ill.   W 10
6/29/28 Santiago Zorilla San Francisco, Calif. W 10
7/10/28 Johnny Vacca Los Angeles, Calif.   W 10
7/27/28 Santiago Zorilla San Francisco, Calif. L 10

1/29/29 Billy Shaw Indianapolis, Ind.   KO 2
1/31/29 Bobby Dempsey Davenport, Iowa   KO 4
2/8/29 Al Singer New York City   LF 4
3/15/29 Al Singer New York City   L 10
4/1/29 Henry Falegano Milwaukee, Wis.   W 8
4/10/29 Young Montreal Providence, R.I.   L 10
4/16/29 Tommy Murray Indianapolis, Ind.   KO 2
6/11/29 Goldie Hess Los Angeles, Calif.   D 10
7/22/29 Andy Martin Boston, Mass.   L 10
9/20/29 Orlando Martinez Evansville, Ind.   KO 4
10/8/29 Earl Mastro Chicago, Ill.   D 10
11/15/29 Santiago Zorilla Chicago, Ill.   W 10
12/27/29 Earl Mastro Chicago, Ill.   TKO by 9

3/20/30 Battling Battalino Detroit, Mich.   W 10
4/11/30 Paul Wangley Minneapolis, Minn.   KO 5
4/21/30 Fidel LaBarba Chicago, Ill.   L 10
6/3/30 Jackie Johnston Chicago, Ill.   KO 2
6/12/30 Johnny Kaiser Springfield, Ill.   TKO 3
7/1/30 Earl Mastro Chicago, Ill.   L 10
7/29/30 Mickey Genaro Indianapolis, Ind.   W 10 (N)
8/18/30 Battling Battalino Hartford, Conn.   L 10
10/1/30 "Soldier" Dombrowski Fort Wayne, Ind.   KO 4
10/14/30 Eddie Edelman Spokane, Wash.   W 8
10/21/30 Santiago Zorilla Seattle, Wash.   D 8
11/10/30 Maurice Holtzer Los Angeles, Calif.   L 10
11/28/30 Fidel LaBarba New York City   L 10

1/13/31	Joe Lucas Indianapolis, Ind.	W 10 (N)
1/30/31	Sammy Hackett Buffalo, N.Y.	KO 3
2/16/31	Benny Bass Philadelphia, Pa.	KO by 2
3/16/31	Lew Massey Philadelphia, Pa.	LF 8

Index of Names

Ali, Muhammed (Cassius Clay), Chap. 9, 22
Amos, Babe, Chap. 49
Anderson, Eddie, Chap. 18, 23
Andrews, Tom, Chap. 11
Anka, Paul, Chap. 8
Anthony, Susan B., Chap. 10
Aragon, Art, Chap. 52
Armstrong, Artie, Chap. 4
Armstrong, Henry, Chap. 51
Armstrong, Neil, Chap. 35
Ash, Frankie, Chap. 17
Asher, Johnny "Babe," Chaps. 10, 11
Avalon, Frankie, Chap. 8
Baer, Max, Chap. 50
Baker, Ed, Chaps. 5,6
Baldock, Teddy, Chaps. 35, 37
Balsinger, Dr. William, Chap. 41
Barnett, Dick, Chap. 6
Barnhart, Jackie, Chaps. 6, 17, 29, 31, 36, 52
Barry, Dave, Chap. 44
Barry, Edwin, Chap. 25
Basilio, Carmen, Chap. 53
Bass, Benny, Chaps. 36, 48
Battalino, Battling (Christopher Battaglia), Chaps. 46, 47
Bayh, Birch Jr., Chap. 50
Bayh, Birch Sr., Chap. 50
Bayh, Evan, Chap. 50
Bayh, Leah, Chap. 50

Bays, Fred, Chaps. 29, 31, 33, 34
Bays, Lee, Chap. 33
Berlenbach, Paul, Chap. 19
Bimstein, Whitey, Chap. 16
Bird, Larry, Chap. 5
Blackburn, Jack, Chaps. 2, 9, 11, 12, 14, 15, 18, 20, 30
Bowles-Wiley, Anna, Chap. 10
Brix, Lou, Chap. 16
Brokaw, Dick, Chaps. 9, 10, 36, 42
Brokaw, Howard, Chaps. 36, 53
Bronson, Ray, Chap. 28
Brown, Johnny, Chap. 16
Brown, Johnny (English), Chaps. 24, 35
Brown, Mickey, Chap. 19
Brown, Norman, Chap. 49
Brown, Paul, Chaps. 17
Brown, Warren, Chaps. 28, 38
Buff, Johnny, Chaps. 15, 17
Burns, Jimmy, Chap. 4
Burrone, Vic, Chap. 28
Callahan, Mushy, Chap. 51
Campbell, Ray, Chap. 18
Campanella, Roy, Chap. 4
Canzoneri, Tony, Intro, Chaps. 28, 30, 31, 32, 33, 35, 36, 42
Capone, Al, Chap. 32
Carey, Max, Chap. 22
Carnera, Primo, Chap. 50
Carpentier, Georges, Chaps. 9, 15
Cayton, Bill, Chap. 53
Chacon, Bobby, Chap. 53
Chaney, Lon, Chap. 14
Chink, Battling (Johnny Samuels), Chaps. 6, 7, 11
Chip. George, Chap. 2
Choynsky, Joe, Chap. 33
Christine, Judy Rutz, Chaps. 51, 53
Churchill, Frank, Chaps. 18, 26, 38
Clabby, Jimmy, Chap. 28
Clark, Jeff, Chap. 3

Cobb, Ty, Chap. 13
Coffey, Joe, Chaps. 13, 15
Collins, Phil, Chap. 45
Comiskey, Charles, Chap. 27
Cook, Charley, Chap. 31
Cook, Earl L., Chap. 33
Cooper, "Farmer" Joe, Chaps. 29, 36
Corbett, George, Chap. 9
Corbett, Jim, Chap. 41
Coughlon, Gene, Chaps. 18, 51
Coulon, Eddie, Chap. 11
Cox, James M., Chap. 4
Criqui, Eugene, Chap. 53
Cryer, George, Chap. 28
Cullum, Dick, Chap. 47
Cummins, Ed, Chap. 42
Curley, Don, Chaps. 2, 5, 6
Curtin, Johnny, Chaps. 16, 52
Curtis, Carlo, Chap. 28
Davis, Ora, Chaps. 12, 15, 20, 21, 28
Davison, "Dutch," Chap. 6
Debs, Eugene V., Chap. 5
Del Rio, Delores, Chaps. 38, 40
Delaney, Jack, Chap. 19
Delaney, Jimmy, Chaps. 30, 32
Dempsey, Jack, Intro, Chaps. 2, 3, 9, 11, 13, 15, 18, 22, 28, 31, 34, 35, 40, 41, 43, 45, 46, 50, 52
Dempsey, Bobby, Chap. 42
Dillinger, John, Chap. 34
Dillon, Jack, Chaps. 2, 8, 38
Donahue, Thomas, Chap. 39
Doyle, Jack, Chaps. 20, 21, 22, 23, 24
Doyle, James E., Chap. 25
Doyle, Tom, Intro
Dresser, Paul, Chaps. 18, 21, 31
Duane, Carl, Chap. 16
Dundee, Angelo, Chap. 53
Dundee, Johnny, Chap. 24

Dyer, Eddie, Chaps. 13, 17, 18, 36
East, Estella, Chap. 1
Eckersall, Walter, Chaps. 9, 17, 18
Eckwart, Whitey, Chaps. 15, 26
Edgren, Bob, Chaps. 22, 23, 28
Edwards, Jack, Chaps. 3, 4
Epstein, Solly, Chaps. 7, 8, 12
Evans, Grace, Chap. 5
Evans, Linus, Chap. 44
Everett, Stanley, Chap. 11
Fabian, Chap. 8
Falegano, Henry, Chap. 42
Farr, Johnny, Chap. 36
Farris, Harold "Bones," Chaps. 50, 52
Fernandez, Ignacio, Chaps. 38, 39
Fetze, William, Chap. 33
Fields, Jackie, Chaps. 23, 51
Firpo, Louis, Chap. 18
Fisbeck, Edith (Taylor), Chaps. 1, 2, 10, 31
Fisbeck, Horace, Chap. 41
Fitzgerald, John M., Chap. 28
Fitzsimmons, Bob, Chaps. 2, 4, 41
Fleischer, Nat, Chaps. 15, 35, 52
Flournoy, Frank, Chap. 15
Flynn, Clint, Chap. 3
Foley, Joe, Chap. 39
Foley, Vic, Chap. 38
Fontaine, Ritchie, Chap. 51
Foster, Bob, Chap. 4
Foster, Charles "Pop," Chaps. 20, 23
Fox, "Tiger" Jack, Chap. 50
Fralick, Dr. William, Chaps. 19, 22, 31
Francis, Kid, Chaps. 37, 39, 44
Frank, Max, Chap. 1
Fraser, Don, Chap. 53
Frayne, Ed, Chaps. 4, 22
Frazier, Joe, Chaps. 1, 22
Fritz, Louise, Chap. 5

Furey, Barney, Chaps. 30, 33, 45
Gallico, Paul, Chap. 2
Gans, Joe, Chap. 3
Garcia, Frankie, Chap. 18
Gardner, Eddie, Chap. 2
Gehrig, Lou, Chap. 41
Geiger, Edward J., Chap. 39
Genaro, Frankie, Chaps. 13, 14, 15, 18
Gerhardt, Louis, Chap. 2
Gerhardt, Mary, Chap. 24
Gering, Walter, Chap. 3
Gibbons, Mike, Chaps. 2, 6, 30
Gibbons, Tommy, Chaps. 6, 13, 15, 18, 20, 30
Gibson, Billy, Chaps. 10, 16
Gill, Mickey, Chap. 26
Gillis, Arthur, Chap. 33
Goldman, Sammy, Chaps. 30, 31
Goldstein, Abe, Chaps. 16, 17, 18, 20, 22, 24, 25, 31, 32, 33
Goozeman, Ernie, Chap. 20
Gordon, Harry, Chaps. 14, 18
Graham, Bushy (Mickey Garcia), Chaps. 22, 23, 24, 27, 28, 30, 31, 39
Grammell, George, Chaps. 2, 8, 11, 13, 15, 21, 25
Grange, Red, Intro
Greb, Harry, Intro, Chaps. 7, 9
Hagler, Marvin, Chap. 53
Hanks, E.Z., Chaps. 20, 21
Hardin, Warren G., Chap. 4
Harper, Ida Husted, Chap. 10
Hart, Marvin, Chap. 2
Harter, Ed. W. "Steve," Chaps. 12, 17, 19
Hellmann, Chuck, Chap. 27
Henke, Frankie, Chap. 9
Herman, Pete, Chap. 9
Hess, Goldie, Chaps. 43, 45
Hettinger, Karl, Chap. 42
Hewitt, John, Chap. 18
Holtzer, Maurice, Chap. 47

Hornsby, Rogers, Chaps. 13, 41
Houck, Leo, Chap. 48
Howard, Kid, Chap. 13
Hughes, Frankie, Chap. 49
Hughes, Johnny, Chap. 32
Hulman, Herman, Chap. 5
Iscariot, Judas, Chap. 42
Jackson, Guy, Chap. 5
Jackson, Peter, Chap. 3
Jeanette, Joe, Chap. 3
Jeffries, James, Chaps. 2, 15
Jeffries, John P., Chap. 10
Jennings, Tom, Chap. 34
Jerome, Frankie (Frank Dougherty), Chaps. 16, 17, 26, 42, 49, 52
Jett, F.W., Chaps. 1, 17
Johnson, Charles "Tex," Chap. 2, 3, 4, 5, 8, 9, 10, 33
Johnson, Jack, Chaps. 2, 3, 15, 30, 35
Johnson, Noble, Chap. 3
Jones, Bobby, Intro, Chap. 21
Jones, Jersey, Chap. 53
Jones, William "Gorilla," Chaps. 50, 51
Jones, Jimmy, Chap. 36
Jones, Morgan A., Chap. 16
Joyce, Billy, Chap. 33
Julian, Rose, Chap. 41
Kane, Eddie, Chaps. 6, 9, 11, 13, 14, 17, 18, 20, 27
Kansas, Rocky, Chap. 27
Kearns, Jack, Chap. 2
Kellett, Andy, Chap. 50
Kelly, Jimmy, Chaps. 9, 10, 11, 12, 13
Kennedy, Jack, Chap. 43
Ketchel, Stanley, Chaps. 3, 10
Kent, Noel, Chap. 1
Keyes, Jimmy, Chap. 7
Killbane, Johnny, Chap. 2
Killebrew, Harmon, Chap. 4
LaBarba, Fidel, Chaps. 26, 44, 46, 47, 51
LaHood, Dixie, Chap. 27

LaMotta, Jake, Chaps. 42, 53
Lance, Walter, Chap. 38
Langford, Sam, Chap. 3
Langford, Wolcott, Chap. 47
Leonard, Benny, Intro, Chaps. 2, 9, 11
Levine, Hilly, Chap. 14
Levy, Sam, Chap. 31
Lewis, Willie, Chaps. 17, 25
Light, Leo, Chap. 2
Lindbergh, Charles, Chaps. 32, 35
Loi, Duilio, Chap. 53
Long, Billy, Chaps. 3, 10, 11, 52
Long, Eddie, Chaps. 6, 9, 10, 11, 14, 15, 16, 17, 18, 19, 20, 21, 22, 23, 25, 26, 27, 28, 29, 30, 31, 32, 35, 36, 37, 39, 43, 44, 45, 46, 48, 51, 52
Long, Jim, Chaps. 11, 43, 52
Lonsdale, Lord, Chap. 24
Lord, Bert, Chap. 16
Louis, Joe, Intro, Chaps. 2, 22
Lowry, Paul, Chaps. 20, 22, 23, 27
Lucas, Joe, Chap. 48
Lucas, Johnny, Chap. 3
Lynch, "California" Joe, Chap. 27
Lynch, Eddie, Chap. 40
Lynch, Joe, 7, 9, 11, 17, 20, 53
Mace, Lloyd, Chap. 18
Mahaney, Larry, Chap. 3
Mandell, Joe, Chap. 9
Mandell, Sammy, Chaps. 6, 8, 9, 13, 18, 27, 28, 32, 41, 51
Marshall, T.R., Chap. 2
Martin, Andy, Chap. 43
Martin, Eddie "Cannonball," Chaps. 18, 20, 24
Mason, Frankie, Chaps. 4, 5, 10, 15, 33
Massey, Lew, Chap. 48, 49
Mastro, Earl, Chaps. 43, 44, 45, 46, 47, 49
Mauk, Jane, Chap. 2
McAfee, Olin, Chap. 4
McCormack, William, Chap. 16

McDermott, Jimmy, Chaps. 29, 36
McFarlin, Robert, Chap. 36
McGregor, C.V., Chap. 39
McGuigan, Barry, Chap. 53
McLarnin, Jimmy, Chaps. 20, 22, 23, 24, 28, 35, 40, 42
McMahan, Jess, Chap. 36
McVey, Sam, Chap. 3
Medill, Joey, Chap. 31
Meharry, Mickey, Chap. 31
Mercer, Sid, Chap. 15
Miller, Bill, Intro, Chap. 17
Miller, Robert, Chap. 36
Miloslavich, Dr. Edward L. Chap. 26
Montreal, Young (Maurice Billingkoff), Chaps. 28, 42
Moon, Bobbie, Chap. 5
Moore, "Memphis" Paul, Chaps. 7, 9, 10, 11, 12, 15, 18, 30, 31, 32, 33, 36
Moore, Roy, Chap. 15
Moore, Tommy, Chap. 25
Moran, Mike, Chap. 20
Mulkern, Frank, Chap. 26
Mullan, Harry, Chap. 53
Mullen, Don, Chap. 3
Mullen, Jim, Chaps. 9, 14, 20, 25, 27, 28, 30, 31, 32, 33, 41
Murett, Tom "Whitey," Chap. 4
Murphy, "Dynamite," Chap. 20
Murphy, Jimmy, Chaps. 6, 7
Murray, Tommy, Chaps. 13, 42
Nable, Sammy, Chaps. 16, 17
Nash, Eddie, Chap. 9
Nasser, Johnny, Chaps. 41, 43, 46
Nasser, Mary, Chap. 41
Nasser, Saleem, Chap. 41
Nationalista, Young, Chaps. 27, 31
Nehf, Art, Chaps. 5, 41
Nesbit, Bob, Chaps. 15, 20, 49, 52
Norris, Dr. Charles, Chap. 16
Norris, Terry, Chap. 53

Oates, Joyce Carol, Chap. 42
O'Brien, Billy, Chap. 11
O'Brien, Jack, Chap. 3
O'Dowd, Eddie, Chaps. 6, 10
O'Dowd, Phil, Chaps. 17, 18
O'Keefe, Jack, Chap. 6
O'Neill, Ollie, Chap. 9
O'Shea, Leo, Chap. 26
O'Sullivan, Jack, Chap. 16
Oswego, George, Chaps. 11, 12, 17
Pappakeriazes, John, Chap. 3
Patterson, Floyd, Chap. 1
Patton, Blaine, Chap. 42
Pegler, Westbrook, Chaps. 16, 22, 31, 36, 42
Perrill, Adolphus, Chap. 2
Perrill, Catherine, Chap. 2
Perrill, Clifford "Bud," Chaps. 2, 3, 10, 17, 36, 52
Pettingill, Al, Chap. 17
Pfeifer, Carl, Chap. 14
Pfeifer, Florence, Chap. 14
Pfirman, Cy, Chap. 4
Polacio, Tony, Chap. 46
Porter, Don "Kid," Chap. 29
Potter, Paul, Chap. 52
Potts, Joe, Chap. 12
Randall, Jack, Chap. 53
Ray, Terry, Chap. 53
Raycroft, Joseph E., Chap. 2
Raymond, Lew, Chap. 17
Reilly, Tommy, Chap. 48
Rickard, Tex, Chaps. 4, 15, 16, 23, 24, 25, 30, 31, 36, 39
Ritchie, Willie, Chap. 2
Rivers, Georgie, Chaps. 18, 40
Roberts, Donn, Chap. 2
Roberts, Leo, Chap. 2
Robinson, "Sugar" Ray, Intro
Roosevelt, Franklin D., Chap. 4
Roosevelt, Teddy, Chap. 2

Rose, Charlie, Chap. 28
Rose, Chauncy, Chap. 5
Rosenberg, Charley Phil, Chaps. 15, 20, 21, 22, 23, 24, 25, 27, 28, 30
Ross, Ted, Chap. 6
Routis, Andre, Chap. 46
Runyan, Damon, Chap. 28
Ruth, Babe, Intro, Chaps. 2, 5, 6, 13, 28, 31, 41
Ruth, Roy "Babe," Chap. 37
Rutz, Barbara Jean (Taylor), Chaps. 20, 22, 23, 24, 34, 36, 40, 43, 44, 51, 52, 53
Rutz, Charles, Chap. 1, 51, 52
Ryan, "Greek" Jimmy, Chap. 3
Ryan, Joe, Chap. 6
Ryan, Tommy, Chaps. 18, 26, 27
Rychell, Ray, Chaps. 31, 32
Saddler, Sandy, Chap. 4
Sangor, Joey, Chaps. 24, 28, 29, 30, 35, 36, 37, 40
Santry, Eddie, Chap. 11
Sarmiento, Pete, Chaps. 18, 21, 22, 27, 30, 31, 36
Sarreal, Lope, Chap. 53
Saylor, Milburn, Chap. 28
Schaeffer, Herbie, Chaps. 9, 14, 17
Schinner, Arthur J. Chap. 26
Schmeling, Max, Chap. 43
Schreck, Mike, Chap. 2
Schwartz, Izzy, Chap. 26
Scopes, John, Chap. 21
Segal, Harry, Chaps. 20, 21, 22, 27, 28
Selge, Paul, Chap. 52
Sencio, Clever (Sencio Moldez), Chaps. 26, 28, 42, 49
Shade, Dave, Chap. 50
Sharkey, Jack, Chaps. 34, 43
Shawn, Billy, Chap. 42
Shea, Eddie, Chaps. 25, 30, 44, 47
Sheehan, Paul, Chap. 3
Shepard, Johnny, Chap. 13
Shepherd, Everett "Jack," Chap. 3
Short, Jay, Chap. 21

Shumard, Laura, Chap. 44
Silva, Teddy, Chap. 26
Silver, Phil, Chap. 33
Singer, Al, Chap. 42
Sisler, George, Chap. 13
Slaughter, Sammy, Chaps. 47, 49, 50
Smith, Al, Chaps. 3, 31
Smith, Don, Chap. 35
Smith, Ed, Chaps. 7, 9, 11, 12, 14, 22
Smith, Gunboat, Chap. 41
Smith, Harold, Chaps. 7, 9, 11, 15, 26, 27, 30, 32
Smith, James "Bonecrusher," Chap. 15
Smith, Vera, Chap. 20
Smith, William J. "Midget," Chaps. 20, 30
Smith, Willie, Chap. 37
Smock, Jack, Chap. 12
Snell, Doc (Bill McEachern), Chaps. 22, 25
Sparks, Ward "Kid," Chaps. 10, 36
Steeg, Henry, Chap. 2
Sugar, Bert, Chaps. 2, 3, 4, 53
Suggs, Chick, Chaps. 23, 24, 27, 30, 32, 36
Sullivan, Ed, Chap. 42
Sullivan, John L., Chaps. 2, 15, 32
Taylor, Andrew, Chap. 5
Taylor, Barbara Jean, Chaps. 20, 22, 23, 24, 34, 36, 40, 43, 44, 51, 52, 53
Taylor, Bud Jr., Chap. 1, 15, 42, 50, 51, 52
Taylor, Edith, Chaps. 1, 2, 10, 31
Taylor, Ellen (Grabski), Chaps. 38, 40, 41, 43, 44, 50, 51, 52
Taylor, George "Bunny," Chap. 3
Taylor, Iris (Ward), Chaps. 14, 15, 18, 23, 24, 26, 31, 34, 36, 44, 52
Taylor, Lillian, Chap. 52
Taylor, Margaret, Chap. 5
Taylor, Matilda "Tillie," Chaps. 1, 3, 14, 33, 52
Taylor, Orville, Chap. 1
Taylor, Sam, Chaps. 1, 3, 13, 14, 33, 52
Teague, Tommy, Chap. 3
Temple, Shirley, Chap. 40

Templeton, Davy, Chaps. 3, 4, 14
Tendler, Lew, Chap. 11
Terhorst, Margaret, Chap. 44
Thil, Marcel, Chaps. 50, 53
Tierney, Jack, Chaps. 2, 5, 6
Tilden, Bill, Intro, Chap. 21
Tremaine, Carl, Chaps. 18, 27
Tunney, Gene, Intro, Chaps. 15, 22, 28, 35, 41
Vacca, Johnny, Chap. 40
Vaccarillo, Tony, Chap. 19
Valentino, Rudolph, Chap. 8
Van Hook, Ray, Chap. 43
Vaughan, Manning, Chap. 26
Villa, Pancho (Francisco Guilledo), Chaps. 11, 12, 13, 14, 15, 17, 21, 22, 26
Vogel, Benny, Chap. 12
Voorhees, Daniel, Chap. 18
Wadhams, Hayden "Wad," Intro
Wagner, Clarence, Chap. 5
Wagner, John, Chap. 9
Walker, Buddy, Chap. 6
Walker, Mickey, Chap. 9
Wallace, Frank, Chap. 26
Welch, Suey, Chaps. 51, 52
Welling, Joe, Chap. 2
Wengert, Eugene, Chap. 26
White, Ralph, Chaps. 2, 3, 4, 6, 8, 10, 13, 14, 15, 16, 17, 19, 21, 22, 26, 27, 28, 30, 31, 40
Whiteman, Paul, Chap. 21
Whitman, Benny, Chap. 23
Wilde, Jimmy, Chaps. 5, 11, 13, 15
Willard, Jess, Chaps. 2, 17, 50
Wills, Harry, Chaps. 3, 18
Withrow, Ed, Chap. 52
Wolgast, Bobby, Chap. 21
Young, "Bull," Chap. 17
Ziemer, Al, Chaps. 18, 19
Ziff, Sid, Chaps. 11, 47

Zivic, Fritzie, Chap. 7
Zivic, Jack, Chap. 19
Zorilla, Santiago, Chaps. 38, 40, 44, 45
Zwick, Phil, Chap. 37

Printed in the United States
142985LV00012B/39/P